The authors have a lovely way of validating and normalizing the struggles of so many families throughout the book. I can feel their genuine sense of compassion and faith in all caregivers—there's a sense of hope and relief that comes just by reading the book (let alone putting the suggestions into practice). I could hear the authors in my head, and reading this book created a very personal and down-to-earth experience.

—**JENNIFER COMETTO, PhD,** CLINICAL PSYCHOLOGIST, ASSISTANT CLINICAL PROFESSOR, DEPARTMENT OF PSYCHIATRY AND BEHAVIOURAL NEUROSCIENCES, McMASTER UNIVERSITY, HAMILTON, ON, CANADA

This book gives you all you need to know about how to deal with your child's anger and your own. More than anything, it explains why anger is something we shouldn't fight so much as listen to. By means of many examples and descriptions of different methods, it will help relieve you of any guilt and shame you may have about your competence as a parent. We all struggle. Having offered groups and training programs to thousands of parents, the authors really get down to helping the reader deal with anger and provide helpful tools. Do yourself a favor and read this book. You will feel how close to reality what they write about is. You will leave with a greater understanding of what anger is and what to do with it.

—**LESLIE S. GREENBERG, PhD,** DISTINGUISHED RESEARCH PROFESSOR EMERITUS, DEPARTMENT OF PSYCHOLOGY, YORK UNIVERSITY, TORONTO, ON, CANADA

It is wonderful to see the authors embracing anger and providing guidance for how parents can understand and respond to it. So often we fear anger—yet it can be such a healthy part of our growth. This book provides very practical ways for parents to meet their child's anger so they grow up understanding and experiencing anger in ways that will help them meet their needs, rather than suppressing and bottling it up. This will contribute to a much healthier culture around anger.

—**SOPHIE HAVIGHURST, PhD,** PROFESSOR, LEADER AND COAUTHOR, THE TUNING IN TO KIDS PARENTING PROGRAMS, THE UNIVERSITY OF M

Finally, a book that resonates deeply with the angry struggles of our children and of ourselves! *Angry Kids, Angry Parents* reads like a conversation about working with hard feelings in a soft way, compassionately embracing the dirty secret that parents are often angry too. As a researcher and clinician, I was delighted by how this book put solid research into very practical terms. As a parent, I wish I had read this book years ago.

–ANTONIO PASCUAL-LEONE, PhD, PSYCHOLOGIST; PROFESSOR, UNIVERSITY OF WINDSOR, WINDSOR, ON, CANADA; HONORARY RESEARCH PROFESSOR, UNIVERSITY OF LAUSANNE, LAUSANNE, SWITZERLAND; COAUTHOR, *EMOTION-FOCUSED THERAPY FOR COMPLEX TRAUMA: AN INTEGRATIVE APPROACH* (2ND ED.)

Parenting is one of the most important tasks we face. However, we are given little information about how to do it, and the opportunity for vicarious learning within our individualist cultures is limited. Developing emotional intelligence is a key element of parenting. This book is a step-by-step guide to managing one of the most difficult emotions to master—anger. It is written by experts in training emotional intelligence and should be part of every parent's tool kit.

–JANET TREASURE, OBE, PhD, FRCP, FRCPsych, PROFESSOR OF PSYCHIATRY, INSTITUTE OF PSYCHIATRY, KING'S COLLEGE LONDON, LONDON, ENGLAND

ANGRY KIDS, ANGRY PARENTS

;bø **Hagen**

H O L

Joanne Dolhanty

PHD, CPSYCH

ANGRY KIDS, ANGRY PARENTS

Understanding and Working
With Anger in Your Family

 AMERICAN PSYCHOLOGICAL ASSOCIATION

Published by
APA LifeTools
750 First Street, NE
Washington, DC 20002
https://www.apa.org

Order Department
https://www.apa.org/pubs/books
order@apa.org

Typeset in Sabon by Circle Graphics, Inc., Reisterstown, MD

Printer: Sheridan Books, Chelsea, MI
Cover Designer: Mark Karis, Frederick, MD
Translator: Jill Karchmann

Library of Congress Cataloging-in-Publication Data

Names: Hagen, Anne Hilde Vassbø, author. | Dolhanty, Joanne, author.
Title: Angry kids, angry parents : understanding and working with anger in your family / Anne Hilde Vassbø Hagen and Joanne Dolhanty.
Description: Washington, DC : American Psychological Association, [2023] | Includes bibliographical references and index. | Summary: "Everything you need to know about your child's anger and how to manage it"-- Provided by publisher.
Identifiers: LCCN 2023001036 (print) | LCCN 2023001037 (ebook) | ISBN 9781433840654 (paperback) | ISBN 9781433840661 (ebook)
Subjects: LCSH: Anger in children. | Parent and child. | Interpersonal relations. | BISAC: FAMILY & RELATIONSHIPS / Parenting / Co-Parenting | SELF-HELP / Self-Management / Anger Management (see also FAMILY & RELATIONSHIPS / Anger)
Classification: LCC BF723.A4 H34 2023 (print) | LCC BF723.A4 (ebook) | DDC 155.4/1247--dc23/eng/20230314
LC record available at https://lccn.loc.gov/2023001036
LC ebook record available at https://lccn.loc.gov/2023001037

https://doi.org/10.1037/0000359-000

Printed in the United States of America

10 9 8 7 6 5 4 3 2 1

CONTENTS

ACKNOWLEDGMENTS

This book has come about with the help and support of many. We would like to thank our translator, Jill Kirchmann, who navigated the bridge between the Norwegian and the English versions for us. We want to thank the entire team at the American Psychological Association who guided us through the editing and production process with invaluable feedback and advice, and the colleagues and parents who read early drafts and also gave feedback. We thank our emotion-focused colleagues and friends around the world whose own work has made ours possible. We are forever grateful to Les Greenberg for welcoming us into the world of emotion-focused therapy with such generosity and tireless guidance, and for welcoming our branching out to bring his work to parents. We would like also to extend our appreciation to those parents, too many to count, who have allowed us into the world of their families, their children's tantrums, and their own anger, and who have taught us so much. Finally, we would like to thank our children, Alma, Ylva, Johan, Liam, and Rory, for being the best teachers of all, and our husbands, Bjørn and Mike, for supporting and standing by us through every lesson hard-learned and every absence from home occasioned by the work we do.

ANGRY KIDS, ANGRY PARENTS

ANGER CAN BE USEFUL

Four-year-old Vanessa is lying on her bed, kicking her legs wildly. She's crying and shouting that she doesn't want to wear tights. Each time I try to wrangle her into the impossibly small tights, she pulls her foot away. She gets more and more angry, and I'm more and more stressed. The clock is ticking. My first meeting at work is in 45 minutes. We have to get going. But none of this matters to Vanessa. She could not care less about my work meeting. She fights me off every time I come close. I start to get a bit more forceful, more than I feel comfortable with; I'm holding her as I try desperately to shove both legs into the tights at the same time. She screams furiously. Finally, I tear off her half-pulled-up tights, throw them down on the bed beside her, and scream: "If you do not put those tights on right now, you are going to GET IT!"

And there it is. I'm desperate to disappear from the whole situation. I can't bear to look at my frightened little girl. I want to turn back the clock. But even though I'm ashamed, I'm still angry at her. *She* has put *me* in this impossible situation by being so stubborn. If she would just behave, then I wouldn't have to get so angry. I want it to be her fault. In fact, I don't want to feel anything, and I don't want to think any more about what happened. Now it's just about getting us moving and out of the house. "Okay, Vanessa, you don't have to wear tights to kindergarten today. If you come right now, you can have a snack on the way. I've got blueberry muffins."

Anger in children is challenging and exhausting. A child's anger can lead to a lot of painful moments for parents. In our work as therapists, we once met a father who smashed his son's iPad in frustration over the fact that the boy wouldn't get ready for bed. One mother sat in our office and told us that, in a moment of utter desperation, she had turned to her daughter—who was having a tantrum and who had hit her 6-month-old sister—and said, "I wish you'd never been born!" We have counseled parents who have collapsed in tears and fled the house after their child threatened them with a knife, parents who have thrown the remote control at their child in an attempt to get their attention, and parents who have threatened to ground their child for a year after he barricaded himself in his room in anger and refused to go to school for the sixth day in a row. We have met parents who've had to place their violent children in institutions and parents who have been so afraid of their angry adult children that they cut off contact with them. We've talked to parents who have divorced because it's been so difficult to cope with their child's anger while also handling each other's different reactions and strategies.

As parents, we worry, and we sometimes say and do things in desperation that we would never have imagined possible before we had children. It is a massive challenge to be faced with an angry child, a rude and sullen adolescent, or a shut-down and silent adult child still living under our roof. These situations bring up a bunch of emotions for us as parents. We can feel despair and desperation when a child refuses to do what we ask. We can go from feeling frustration to feeling furious. We can even feel hatred toward our child. We can cringe with shame when they behave badly in front of others, and we can feel fear that they will never "grow out of" their bad behavior. Then more shame and despair set in because we haven't been able to find the thing that works to help them and to set our family on a better path.

The feeling that we have failed in our role as caregiver is a heavy burden to carry, and that feeling does not make us better parents. We're exhausted with worry. We feel powerless when strife or even violence has become almost a norm in our home. We feel a pervasive sadness, which has crept into the chasm between us and our children. All these emotions affect our behavior. They cause us to pull away from our children, to cry, to criticize, or to use force and, for example, grab them roughly by the arm. But these painful feelings, although they lead to behaviors that aren't good for us or for our kids, can actually be helpful.

WAIT—ANGER CAN BE HELPFUL?

Emotions give us information about what we need. We can listen to our emotions and use them in a way that helps us get our needs met. With new information, and a deeper understanding of our own feelings and reactions and those of our child, emotions can help us understand what we and our child need. Use your discomfort, shame, guilt, and sadness. Draw strength from these feelings so that, the next time you are faced with your angry or aggressive young child, your furious teenager, or your dismissive adult child, you can do something different. The most important thing is not what happens, it's what happens next! It is never too late to repair a relationship, and it's never too late to meet your child's feelings in a new way.

Anger is incredibly difficult to deal with. Angry children are difficult to deal with. It's exhausting to deal with constant blow-ups, especially when parents are overloaded with a million other things to get done in a day. When a child is angry and aggressive, parents can also begin to worry about the child's future: "What's going on with them?" "I'm afraid they'll end up in jail." "She'll never make friends." "Doesn't he have any empathy?" "Is she just a little psychopath?"

To make things more complicated, anger never comes alone as a single feeling. A child can alternate between being angry and sad and between being angry and ashamed. Anger and laughter can even occur together. But our own emotional reaction happens despite the fact that, under their anger, our child may be hurting. When we are already stretched beyond our limit, we react to their anger by getting angry ourselves. We can then end up criticizing, ridiculing, or rejecting the child, or just giving up. Our child's anger can also lead us to despair. It is painful to watch your child struggle. It's no wonder it can be hard to cope with an angry child when our heads are filled with worst-case scenarios.

The key lies in knowing more about how anger works and understanding that behind aggressive behavior often lie feelings of vulnerability. An angry child is often a child who is embarrassed, ashamed, or disappointed or who feels small, stupid, or "not enough." A child's anger can be an expression of sadness, loneliness, or fear. You, as the adult, need to be aware of what feelings their intense anger can evoke in you, and you need help figuring out how you can work with your own feelings—feelings that can keep you from doing the vital work of being emotionally present for your child.

Anger is the emotion in children that creates the greatest level of frustration in caregivers. Anger, along with shame, is the most misunderstood feeling. Anger has gotten a very bad rap; it often has only negative connotations, associated with aggression and violence, and is considered undesirable overall. Who hasn't heard a million times, "You don't need to be so angry!"

This book shines a light on anger and reminds people why it is an important and essential emotion. Anger has a crucial social role, allowing us to create boundaries and defend ourselves. Without anger, life would be very problematic. Without anger, others could do what they wanted to us and to what is ours: run us down, invade and rob us. We'd be defenseless without a healthy dose of anger!

I JUST WANT MY CHILD TO BEHAVE

Understanding your child's anger is all well and good, but at the end of the day most parents want their kids to behave. How can we get them to stop yelling at us or acting out? How can we get those tights on our daughter so that we can get to work on time and not end up acting either like Godzilla-Mom or like a total doormat with zero boundaries?

This process starts with understanding. Parents can learn to handle children who are aggressive or violent by understanding more fully what anger actually is. Just as important, they can learn what to do when things still (despite the parent's new learning) go completely off the rails—because that *is* going to happen, regardless of how much information and knowledge we have about emotions and child rearing. It is possible to get through the catastrophically bad days with our self-respect, and our relationship with our child, intact. This is even possible for parents whose children react with anger in almost any and all challenging situations. What does a child who is making threats and giving you the evil eye actually need? And how can parents who have almost completely given up regain faith in their ability to handle their child's anger?

This book gives you all you need to know about your children's anger and aggression—the good, the bad, and the ugly. We'll show you how anger can help you stand up for yourself, create healthy boundaries, and protect yourself against situations that are unfair or threatening. We'll also show you ways to respond when your child's anger shows up as rage, sharp criticism, intimidation, hate, screaming, biting, punching, and kicking. By helping your child understand and verbalize their needs, you can help them grow and strengthen their self-control and assertiveness. This will help them be better equipped to handle their anger in the future.

This book is not about giving your child whatever they want, and it is not about allowing aggressive behavior. We'll teach you a new approach to maintaining healthy boundaries that will allow you to set limits effectively while also understanding your child's emotions. The newsflash is that understanding emotions—your own and your child's—is the key that will help you rock the limit-setting.

This book is for all parents who would like to understand more about their child's anger and their own relationship with anger. Not all parents have children who are particularly angry, but all parents have children with a nervous system, a stomach, and a brain that can experience anger. This book is therefore not only for the parents of "angry kids" but also for parents who are simply curious to learn more about how to help their child develop a good relationship with anger. This book is for all parents who like to read and are hungry for knowledge.

THE APPROACH WE TAKE

We, the authors, are psychologists with many years' experience working with children, parents, and families. We specialize in a counseling model called *emotion focused skills training* (EFST; Dolhanty et al., 2022), which is based on the emotion-focused therapy model developed by Leslie Greenberg. EFST is a method whereby, instead of us jumping in to "treat" your child, we focus on supporting and guiding you, the parent. We believe you are the best one to help your child with their emotional and behavioral difficulties. We use the bond you have with your kids (and, if that bond is bent or broken, we help you repair it), and we teach you, so that you can teach them, ways to deal with emotional difficulties and solve problems. Lots of research shows that this way of working with families and emotions is effective (Ansar et al., 2021; Foroughe et al., 2018; Havighurst et al., 2015; Lafrance Robinson et al., 2013). The most important study of EFST showed that it makes a big difference in children's symptoms of anxiety and depression and behavioral difficulties (Ansar et al., 2022).

Joanne is the original founder of EFST for parents, and Anne Hilde has been a close collaborator in developing the approach. Although both of us have trained hundreds of parents and professionals in the method, this is our first book written for everyday parents. We hope to help you regain faith in yourself so that you can help your angry child to live in harmony with their emotions.

After helping hundreds of families, we know that massive change can occur when parents delve into understanding their children's emotions and when they genuinely convey to their child that "Your feelings are valid." It may sound banal and easy to say, "Of course you feel the way you do, because . . .," but this isn't easy to do when you're standing in front of a 5-year-old who smashes her toy to the floor, saying no one will play with her, or a 10-year-old who angrily yells that he hates his teacher and refuses to go to school. When feelings are acknowledged and allowed to function as intended, children learn that their emotions give them important information and help them to get what they need. This kind of emotional competence will change behavior, thoughts, and relationships. However, it isn't the behavior or thoughts that we want to help parents target. The goal in EFST, and of this book, is for parents not only to help their children feel better but also to help their children get better at feeling—both the painful and the pleasant feelings.

This book will also help you relate differently to your own feelings as well as to those of your child. We will help you regain your faith in yourself, knowing that you are the best person to help your children. Like all parents, you need to forgive yourself for any past mistakes. You need to quiet your inner critic and get in touch with your own old, unmet emotional needs and fears that are competing for attention and that can interfere with parenting (Greenberg, 2002, Chapter 12).

EFST is an *experience-based* method, which means that parents learn not only by acquiring knowledge but also through practice, experiences, and being emotionally activated during the learning process (Greenberg et al., 2007; Greenberg & Goldman, 2019). Therefore, the chapters in this book include experience-based exercises that can help you, in addition to reading the book, of course. These exercises each begin with the heading "Experience It." We urge you to put in the effort to complete them. They'll help you get to know your own emotions as well as connect you to your child's. They also will help you learn on a deeper level than simply reading the text will. It's worth the time and effort because, with emotion, "You gotta feel it if you want to deal with it."

The book is divided into three parts. The chapters in Part I examine anger as an emotion: What is anger, how does the feeling work, and when does it become a problem? Part II teaches you how to respond to your child's anger with empathy. This includes empathically validating their anger (but not their misbehavior!) and, if necessary, helping them problem solve. You will learn how to manage your own emotions as you deal with your child's anger as well as how to apologize when it is necessary to repair the relationship. Finally, the chapters in Part III teach you how to create and set healthy and flexible limits.

I

THE POWER OF ANGER

INTRODUCTION: THE POWER OF ANGER

We have met lots of parents with kids whose anger seems out of control. Children swearing, hitting, kicking, and flinging things around their rooms. No matter what the parents say to them, it only makes it worse. There's no way to reach them—the door has slammed shut, literally and metaphorically. It is depressing, painful, and exhausting for everyone involved.

Why do we need the emotion of anger? Wouldn't it be better if kids just never got angry? Wouldn't the whole world be a better place without this feeling? We might have avoided wars and violence. We'd probably feel like much better parents. Is it really necessary to be angry?

The answer is yes, we need anger. Anger is the extra "oomph" we need to be self-assertive, to stand up for ourselves, to express our needs and wants, and to defend ourselves and the things that are important to us. Anger allows us to say "no" and to create boundaries. When someone gets in the way of us reaching an important goal, it's anger that clears the way. Anger, however, can be destructive as well as constructive, and it comes in many different forms.

In Part I of this book, we describe constructive versus destructive anger and then lay out four challenges we face when we're dealing with angry kids. The first challenge is when anger works as a "cloaking device," hiding our child's more painful emotions and the emotional needs that come with them. The second challenge is when anger that shows up in the present is really about old anger from the past and from past relationships. The third challenge is how to handle it when our kids seem to "fake" being angry—what we call "adopting the stance of anger." Finally, we address the big challenge of what to do when your child's anger gets aggressive and even physical.

CHAPTER 1

CONSTRUCTIVE VERSUS DESTRUCTIVE ANGER

Anger is one of our seven basic emotions. In addition to anger, we feel joy, sadness, shame, curiosity, disgust, and fear. We also have a number of complex emotions, like jealousy, envy, melancholy, and love. We have this innate emotion of anger so that we can defend ourselves, and those we care about, when we are threatened, when our boundaries are trampled on, when things that are ours are taken from us, or when we are prevented from doing something important.

Think of a big brother who steals his little brother's candy. The most likely reaction for the little brother is to get angry, to express that anger verbally and make an angry face, and to fight to get the candy back. The younger brother might also go to his parents, who may intervene and speak with their older son. The idea is for the big brother not to steal the candy again, at least not without a second thought, because he didn't get away with it. In this example, anger functioned in the way it was intended, giving the little brother the direction and power to act and to defend himself.

In truth, anger can have either constructive or destructive effects, depending on how it is used. In this chapter, we explain the difference between the two. We also discuss the role of parents and why some kids might be angrier than others (hint: It's not just about what parents do!).

HOW ANGER CAN HELP US

Anger is activated when someone does not respect our boundaries or our wishes, prevents us from achieving an important goal, or treats us or those we love unfairly. A young person will be angry if their parents read their private journal, because that does not respect their personal boundaries. If a child wants to play soccer, but the parents make her take swimming instead, the child will feel anger that her wishes were not respected. A child playing their computer game will be highly invested in their efforts to achieve an important goal in the game. They are fighting the battle of their life, about to slay the last dragon in the final level of the game. Dad comes along and pulls the plug out without any warning, because the agreed-upon time limit is up. The child blames Dad for ruining the chance to complete the game, and feels angry. Kids get angry when they feel that siblings are treated differently. The little brother is allowed to sleep in his parents' bed when he's sick, but his big sister, a year older, is not. It feels unfair, and she feels angry. Note that we're not saying who is right and who is wrong in any of these situations; we're just talking about how understandable it is for any of us to feel angry when we believe that someone is treating us unfairly or thwarting our efforts to achieve a goal.

Anger Helps Us Be Assertive

There are lots of everyday situations that lead to understandable and justifiable anger in children, where it is good for the child to get angry and where the child needs to stand up for themselves and speak up. In these cases, the anger is *adaptive* (Greenberg, 2017), meaning it is fresh and new, it fits the situation, and it gives us important information. Adaptive emotions tell you about important emotional needs and what you need to do to get those needs met. Because adaptive anger helps people assert their needs, we also refer to it as *assertive anger*.

We want children to have a good relationship with anger. We want them to allow themselves to be angry when it is appropriate and to stand up for themselves and for their siblings and friends. Children who don't get angry may struggle with assertiveness in situations where it's needed. We need to applaud and praise our kids when they are angry and assertive in situations where they, or others, are being walked over or treated poorly. It takes guts to be assertive, and that courage needs to be recognized. When your child clearly expresses anger—for example, when they disagree with you or tell you something is unfair—they're giving you good information that can help you navigate the conflict and prevent it from escalating. They're telling you about their feelings, their boundaries, and their needs. This gives you an opportunity to validate, and maybe even meet an emotional need. The child's expression of anger is thus a "win" for both of you.

Anger Protects Us Physically

Children can also learn to use their instincts regarding when and how to use their anger in a way that keeps them safe, and this can be very different depending on the situation. Anger can come across as power to others, and it can help us to stand up for ourselves. It can stop us from being bullied or prevent the bullying from happening again. We can use anger to assert ourselves, speak up, and say, "No! Stop! Don't! I don't like this!"

Anger Helps Protect Our Self-Image

Even when anger doesn't show on the outside, it can have an important internal function. Sometimes it can be ill advised to speak up in the moment and we don't dare stand up for ourselves or show our anger. Consider a serious situation in which a child is being bullied, beaten, threatened, or sexually abused. It could be reckless to express anger. It could expose the child to more danger and bring the risk of more physical harm where they end up taking even more of a beating or more psychological humiliation. The most important need in this case, more important in the moment than self-assertion, is for the child to protect themselves. In such situations humans have an innate protective strategy to freeze and not say or do anything. To play dead. Evolution has taught us that we are more likely to survive, even if we are hurt, if we submit to the one who is dominating us and who has the upper hand.

In situations where they are overpowered and where they outwardly submit, some children will still feel angry inside. Although they may not dare express it in the moment, the anger they feel has an intrinsic value and works to protect them against a damaged self-image. Even if the child isn't able to speak up at the time, being able to feel the anger, in the situation or afterward, will protect them against further negative effects. To feel anger, even if it is not expressed right then and there, increases the chance that the child will tell someone afterward and that they will think "That was not my fault." Anger can protect the self and our self-esteem and prevent us from becoming overly submissive and feeling guilty or self-critical.

Imagine a child surrounded by four older children who are pelting him with pine cones. The big kids laugh out loud as the pine cones smack the smaller boy's head. Picture the smaller child's look of fear. He stands with his hands over his face, trying to protect himself the best he can. Imagine that we can connect with that small child and know his feelings and thoughts. Let's imagine that the first thing we feel is fear of the other kids and shame at being humiliated in front of them. But there is also a growing spark of anger. The child feels the physical pain, and the hurt feelings, but the pain and hurt start to alternate with a feeling of anger. Picture the anger as it begins to grow and take up more space in the child's mind. Imagine that the child stands in the middle of that circle, protecting his face, but inside feeling rage and thinking, "Just wait until I get bigger. I'm gonna whip those pine cones at you! Jerks!"

The child in this example risks an escalation of the situation if he shows his anger. It's four bigger guys against one smaller one, so the odds are not in his favor. But the most important thing is that anger is present in situations where others are bothering us or are treating us badly, even if it isn't wise to express it. By feeling anger internally, and by thinking self-assertive thoughts, we protect ourselves from destructive feelings of shame or inferiority. The protection is even better if we can also put the anger, and any other feelings we have in the situation, into words once we are out of danger and in a setting with people where we feel safe.

Children who are bullied but do not experience internal assertive anger can end up feeling "I'm a loser," "I'm an idiot," "No wonder they put me down and push me around." These children tend to grow up with low self-esteem and can be socially insecure. The shame makes them want to hide and become invisible. Conversely, think of the child who feels anger and pride, in addition to the fear and shame. This child might be inclined to think, "What a bunch of idiots! They're so immature. I didn't deserve that. Now that I'm older, I'm not going to hang out with jerks like that. I don't need them in my life." These children will likely grow up with a different story and a more nuanced image of themselves than the kids who haven't felt angry.

EXPERIENCE IT: YOUR ASSERTIVE ANGER

Let's do a little exercise so that you can start to get a picture of your own, and your child's, relationship with assertive anger. Can you be assertively angry?

Take a minute and think of a situation where you were angry, and with good reason, a time when you felt you were treated unfairly or when someone prevented you from doing something important or crossed your boundaries. In this situation, you're quite sure that someone else would understand why you were angry and would think it made sense. Take a minute or two to think of a situation before you read further.

Once you have the situation in mind, sit with it for awhile and notice whether the angry feelings arise again. If they do, sit with them for a bit. Allow the anger to be in your body for a few minutes. Let your body and the anger speak to you: What do I need in this situation? What do I need from myself? And what do I need from others? Take some time and see if you get some answers before you move on. Close your eyes while you sit with this.

Once you're done, think about this: Did you get what you needed, emotionally, in the situation or afterward? Were you assertive? Did anyone else stand up for you?

It's totally normal if one or more emotions other than anger showed up during the exercise. Just be curious and open to what comes. These other feelings might be able to give you important information about your needs. If you feel really angry, you can come back to this exercise later.

If you weren't assertive in the situation you're thinking of, what was stopping you? What stopped you from feeling and expressing anger? See if you can accept the absence of anger and be curious about it.

Take some time to answer these questions before you end the exercise.

EXPERIENCE IT: YOUR CHILD'S ASSERTIVE ANGER

Take a moment to recall a time when your child was angry, and with good reason, a situation where, when you think about it now, it is easy for you to understand your child's anger and you realize it was appropriate. We want you to think of a time when your child felt unfairly treated, or when someone stopped your child from doing something important, or crossed their boundaries. Take a minute or two to think of a situation before you read further.

Once you have the situation in mind, sit with it for awhile. Imagine you are your child, that it is your body, your things, or your integrity that were offended or violated and disrespected. Notice whether the angry feelings arise again here and now, as though you are your child. If the angry feelings arise, sit with them for a bit, and allow yourself to feel them. Let your body and the anger speak to you as if you were your child: What do I need in this situation? What do I need from myself? And what do I need from others? What do I need from my parents? Close your eyes and see if you are able to feel your child's needs.

Once you're done, and still thinking as your child, think about this: Did you get what you needed, emotionally, in the situation or afterward? Were you assertive? Did anyone else stand up for you? How did your parents react to your anger? Take some time to reflect and see if you can come up with some answers before you go on.

If the child was not able to be assertive, continue to imagine that you are your child and think about how your tummy and chest must have felt at that time. What stopped you? What stopped you from feeling angry and expressing your anger? As an adult, see if you can meet your child's resistance or avoidance of anger with a gentle curiosity. Take your time before ending the exercise.

HOW ANGER CAN HARM US

Just as anger can help us meet our needs, so too can it cause harm when it is not used properly. The same physiological changes that help us be assertive can negatively affect our health and well-being.

Anger Decreases Our Ability to Think

Our hearts beat hard and fast when we're angry. It feels like our blood is boiling, and our head and body temperature rise, seemingly instantly, to a thousand degrees. We lean forward, and our bodies puff up and take up more space. We glare straight ahead, furrow our eyebrows, and clench our fists and our jaw.

Anger activates the part of our brain that is involved in our emotional system before we even know we're angry. The most well-known and central brain structure that is activated is the *amygdala*. It turns our body's stress system on and off. When we are stressed, our body's nervous system secretes different hormones, such as adrenaline, norepinephrine, and cortisol. These stress hormones have an effect on the cells and neurons in our brain and body. They cause blood to flow out of the stomach and into the muscles so that the body is prepared to act physically, and fight if needed. Our heart pounds, our blood pressure rises, our breathing becomes more rapid, our body temperature increases, and we begin to sweat. Our senses become razor sharp. In other words, a lot of good things happen in our bodies when we're angry. Our body mobilizes our physical power so that we can stand up for ourselves, speak out, and fight to defend ourselves if we have to.

If your child gets angry too often, though, then the anger can be harmful. Elevated levels of one of the stress hormones, cortisol, can cause brain cells to become overactivated. Children who are often really furious cannot think as clearly as kids who are calm. If brain cells in the frontal lobe and hippocampus are activated too often by stress, they can become impaired. Fortunately, lost functions can develop again when the brain is rested and no longer in an overactive mode.

The *frontal lobe* is the part of the brain that accounts for our most advanced thinking and it, more than any other part, separates us cognitively from animals. The frontal lobe helps us to organize, plan, and make smart choices. It is a counterweight to impulsivity. In humans, the frontal lobe is the part of the brain that develops last, and it is not fully developed until we are well into our 20s (Johnson et al., 2009; Siegel, 2015). When the frontal lobe is not working as it should, or when the amygdala is very activated, the child is unable to reflect on their own or others' actions. They're also unable to make good decisions, consider consequences, or plan well for the future. Intense anger can actually stop us from being able to think. When a child can't think straight, then you have a child who is typically not receptive to talking or instructions and who will keep acting out even though they know better. In children and adolescents, whose frontal lobes are not fully developed, anger causes the brain to stop working properly even faster than it does for adults. It's like the door slams shut and the lights go out.

Anger Compromises Our Memory

The *hippocampus* is the part of the brain that, among other things, affects short-term memory and acts as a kind of library or archive that helps us sort out what is and isn't dangerous. A furious amygdala makes the hippocampus think that the situation is dangerous or threatening, and so it is harder to remember, and to store, new memories or experiences. When a hyperstressed amygdala and hippocampus are wearing the "You gotta protect yourself" glasses, it means that neither you nor your child will remember what should be said during an important discussion or confrontation. It is precisely this kind of overactive hippocampus that also prevents us from remembering accurately what was said and done in the middle of a conflict.

Anger Causes Health Problems

The constant flow of stress hormones that accompanies persistent, ongoing rage can harm a child's body in a variety of ways. It's not dangerous to be temperamental or to feel intense anger in certain situations, but damage can occur when anger doesn't function as it's meant to and becomes intense and long-lasting. The short- and long-term health problems associated with persistent rage include headaches, stomach pain, poor sleep, high blood pressure, and eczema. In adults, very extended periods of anger can ultimately result in a heart attack (Al Majali & Ashour, 2020; Thomas, 1997). Too much cortisol can also reduce the production of *serotonin*, the hormone that plays an essential role in feeling happy. Many of us who work as therapists have witnessed that clients who have extensive unprocessed and uncontrolled anger over a long period of time can have mental health challenges such as anxiety, depression, and aggression.

WHY ARE SOME KIDS ANGRIER THAN OTHERS?

Although the benefits and drawbacks of anger can apply to anyone with anger, some people are naturally angrier than others. This is true for adults as well as children. We all have different innate qualities and sensitivities, in our temperaments and personalities and even in our cells, that affect our expressions of anger. More than anything, genetics make some children more prone to be easily upset and aggressive than others.

Temperament is an organic and fundamental part of our personality that provides emotional color to our experiences and social interactions. We can think of our temperament as the way we tend to react emotionally to different situations. Some people have very calm temperaments; it takes a lot to get them angry, and their expressions of anger are low key. Others are more quick tempered, easily angered, and can fly into a rage over something that seems insignificant to others. Our temperament is largely innate, even though scientists know of no specific genes for temperament. We seem simply to be born with a certain temperament.

A person's temperament is generally stronger and more distinct during their teen years, so it is no wonder that's a challenging time for both kids and parents. To make matters worse, the teen brain is not yet fully developed, and teens can swing from being a rebellious anarchist one day to a goody-two-shoes the next. Fortunately, we know that children and teens with intense temperaments usually mellow out as they get older.

If you have a child who is far to one end of the temperament scale, it's important to focus on how to highlight and play to their strengths. To dismiss or criticize a child's temperament is the opposite of accepting that they are who they are. It will likely have little effect on their temperament and could even heighten those particular traits and the child's ways of dealing with emotions. Kids with powerful and intense temperaments often need boundaries that are well-thought-out and adaptable, as well as a good amount of structure and predictability. Some parents believe that if they don't take a hard stance with such kids, it amounts to letting the child set a negative tone and create an unpleasant, and even dangerous, situation in the family, especially in regard to younger siblings. In this book, you'll get lots of specific tips on how to set limits on your child's problematic behavior without sacrificing the need to acknowledge their temperament and emotions.

It is tiring to be the parent of an explosive child who is learning to manage their emotions. However, although having a strong temperament may be a risk when it comes to compromising good social engagement, a strong temperament does not equal aggressive behavior and lost friendships. Children with a strong temperament have an inner energy that can be a powerhouse of productivity and play, and that can be a great asset both when working with and competing against others, as long as they feel safe and good about themselves.

Although temperament is mostly innate, it can change as a result of environmental influences. Early in life, various genes turn on and off depending on whether or not they are stimulated. When a person goes through challenges and struggles, these events can camouflage, dampen, or intensify the person's natural temperament. In other words, how quickly your child gets angry and the amount of stress hormones their body produces are also related to what your child has learned through experience. If a child has experienced that getting angry works well in the short term, to get attention or get their way or feel loved, their brain will actually produce anger hormones faster, and they will often become angrier than children who have received help in dealing with difficult emotions at home and at school. Children who grew up in homes where adaptive anger was accepted will often be more assertively angry than children who grew up feeling that anger was forbidden or dangerous. The environmental influence on genes is called *epigenetics*. Genes, environment, and our learning history all contribute to who we are, and they contribute to our relationship with anger.

It is important to note that children who have very mild temperaments need as much time and attention as the intense ones. These children can be easily overlooked in the midst of a hectic day. Children with mild temperaments need adults to be able to pick up on small nuances in their emotional expressions, and they need to have their anger accepted when it shows up in its mild form. Their anger could take the form of a silent protest, a furrowed brow, crossed arms, or becoming quiet and withdrawn. The strength of kids with mild temperaments is that they are often perceived as socially adaptable, and they are well liked. Our experience has been that parents who describe their children as having mild temperaments also say that these kids are resilient. They are generally in a good mood and don't feel things so intensely. They are easy to deal with, and they take life in stride. Whereas an intense temperament increases the likelihood of more extreme behavior, a mild temperament increases the likelihood of being passive and not maintaining sufficient boundaries. In both cases, it's important to challenge or correct the behavior rather than the temperament or personality.

Who your child was when they came into this world also plays a crucial role. Some children have intense temperaments because of sensory hypersensitivity, which means that they react more than others to things like loud noises, bright lights, and even itchy fabrics. Some might have gastrointestinal problems, migraines, or other physical issues that can lead to more frustration and anger. It's important to figure out what triggers your child's anger. Sometimes, simple preventive or practical measures can be used in critical situations to avoid intense outbursts and conflicts at home and at school. A child who is sensitive to sound and crowds may need help getting back to the classroom after recess, so that they aren't with all the kids who are running and shouting through the hallway at the same time. If you have a child who is bothered by itchy fabric and seams in their clothing, finding clothing that is soft and loose fitting can help. It's important to point out that these specific examples are not the most common causes of a child's anger.

EXPERIENCE IT: YOUR CHILD'S TEMPERAMENT

Where does your child's temperament fit on a scale of 1 (*mild*) to 10 (*intense*)? Here are some questions to guide your rating:

- How does your child's temperament affect them? What happens to their voice and body language when they're angry?
- Is your child familiar with the feeling of anger? Do they feel bad after they've been angry?
- When does your child's temperament, whether it's mild or intense, create problems for them?
- What does your child need when their temperament causes problems?

THE ROLE OF PARENTS

In light of the potential for anger to be helpful or harmful, what role do parents play? As parents, one of our goals is to help our kids use their anger constructively. To do that, we must teach them to identify the unmet need underlying the anger. All basic emotions have an associated emotional need. The emotions act as a signaling system for the needs. They tell us something about what we need from ourselves and others and what actions we can take to get our emotional needs met. When we're sad because we've lost someone or something important to us, we need comfort, care, and closeness. If we're afraid, we need to feel safe or reassured. If we're ashamed because we've said or done something wrong, we need help to restore our damaged self-image and to be invited back into the circle of family or friends through being acknowledged and having our feelings normalized. If we feel disgust because we've been confronted by something or someone we really don't like, we need to put distance between ourselves and that person, remove ourselves from the situation, or get away from the object that makes us feel sick. When we're surprised or curious when faced with something unknown, a particular problem, or a new situation, we need time to explore, play, learn, and find solutions to the problem. If we're angry because someone has treated us badly, we have a need to stand up for ourselves, speak up, and maintain our boundaries. We often experience joy once we've met an important need. Joy can take many forms, from pleasure and feelings of peace to happiness and ecstasy. We experience joy when we've been desperate to pee for 3 hours and finally get to the bathroom. When we've experienced something fun, or feel that something is meaningful or serene, we feel joy. For some of us, it's important to share joy with others, while others like to revel in the joy alone.

If we can't meet our emotional needs, we need to seek help from others. Children will need help consistently until they are able

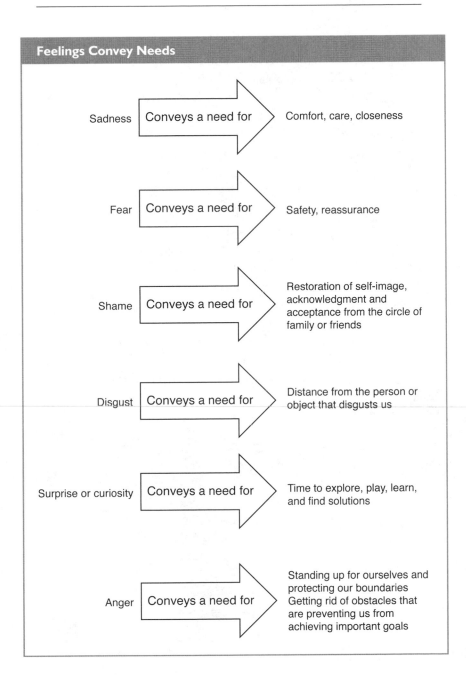

Feelings Convey Needs

Sadness — Conveys a need for — Comfort, care, closeness

Fear — Conveys a need for — Safety, reassurance

Shame — Conveys a need for — Restoration of self-image, acknowledgment and acceptance from the circle of family or friends

Disgust — Conveys a need for — Distance from the person or object that disgusts us

Surprise or curiosity — Conveys a need for — Time to explore, play, learn, and find solutions

Anger — Conveys a need for — Standing up for ourselves and protecting our boundaries Getting rid of obstacles that are preventing us from achieving important goals to behave in a way that gets their own emotional needs met. When children are angry, they need help to understand their emotions so that they can begin to connect with those needs. Once they know what they need, they can begin to solve a problem on their own initiative. If they aren't able to manage that, then they also need help in solving the problem. As the child develops, and as new and bigger challenges arise, they will frequently need help from adults. Children are learning how to deal with situations that will become even more demanding and complex as an adult. If a child manages to say that they don't like to be treated unfairly, or walked all over, or be stopped from reaching goals, then they're more likely to be the kind of adult who is clear on the way they want and deserve to be treated. This doesn't mean that they won't have challenges in life, or that they'll always be able to assert themselves when needed, but being allowed to be angry, when it's appropriate, is an important factor that increases the chance that a child will get to know their own boundaries and self-worth. Kids need help from adults in their lives to know how to use anger in a good way. They need strong role models and adults who can acknowledge anger and show that it is normal and valid and good.

CHAPTER 2

CHALLENGE 1: ANGER AS A CLOAKING DEVICE

Up to this point, we've been talking about anger in its purest form: as assertive and understandable. But this isn't usually where the trouble starts when it comes to our children. As parents, it's easier for us to relate to our child's anger when we "agree" with the anger and with the degree of their anger. It's easy to understand when a teenager is angry with a friend who broke their trust and shared a secret with someone else. It makes sense that the teen would be angry when they talk about it at home and when they say they don't want to talk if that friend calls or comes by. It's much more of a challenge when we think the anger is exaggerated and not in keeping with the situation, or when we simply have no idea why the child is angry in the first place. There are four main scenarios when this is the case. In this chapter, we cover the first scenario: when anger is a cloaking device that covers other emotions.

HAS SOMETHING LIKE THIS EVER HAPPENED TO YOU?

A 10-year-old girl is struggling at school, especially in math and English. She is restless and has trouble concentrating, except when she's playing her favorite video game. She's constantly fighting with her 8-year-old brother, who does well both in school and socially.

Cloaking Anger

There are frequent conflicts between her and her parents. She doesn't listen to what they say and gets angry any time they try to set a limit or impose an expectation.

It's dinnertime, and the little brother comes into the kitchen. His mom walks over to him and strokes his head. They smile at each other. The daughter comes into the kitchen, full of energy, and sits at the table, bouncing in her seat, in her usual restless way. Mom asks her, gently, to sit still. Her little brother puts a piece of chicken on his plate and then takes a bite without his mom seeing. His sister puts one, two, then three pieces of chicken on her plate and takes a bite. Mom sees and says, firmly, that she's taken too much and that she needs to wait to start eating. Mom lets out a big sigh. Her daughter is instantly enraged. She throws a piece of chicken on the floor and screams, "I hate you!" She storms out of the kitchen. Her mom goes after her, confused about why she's so upset. The little girl is sitting in her room, crying. She's now clearly more sad than angry. Mom is gentle and asks, curiously, what is going on. The little girl says that she feels like she's always doing something wrong and that she's the only one who gets yelled at. She thinks that her mom and dad love her little brother way more than her.

Think about this story and focus on the emotions. What is actually going on? We assume that the little girl was feeling fine before she walked into the kitchen. She sees her mom stroke her little brother's head. Maybe she's a bit jealous? Maybe she wishes that her mom stroked her head that way? When her mom asks her to sit still, maybe she feels it's unfair and critical, too, as if there's something wrong with her because she can't sit still. When her mom reprimands her, she gets angry because she feels like it's unfair that she's the only one who gets in trouble. When her mom sighs, her daughter feels small, ashamed, as if she's not good enough. In this example, shame is the first emotion that shows up when the situation suddenly reaches its peak, and it's the one she feels most strongly—the feeling of having done something wrong and of being "wrong" in who she is. The feeling of shame is painful and unpleasant, and the little girl has no words for that emotion. Anger, in this context, is a great solution. Anger covers shame like a blanket and protects her from it. In the choice between two "evils," anger is easier to feel than shame. Shame is her primary emotion, and the anger functions as a cloaking device to cover the shame. Anger protects her from the feeling of being somehow all wrong and of being a disappointment. Anger also hides the shame so her mom and her brother can't see it. Anger in this case is thus a misleading signal—the child shows anger to others when shame is the more painful feeling. She needs help with the shame but, out of a sense of shame, she draws attention to herself with anger. Anger provokes a reaction and, as we've said, none of us tend to react well when anger is directed at us. When the girl leaves the kitchen so that she's no longer seen by the others, the shame returns. The anger kept the shame away for only a short time, but at other times the anger can last longer. It's not always easy to understand in the moment that a child who is furious can be feeling very small and vulnerable on the inside, but it is often the case.

PRIMARY AND SECONDARY EMOTIONS

In emotion-focused therapy, we call feelings that disguise, cover up, or cloak other feelings *secondary emotions* (Greenberg, 2017). They come in response to a different primary emotion. All emotions can cloak others, and all emotions can be cloaked. Someone who thinks being sad is a sign of weakness may show anger as a way to hide that sadness. Someone who fears or avoids confrontation and anger may spontaneously cry and show sadness when underneath they feel a seething and unwelcome anger. The two most common emotions that we use as cloaking devices are worry (which we can also think of here as anxiety) and anger. With worry and anxiety, it's as though, for some people, letting the mind spin with worst-case-scenario thoughts is less painful than allowing themselves to feel sad, lonely, or ashamed. For others, anger is their go-to best protection against those vulnerable primary emotions.

Sometimes even adaptive and typically positive emotions, like happiness, curiosity, joy, and excitement, can be scary and make some people feel too vulnerable. Showing these emotions can let others see our inner self, and this can make some people feel exposed. Some children may have had the experience of others not liking a display of these feelings. They may have been told they look silly jumping around excited. They may have sensed that the commotion and racket of their upbeat emotions has made their parents feel awkward or on edge. Most of us as parents have had the experience of cringing a little with embarrassment when our kids acted too silly, too noisy and rambunctious, or "too much" for a given social situation. Out of our own embarrassment we may convey our disapproval, which the child picks up, or we may reprimand them in front of others. The child may feel rejected, criticized, ridiculed, or shamed and end up not having their emotional needs met. Yes, even pleasant emotions have associated emotional needs!

Pleasant feelings, like happiness and curiosity, can also work as protectors when they are used in a clowning way, ironically, or in an exaggerated way, such as when a child throws themselves into hobbies or homework so that they don't have to think about painful feelings, or they become the one who cheers up the adults in the family.

We also need to be aware of gender differences, even though many of us may be working hard not to be confined by gender stereotypes. There are still implicit and explicit messages, for example, that big boys don't cry and good girls don't get angry. Each of you as a parent, and in collaboration with your kids as they develop, will find where you fit in the gender roles that work best for you. We believe that wherever that place is, we all still need to grapple as parents with the messages that exist. It is still more common that men cloak sadness with anger and women hide their anger behind sadness. The world has certainly evolved when it comes to accepting emotions in general and in terms of defining gender roles, assessing stereotypes, and redefining what is and what is not acceptable. However, experiences in day care, at school, and at home will still communicate values to your child. The fact is that observed overall differences in emotion expression between boys and girls remain. Each of us as a parent hopes to help our child navigate their emotional world, including as that world interacts with their gender identity, in the way best suited to that child.

We want to make clear that any feeling can be a primary emotion, and any feeling can be experienced as a vulnerable emotion. It depends on our temperament and what we learn through our experience with emotion in our early relationships. It's also important to note that it is rarely, or maybe never, a conscious choice to protect ourselves by cloaking our emotions with other emotions. Our emotions organize themselves automatically on the basis of what we've learned through experience, including which emotions are acceptable and which are not. The feelings that we cloak the most are sadness, anger, shame, and fear. Some children and adults get angry when they're actually sad, and some get sad and start crying every time they feel angry.

We need this ability to use feelings as a cloak to hide our more vulnerable emotions. Evolution has allowed us to develop in this way so that we can protect ourselves when faced with our enemies or with people who don't have our best interests at heart, or when it's just not the right situation to show vulnerability. In different contexts, it may be smart to play the angry card or to put on a happy face. All of this suggests that it is normal for us to cloak and hide our vulnerable emotions. We would be overly exposed if we strolled around always showing our true, vulnerable feelings to everyone in the world. We return to a discussion of cloaked anger later in this chapter. First, though, we must ask, When does it become a problem to cloak our emotions, and why?

WHEN ANGER AS A CLOAKING DEVICE BECOMES PROBLEMATIC

Using anger as a cloaking device can become problematic, especially in our closest and most important relationships—with family, friends, and teachers. Remember that our emotions are the way we discover what we need; they act as signals, directing us to a particular need. Primary emotions carry this information about our needs, and they signal us to pay attention to them. In a cloaking emotion, however, the only need inherent in the emotion is the need to hide the primary emotion—the one we don't want to feel. Cloaking emotions in kids are thus an indication that the child needs to be seen.

They signal the adult to look for the feelings and needs that lie underneath the child's cloaking emotion. Anger as a cloak is a reaction to the first—and likely more genuine, but also painful—feeling. The core emotional need is always connected to the first emotion that is activated in a particular situation. It's also this genuine feeling that gives you information about what you need emotionally from yourself and those around you.

As parents, our goal is to grasp the feelings that lie underneath the cloaking anger so that we know what our kids actually need from us. If a child is sad, they need comfort. If it's actually fear, then the need is for safety and protection. But when cloaking anger hides the sadness or fear, we get the wrong signals about what our child needs, and the real needs are hidden. When you see that anger in your child, you might think they need space, some time to themselves, and maybe a clearer framework of limits and expectations. But if the anger is a cloaking device and what the child is actually feeling is sadness, then what they need are comfort and closeness. If a child goes a long time feeling sad and the parent isn't able to see it, the sadness can turn into a more persistent loneliness or a fear of being abandoned. If a child uses anger to cover shame or guilt, then the emotional need for acknowledgment, normalizing, and help to restore self-esteem, could be overlooked. If a child does not receive help from an adult to handle shame and guilt over a long period of time, then there is an increased risk for the child to develop a tough inner critic or a feeling of self-loathing.

In other words, a child will not have their emotional needs met by the parents if that child is mostly expressing themselves with cloaking anger, unless the parents can discover the underlying, genuine, and vulnerable emotions. If you think this seems like a maze—you're right! Let's keep thinking about how we can do this.

Note that it's not just the feeling but also the emotional need that is cloaked when a child covers up their true, vulnerable feelings with anger. Thus, two things happen for the child when they resort to cloaking anger as a way to hide and protect themselves from their primary painful emotions. One is that, as parents, we react negatively to the cloaking anger, and it's understandable that we do. The anger is out of proportion to the situation, and it's annoying. Second, we aren't able to meet the child's important needs associated with their primary painful feelings because the cloak has hidden the needs along with the feelings. But having their needs not met can lead kids to behave in a way that generates even more conflict, and it can become a vicious circle. Conflict, loneliness, low self-esteem, unresolved challenges, and hopelessness can develop, and these can escalate the child's emotional and behavioral problems.

It's very common for children to express cloaking anger and other cloaking emotions, even in close relationships. How can parents figure out what their child's real feelings are? How can you talk about this without imposing your own view on the child or pushing them too much? Luckily, it is possible to learn how to navigate your child's cloaking anger. We'll get to those answers in a later section on validation.

EXPERIENCE IT: YOUR CLOAKING EMOTIONS

When did you last feel angry and blame or criticize someone? Was the anger directed toward your child, your partner or coparent, or someone else? Think of a specific instance when you weren't sure if others understood why you were angry. Maybe you don't even totally understand it yourself. It's important here to pick a situation where the reason for your anger was unclear to others and/or to yourself, and not one where you had an obvious and clear reason to be angry but reacted out of proportion to the situation. When you have thought of an example, continue reading.

Try to put yourself back in the moment and feel the blaming or criticizing anger again. Get in touch with this feeling before you go further.

Once you're in touch with the anger, allow yourself just to feel it for a moment. Maybe you feel like you want to defend yourself and continue with the accusations. Maybe you feel ashamed that you got so angry, or you already realize that it was about more than anger. All the emotions that come up are normal. See if you can approach your reaction of anger with a gentle curiosity. Take a few minutes to try this. Close your eyes if it helps.

Now imagine yourself back in that situation when you were angry. Are there other, more vulnerable feelings underneath the anger? Look inside. Be curious. Did something happen that actually made you sad or hurt? Did you feel dismissed? Lonely? Criticized? Did you feel small or ashamed? Were you, in fact, angry? Did something happen before this situation occurred that made you feel vulnerable? Take a few minutes to think about these questions before continuing.

If a feeling of being hurt comes up, let that feeling sit in your stomach or chest and let it just be for a bit. What does this feeling tell you about what you need? What do you need from yourself or others? Do you need comfort, closeness, protection, acknowledgment, or to have your feeling normalized? Sit with this before you move on.

If you know what you need, is there something you can say to yourself, or do, to meet that emotional need?

You may have a sense of what that important need is but then have a negative reaction to it. You might think it's childish, that you should be okay without it, or that you don't deserve to have that need met. If this happens, be very curious about where the negative reaction to this need comes from. Where did you learn that you don't need, shouldn't need, or don't deserve to need? Allow yourself lots of time to feel into this before you end the exercise.

EXPERIENCE IT: YOUR CHILD'S CLOAKING EMOTIONS

When did your child last feel angry and blame or criticize someone? Think of a specific instance when you didn't understand why your child was angry. Once again, avoid a situation in which they had good reason to be angry but reacted out of proportion to the situation. Think of an example and imagine that you are your child. Try to put yourself into the feeling of the anger that is leading to blaming and criticizing.

Once you're in touch with the anger, keep imagining that you are the child. Are there other, more vulnerable feelings underneath the anger? Look inside. Be curious. Keep imagining that you are your child. Did something happen that actually made you sad or hurt? Did you feel dismissed? Lonely? Criticized? Do you feel unimportant? Do you feel like no one likes you? Are you actually afraid of something? Do you think your parents love your sibling more than you? Did something happen before this situation occurred that made you feel vulnerable? Take a few minutes to think about these questions before continuing.

If a feeling of being hurt comes up, let that feeling sit in your stomach or chest, as if you are your child, and let it just be for a bit. What does this feeling tell you about what you need? What do you need from yourself or others? What do you need from your parents? Do you need comfort, closeness, protection, acknowledgment, or to have your feeling normalized? Close your eyes and see if you can feel the answers to these questions.

If you are able to connect with an important need for your child, you may also feel a resistance to being able to meet that need. Maybe you're afraid to make things worse for your child if you meet that need. Maybe you're afraid you can't do it. Maybe you're afraid of babying your child and that they won't become independent. Or maybe you're afraid that if you focus only on the painful feelings, your child won't understand that they've done something wrong and that it's not okay to get so angry. If this happens, be very curious about where these reactions come from. Which emotions in you are behind them? Worry or fear? Anger or irritation? A feeling that you can't manage? Perhaps you can't bring yourself to speak about what is painful? Take this important knowledge about yourself with you as you read further in the book.

HOW DO WE DISTINGUISH SELF-ASSERTIVE ANGER FROM CLOAKING ANGER?

Self-assertive anger can take various forms. A person who is assertively angry talks clearly, in a grounded voice, conveying a sense of something we might call *personal power*. They may have their arms crossed and be standing tall. Self-assertive anger can also be expressed in a less reserved way. There may be some strong words with a dirty look and a flip of the finger. There's something very genuine about assertive anger, and it often evokes understanding, empathy, and respect. When we are assertively angry, we usually start with the word "I" and speak mostly about ourselves. We can be specific about what we are angry about because we know very well why we are angry. We often speak in clear sentences with specific points, as though we are listing important things. The situation doesn't have to end in screaming or losing control. This kind of healthy, primary self-assertive anger feels fresh and new, and it matches the situation. It gives those around us very clear information about our assertive need for respect, and it communicates a boundary.

When adults are assertively angry with a child, it can sound like this:

> I get angry when you do something that is completely different from what you were told to do. I said to be home by 7, and

Assertive Anger Versus Cloaking Anger

How can we tell the difference?	Assertive anger	Cloaking anger
What do we see—body?	• Strong • Grounded	• Out of control
What do we hear—words?	• "I" statements • Specifics	• "You" statements • Generalities
What do we hear—tone?	• Confidence • Personal power	• Accusation • Complaint
What shows us if they're having the anger or if the anger is having them?	• Not taken over by the anger (not a tsunami) • Able to communicate while showing feeling	• Volatile • Communicating feeling without message
What do we understand—what is the message?	• Clear message of what they're angry about	• Vague
What do we sense about the message?	• Genuine • Fresh, new	• Stuck, repetitive
How do we feel in reacting to it?	• Respect	• Defensive • Frustrated

it's 8. I get worried when you don't come home, and it really makes me mad that I have to go out and look for you. It's really important to me that you stick with the rules we make, and that I can trust you to follow them.

Children who are assertively angry may sound like this when they speak to their parents:

I don't like you lending my things without asking me first! You could have asked me! I get to decide about my stuff. Those are my stickers! I made that butterfly sticker, and I didn't want Anna to put it on her drawing. Don't give my things away without asking me.

A person using anger as a cloaking device, on the other hand, may start off shouting right away or may come across as whining and complaining. Cloaking anger is often more volatile than assertive anger and can quickly boil over into rage. It has a blaming and attacking feel to it. The complaints may be general and not clearly connected to the situation where the anger was triggered. In many cases, we may not even know exactly why we are so angry and why there isn't necessarily a reason to be angry. This is even more true of children; their brain, insight, and emotion awareness are still developing, and so they can be even more unsure than adults about what they're feeling and why. This can make it especially frustrating to deal with cloaking anger in our kids. In fact, it's difficult to understand, empathize with, and respect cloaking anger in anyone. We're usually put off by it, whereas with assertive anger, we're more inclined to think, "Wow, that was powerful!" When we show cloaking anger, we usually begin our statements with "you"; we use a more vague and accusatory tone; and we speak mostly about the target of our anger, be it an object, a situation, or a person. It can involve finger-pointing and lecturing. Cloaking anger does not give good information about our needs in the situation, and thus it can be confusing for ourselves as well as give incorrect signals to others.

In adolescents, cloaking anger might sound something like this:

> You are such a frickin' idiot. You don't get it at all! If you don't let me get this sweater then I am seriously going to lose it. None of my friends' parents suck as much as you do. Literally all the other parents are cooler than you. You—you are ridiculous. It's all your fault that my life sucks. You're way too strict, and you're a total idiot.

Parents who are expressing cloaking anger might sound like this:

> If you can't act appropriately then you can just forget about shopping and going to a birthday party today. You are impossible! What am I supposed to do with you? You don't listen to anything I say, and you don't follow any rules. You have no idea how lucky you are. We give you everything. I am so disappointed in you.

Even though cloaking anger is secondary and functions to hide other painful emotions, when our kids show it, they still need us to help them through it. We can view their acting out in anger as a test for us to reassure them that we love them and that we can tolerate their difficult feelings. A child might storm into their room but then check to see if their parent is following them. Behind the anger lie other emotions and emotional needs. Our angry reaction to the anger they show us on the surface can lead them to have an image of themselves as mean or bad. Children typically believe that being angry and being "bad" are the same. They can believe they're bad if they are angry, because anger elicits a lot of criticism.

Children who perceive themselves as bad or mean can also then develop a strong inner critic who tells them that they are bad because they do bad things and that no one likes bad or mean people. All of this leads to a poor self-image and to destructive shame. We call this kind of shame "old shame," because it is a result of old emotional wounds rather than what is happening in the present situation. We discuss this challenging scenario in the next chapter.

CHAPTER 3

CHALLENGE 2: NEW DAY, SAME OLD ANGER

Imagine a child in first grade being bullied. Her classmates tease her at recess and say mean things about her appearance. She's angry, and she's embarrassed and upset. She learns to hide the angry and vulnerable feelings behind jokes and making fun of herself, so it looks like she doesn't care what they say. It's actually an ingenious strategy. Suppose the adults at home and at school realize that the child is having a rough time and that they get it that she has hurt feelings and anger behind the smiles and jokes. Suppose, though, that when talking to her about anger, they say things like: "It doesn't help to get angry," "It's important not to want to get even," "It's not good to be angry." Getting the message that it's not okay to be angry can result in the child still being angry but not getting help to meet the need for self-assertion and for standing up for herself. Long after the bullying has ended, the child may get very angry when a situation arises that reminds her of it. She ends up carrying the anger for longer. She might react with intense rage if the old anger is triggered, when she sees other kids teasing a friend, or if someone makes an innocent comment about her appearance.

We had a family in counseling where the son had been bullied at a previous school. The kids excluded him and would take his things and hide them. As well as being scared and upset, the boy had good reason to be angry. He had a need to stand up for himself. But he wasn't able to defend himself, and his anger was never allowed to surface. He got lots of understanding from his parents about being scared and about how upsetting it was not to have friends at school. His parents even took control of the situation and moved him to a new school. But although he was removed from the difficult circumstances, he didn't get help to deal with his anger about being bullied. In all their efforts to help, the parents had simply not realized that anger is an important emotion that needs to be expressed. And how would they have known? Anger was not the feeling that the boy expressed at the time that he was being bullied.

After some time, he began feeling angry a lot, at school and in social situations outside of school. It was hard for his parents to understand why he was suddenly so angry and for no apparent reason. He began to take offense at every little thing. There had been an unmet need to stand up for himself and to defend himself against the bullies at his old school, and very likely some shame as well at not having been able to defend himself. His anger started to show up in his new circumstances and relationships. Old wounds connected to the bullying were opening up again, but in situations where, to others, it didn't make sense to get so angry. At his new school, the class was welcoming and comfortable. The kids were not mean, and they included him. But the old anger surfaced. He would become intensely angry in vaguely confronting situations. He got invited to birthday parties with his new classmates but would become angry at the smallest thing. At one party, seemingly out of the blue, he threw an unopened gift at the birthday boy. When his parents asked him what was up, he said that the birthday boy had taken the present he was going to give him before he'd had a chance to give it to him, and that, to him, that was stealing.

Kids can experience old anger that never got resolved and feel a need to defend themselves in response to a present situation where there is no threat and no one is being mean to them or excluding them. This boy would become furious and act out any time he felt that he was being treated unfairly. The old anger continued to fuel the fire of any new anger, making it more and more intense and out of proportion to any current situation.

MALADAPTIVE PRIMARY EMOTIONS

In emotion-focused therapy, we call old anger a *maladaptive primary anger* (Greenberg, 2017). A maladaptive primary emotion, like adaptive primary emotions, is a first emotion that comes up in a given situation. But the maladaptive ones are old emotions that first occurred in response to past injuries. If we didn't deal with them in the past, they will keep showing up in the present. In other words, maladaptive primary emotions are old, stuck emotions.

New Versus Old Anger

How can we tell the difference?	New anger	Old anger
The cause or reason for the anger feels . . .	Meaningful	On autopilot
The way the individual proceeds through the anger . . .	Fluid	Stuck
The quality of the anger expressed . . .	Fresh	Stale
The degree of the anger expressed . . .	Makes sense, appropriate to the situation	Doesn't make sense, out of proportion
The purpose of the anger . . .	Helpful purpose, protective	The purpose it serves is outdated

All basic emotions can become old, maladaptive primary emotions. It happens when we don't sort through and deal with painful emotions and don't meet the needs associated with those emotions. If a child is repeatedly left alone, feeling unsafe and afraid, then as an adult that person may be more fearful of being on their own. Logically, they don't experience being alone as unsafe, but the old feeling can resurface, and they can get anxious. Suppose a child says, "I don't want you to brush my teeth; only Daddy is allowed!" Kids do say such things, and parents for the most part try to take them in stride. But a mother who was abandoned and left alone as a child might fear losing her closeness with her child when she hears this. She might react by withdrawing from the entire bedtime routine rather than face down her fear of losing the connection with her child. The signals that the mother's body and brain send out, telling her that she is at risk of losing her loved one, are out of proportion to the bedtime routine's harmless tooth-brushing situation. In this case, the mom's old fear of being abandoned is triggered.

How New Anger Becomes Old Anger

How the anger was dealt with in the past	What happens in the present
Suppressed, ignored, avoided	Triggered by events in the present
Unresolved	Fuels fire to intensify and toxify anger in present
Didn't get healed	Gives us signals that there is an unhealed wound
Emotional needs of the anger not met	Directs us to unmet needs

Anger is not the most common emotion to occur as an old, maladaptive emotion. The most common old emotions are fear of being physically hurt and mistreated, fear of loneliness and abandonment, and shame for feeling not good enough. An old fear of mistreatment and injury comes from experiences of you or someone close to you having been exposed to violence or other serious trauma. An old fear of loneliness and abandonment develops when one has lacked sufficient closeness and a sense of belonging as a child or adolescent. It can be due to the death of a close family member or to parents not being present for the child for various reasons. Old identity shame, meaning shame over who you are, can be the result of two pathways. One is where the child or adolescent has received criticism that left them feeling humiliated, or they have been prevented from exploring and expressing themselves, and they have not received enough acknowledgment for who they are. This may be the case if parents have a strong drive to ensure their child does right and ends up on the right path and believe they must push them to develop what it takes to be successful. The other pathway to the child's developing primary maladaptive shame is when the child feels coddled or cushioned, physically or emotionally, giving them a feeling that they are not trusted to be able to be strong and make good decisions and even make their own mistakes and get back up. The rule of thumb with this is that one should not do something "for" someone that they could do for themselves unless they are an infant, ill, or very old— and even then, only with careful consideration. We can see that in both cases, parents can have the best of intentions, from wanting to toughen their kid up so the child is ready to deal with what life throws them, to wanting to protect them from hurt and emotional pain. These different approaches by parents are usually related to the parents' own experiences, upbringing, and unmet needs.

Maladaptive primary emotions occur in both children and adults. They start out as helpful, new primary emotions. They get stuck and come back to haunt us later in life when something goes awry at the time when they first occur. Maybe we were insulted, scared, or abandoned, without anyone to stand up for, protect, or be there for us. When we don't get help to articulate and handle our emotions, and we don't get our emotional needs met, the emotions go from meaningful and helpful to being repetitive, entrenched emotions that no longer make sense when they show up in the present moment. As we saw in the examples given earlier, these emotional reactions would have had a helpful function in the past, but they no longer protect us. In the present, they can do more harm than good and can even lead to symptoms of mental illness. Old stuck emotions such as fear and shame can be the driving force behind addiction, self-harm, and suicide. What can we do to prevent such serious problems when we all have these old emotions? We can use them, in ourselves and with our kids, as signals, telling us that something from the past is unresolved and needs attention. They can signal us to know that under our child's anger, and our own, lie vulnerable feelings and needs.

RESOLVING OLD, STUCK EMOTIONS

When we work with parents, one of our goals is to teach them how to prevent their kids' feelings from turning into old, stuck emotions. If this has already happened, then our goal is to support parents to help their child experience the feelings while knowing their parent is with them to help with the feeling and to meet the need. This process allows the child to get access to new adaptive primary emotions, such as assertive anger and compassion. These new feelings transform and replace the old unhelpful ones. The parents' and child's assertive anger in the present, in regard to the child having been scared or criticized in the past, can transform the old fear and shame. Grieving the fact that one has been in pain for a long time, and compassion for the child's experience, can help soothe old wounds and enable us to move on.

An example of this in a therapy context would be a child who was sexually abused and who did not receive adequate help to deal with the trauma and feelings connected to the abuse. Shame and fear are natural and useful during the abuse itself. Shame makes the child submissive, which reduces the chance of being harmed even more. Fear signals danger and the need to escape. The child needed help from an adult to get to safety and not be exposed to further abuse. The child also needed help to correct the damage done to their self-worth. If this child does not get help to cope with the shame and fear in the aftermath of the abuse, then the feelings of shame and fear will not go away, even though the abuse has stopped. When the child is a teenager or an adult, old fear and shame will show up in new situations when they are reminded of the abuse. This could be as simple as someone flirting with them, or raising their voice, or even a smell that takes them back to when the abuse took place.

It is possible to rewrite the story of that old shame and fear when the child is an older youth or adult. They can get help to change the story and correct misconceptions from that past experience. We can set the record straight with empathy for the child's suffering, with accurate assigning of who was at fault, and by directing the anger that has been floating in the child's life up to now, to where it belongs—at the abuser.

Let's look at how this works. We call it "changing emotion with emotion." The good news about emotions is that we can use them to heal other emotions that are old, painful, and stuck. Let's continue with the example of the child who suffered abuse. Often, parents feel hopeless despair when they discover this or another painful experience that has happened to their child. We can't imagine what will ever make it better and make our child's pain go away.

But let's look at this idea of changing emotion with emotion. As a parent, we feel anger toward the abuser. We can feel that this is a healthy response. We learn that the child, instead of having access to feelings of anger, was made to feel ashamed and maybe even at fault. If an adult can support a child to find within them the assertive anger that was not allowed a voice at the time, think about what happens. You can't in the exact same microsecond feel both ashamed and angry. Every second that the child can feel that healthy assertive anger, shame is pushed a little further out of the picture. As adults, we also feel compassion for the child. We see that the child has developed a feeling of disgust toward themselves over what happened. If an adult can support the child and help them find compassion within themselves for what they suffered, then compassion starts to take up room and squeeze out and make smaller the disgust—again, because you can't feel compassion for yourself and disgust for yourself in the exact same microsecond. Your brain just can't do both at the same time.

There is, therefore, a lot of hope for getting over past difficulties when you have emotion tools and skills to use them. When you help the child to feel self-assertive anger and compassion, these take up more space so that shame and fear will have less space. Sometimes the old, painful emotions can even disappear completely. Grief over what happened, care and concern for the child who was injured, and self-assertive anger and disgust toward the person responsible can replace the old, stuck, unhelpful bad feelings. The person transforms the inner perception of themselves. They no longer feel revolting or inferior, and they no longer blame themselves for what happened. They can have a new feeling of being safe with others and more content with themselves. They can feel that the blame truly is on the abuser. This person can be proud of having survived the trauma rather than feel ashamed of what happened.

EXPERIENCE IT: OLD ANGER IN ADULTS

Think back to a time many years ago—if possible, back to your childhood and the years that formed who you are. Think of a time when you were very angry, and for good reason. Was it a time when you didn't stand up for yourself and you didn't get help or support from others to be able to? Were you exposed to abuse, threats, or bullying? Did someone not respect your limits and boundaries, or did they prevent you from doing something you wanted to do, or from reaching your goals, without you being able to be assertive and say no? Did you feel unsafe because it was physically or emotionally dangerous for you to get angry? Was there no one around who could stand up for you? And have you never been able to express your anger to the person or people involved, nor able to talk to others about your anger?

Once you have a specific memory of someone insulting you, hindering you and your goals, or when you couldn't stand up for yourself, and when no one helped you, or you're unsure whether you got help, then really focus on that time. Imagine that you can see it as an observer and see how you, as that child, adolescent, or adult were feeling in that situation. Close your eyes and picture the scene.

Imagine that you are yourself in this demanding situation. Imagine how it feels to be in this situation. Notice how it feels in your body to be aware of this.

As the little child or vulnerable adult that you're imagining, feel into what you needed to have happen, what you needed someone to say or do in the moment or afterward.

Put words to what you need in the situation. "I need . . ."

If the need for self-assertion was not met, feel what that is like. Maybe there is some grief about that? Maybe hopelessness? Shame? Anger?

Whatever feeling arises, be curious about it, in a kind way. How do you carry this unmet need now, as an adult? Is there someone you can talk to about your old anger? Is there someone who can help you to get in touch with this old emotion?

Later in this book, we explore how to work with children's old anger and unmet needs for self-assertion, and then maybe you can use some of that new knowledge to meet your own old anger. It is valuable to know if you are carrying old anger and, if you are, how it is affecting you today.

If you can't come up with a specific memory, that's okay; that can happen. You can come back to this exercise another time.

EXPERIENCE IT: OLD ANGER IN CHILDREN

Think back in time, from years ago right up until yesterday. See if you can think of a time when your child had good reason to be angry but they weren't able to express it and you can't remember if you or any other adult stood up for your child. There are many valid reasons why an adult is not able to meet a child's emotional needs, and we get to that later in the book. For now, we want to investigate how it is for the child.

Has your child been exposed to abuse, threats, or bullying, by you or someone else? Have you or someone else been invasive and not respected your child, or prevented them from achieving their important dreams and goals? Where the child had no room for self-assertion or no option to set limits and say no? Where there was no reassurance for the child that it was physically or emotionally safe to be angry? Where you or someone else did not stand up for the child, or apologize for what happened? Where the child was unable to express their anger to you or to someone else or was unable to talk to someone about why they were angry?

Once you think of a specific example of when the child was insulted, or hindered, or where there was no room for them to get help, or you are not sure if they received help, then focus on this situation. Imagine that you are seeing it from the outside, as an observer. What do you observe about the child or adolescent in this situation?

Imagine that you are the child in this challenging situation. Feel what it's like to be them. Notice how it feels in your body.

As the child, imagine what you wanted to have happen, or what you wanted someone to say or do, in the moment or afterward.

Think about what you need in the situation and put words to it. "I need . . ."

If the need for self-assertion was not met, feel what that's like for the child. Maybe there is some grief that arises for them? Maybe a feeling of hopelessness? Shame? Anger? Whatever feeling shows up, be curious about it in a kind way.

How does the child still carry the unmet needs from this situation today? Is there someone they can talk to about their old anger? Is there someone that can help them to connect with this old anger? Can you help your child?

You will get advice on how you can do that in Part II of this book.

If you are not able to come up with a particular example, it could be because your child is good at being self-assertive and there are not many times when that need for self-assertiveness was not met. Can you think of a time when your child was able to assert him- or herself? Try to imagine a situation you remember, and play it out like a film in your mind. What do you see? Imagine you are your child in this situation. How does it feel in your body? What happens with your heart and muscles? What do you feel? What do you want to do? What do you say and do? How does it feel? Praise the child for being able to assert themselves, and remind them that it's very important that they be able to do this. Do this as an exercise for yourself, but also tell your child this the next time that you are talking with them about being angry.

HOW DO YOU DISTINGUISH OLD ANGER
FROM CLOAKING ANGER?

Both old anger and cloaking anger can give the wrong information about what you need in the present moment. However, old anger belongs to the past and is attached to an old, unmet need. The old, unmet need may be to create a protective boundary, to be self-assertive, or to remove obstacles that prevent you from reaching an important goal. For children, there can also be an unmet need for someone else to come in and create the boundary, remove obstacles, or be assertive on the child's behalf.

On the other hand, cloaking anger is anger that protects you from feeling both old and new painful emotions. This form of anger can also sit on top of, and cover up, old anger. Cloaking emotions are not connected to their own emotional needs. In other words, old anger is connected to the original wound that never healed, whereas cloaking anger protects you from feeling the old wounds. Cloaking anger sends the wrong signals to those around us and is confusing for everyone.

Old anger acts like fuel on a fire when the person, in a new situation, is being unfairly treated or prevented from reaching an objective. The new situations are often a reminder of the original, old wound. Cloaking anger tends to hide more vulnerable feelings, like loneliness, shame, or fear.

Old anger and cloaking anger have different functions and origins, but both types of anger can create problems. The two kinds of anger are not always easy to distinguish, especially when you're face to face with a raging 10-year-old or a furious teenager.

It's helpful if we can understand simply that anger is not just anger. Being curious about where the anger comes from, and what role it plays, can provide important information about your child and their needs. Is your child trying to meet an old unmet need for self-assertiveness or limit-setting that belongs in the past or to another situation or relationship? Or is your child trying to protect themselves from other emotions that are difficult to feel and that they don't know how to deal with?

In terms of how they are expressed, old anger and cloaking anger are quite similar. Both can seem "inappropriate," out of keeping with the situation, and difficult to understand. Both can be accusatory and intense. It can be challenging to feel empathy for old or cloaking anger. In spite of their similarities, it is still possible to distinguish between them if you look closely. Old anger is marked by the fact that it is always the same old story being told. "I'm always so unfairly treated"; "I'm never picked first"; "People always ruin things for me." Cloaking anger, however, is always accusatory against the other (e.g., the parent), a thing, or an occurrence. "You are so unfair"; "I hate you!"; "You are so mean." The most important thing, in both cases, is to put the emotional reaction into context and explore with the child what the difficulty is. You can also have this as a rule of thumb: If you are in doubt, it's likely cloaking anger. Cloaking anger is much more common than old anger.

Sometimes children aren't really angry at all, they just act angry. This confusing scenario is the topic of the next chapter.

CHAPTER 4

CHALLENGE 3: ADOPTING THE STANCE OF ANGER

Have you ever had the experience of your child adopting a stance of anger, when your gut tells you they aren't really having a primary emotion? When you sense that they aren't actually angry? Have you noticed them almost pretend to be angry or offended in order to achieve a goal? Maybe because they want something or a reaction from someone? Imagine a small child standing with her arms crossed, very upright, furrowed brows, narrowed eyes, and a clenched jaw—angry! The child says: "I want another brownie! You are so mean!" Dad responds, "So, you want another brownie, angry monkey?" and he tickles her on her side. The little girl's face instantly transforms and breaks into a massive smile. She laughs and says, "Can I have another brownie?"

The tale of the brownie is a common, everyday example of the third challenging scenario: what we call *instrumental anger* (Greenberg, 2017). It's a kind of anger stance that is not completely genuine and that comes up in situations where the child is adopting the stance of anger as a way to communicate what they do or don't want. With very young children, it can even be kind of cute. Children learn what works. They might have figured out that, as parents, we don't always have the strength to deal with their anger and that we give in pretty easily when they are angry.

Other kids have found that their parents are a bit uncertain or afraid when their child gets angry, and so the kids can then get out of doing things they don't want to do. Note that we're all different, and other parents are more likely to give in when children show vulnerable instrumental emotions, like forcing out some crocodile tears.

INSTRUMENTAL ANGER

Instrumental emotions do not have specific emotional needs associated with them the way primary emotions do; instead, they have a dual function of, on the one hand, accomplishing or achieving something, and on the other hand, of being indicative of the child's not having found a more direct way to have their needs met. These adopted feelings are a normal part of a child's development. It's also the case that kids learn which ones work through interactions with us, their parents.

Although a child may occasionally be deliberate in adopting an anger stance, for the most part it is an automatic, learned response. An example of a more deliberate use of adopting an anger stance might be when a teen is tired of the interaction the parent is trying to have with them. Suppose the teen knows that this parent does not do well with confrontational anger. The teen adopts an anger stance, the parent reacts by giving up and walking away, and the teen has accomplished the goal of getting the parent to stop bothering them. On the other hand, if a child grows up in a family where others use anger to be heard or to make something happen or stop from happening, or if anger is the only emotion that seems to work and get a response, then the child may develop an automatic tendency to react with anger when they are wanting to express their needs and wants. In both cases, it can take us down the wrong path to see the child as intentionally trying to manipulate the situation.

Seeing children as manipulative can be like seeing parents as unmotivated—we don't think either is accurate or helpful. We see instrumental anger as a sign that parents and their kids haven't had the chance to figure out how the child can express needs in a way that parents can hear and respond to and how parents can meet their kids' needs while still protecting their own well-being—and their sanity!

Instrumental anger can also serve a useful social function. Imagine that your child's friend is furious with his older brother. Even if your child doesn't really get why his buddy is mad, it can be strategic to seem mad on his friend's behalf. It shows that he supports his friend and may avoid having the friend get mad at him, too. At other times, a child may adopt a stance of instrumental anger out of loyalty, fear, or to avoid being shamed. For example, youth who are prone to getting into fistfights as a group often do so when in fact only one of them has an issue with the opponent. The others may jump in for the reasons just described—they may adopt an anger stance with the opponent even though they feel no actual anger toward them. This may, again, be out of loyalty to the group; out of a fear of being targeted themselves; or out of a fear that, were they not to show anger at the opponent, they may risk being shamed for being seen as a coward or as disloyal. In this way, instrumental anger can protect the child socially, even if others involved may pay a price.

As adults, we use instrumental anger quite often when we parent. This can be useful and is not necessarily a bad thing. We once worked with a mother whose two kids were very responsible and rarely acted out or were disobedient. She had begun to worry that they were too responsible. One morning, Mom went into their bedroom and saw that they'd scribbled over the entire wall with a marker. Mom did not feel angry. In fact, she felt a bit proud. She valued a bit of rebelliousness and had been concerned that her kids' tendency to comply could end up being problematic for them. She was therefore happy and relieved that the kids had a mischievous side. She knew it would be absurd to praise them and tell them it was great that they had drawn on the wall and that it might even take away from the mischievous quality if Mom were to approve. In the absence of feeling actual anger at the kids, she adopted an appropriate stance of anger and scolded them for drawing on the wall.

One father told us that his son, who had been bullied quite badly over a long period of time, had finally beaten up one of his bullies. At the request of the school, the father spoke sternly to his son, although he was not actually angry with him. He understood his son's actions and thought it was good that he had stood up and defended himself. He pretended to be angry with the boy to appease the teacher and principal, out of his own fear of what they would think of him if he didn't. That then became the issue that this dad wanted to grapple with and what we often face in our parenting; that is, how do our own feelings interfere with doing what we want and need to do for our children? This dad wanted to support his son's self-assertive anger but felt he had caved to the pressure of the school rules. He ended up apologizing to his son for the reprimand, which, although more symbolic than severe, still conveyed a message that his son had been in the wrong. The dad returned to the school and told them that they and he had been wrong to correct his son. He pointed out that he had tried to get the school to intervene with the bullying, but the school had said that kids must learn to sort out schoolyard challenges for themselves. The father made the case that if the school was going to leave it in the kids' hands, they could not then fault the kids for the way they dealt with it. The school staff conceded that it was a good point, the matter was dropped, and the son had his father's support in having defended himself with self-assertive anger.

HOW DO YOU DISTINGUISH ADOPTING A STANCE OF ANGER FROM CLOAKING ANGER?

It can be difficult to distinguish instrumental anger from cloaking anger, even though they have very different functions. Both types of anger can be intense. Anger that works as a cloaking device is, to a greater extent, a feeling one has, whereas instrumental anger is a feeling one takes on or adopts. Instrumental anger can come across as such—as artificial—and not as genuine as cloaking anger. Having an empathic connection with someone who is adopting an angry stance that seems fake is even more difficult than with someone who protects themselves with anger as a cloak to hide their true feelings. Instrumental anger can disappear from the facial expression and body in an instant. You can see a rapid shift in the emotional expression of a child who is instrumentally angry. They can suddenly go from being furious to neutral, or even cheerful. Other kinds of anger often linger a bit longer in the facial expressions and in the body, as if the feeling takes time to leave the person. Authentically angry eyebrows take longer to smooth out than the posed, even comically wrinkled eyebrows we see with instrumental anger, especially in the young child who tries to feign anger. The body takes longer to relax and to feel light and free with other types of anger, whereas with instrumental anger the posture can change very quickly. Instrumental anger can flip on and off like a switch.

WHEN ADOPTED ANGER BECOMES A PROBLEM

It can be unpleasant, even frightening, when young people or adults use instrumental anger to achieve a purpose. Instrumental anger is sometimes paired with a feeling of superiority and bravado. An extreme example would be Tony Soprano, the crime boss from the TV show *The Sopranos*. It's easy to imagine him hurting someone,

Cloaking Anger Versus Adopting the Stance of Anger

How can we tell the difference?	Anger as a cloaking device	Adopting the stance of anger
Intensity	Intense	Intense
Way the individual experiences it	The feeling happens to me	I adopt or put on the feeling
Genuineness	Comes across as genuine	Comes across as fake
How we react to it	Hard to have empathy	Harder to have empathy
Duration of the feeling	Gradual shift toward recovering equilibrium	Sudden shift, like an on/off switch

not because he is authentically angry but rather to demonstrate his power. If children or adolescents use a lot of instrumental anger with parents, siblings, and others, in combination with aggression and acting out, it can be harmful to the child and difficult to deal with for those around them.

Children who use a lot of instrumental anger will be in danger of not being liked by their peers. It can lead to them getting a lot of negative feedback, making it even more difficult for the child to express their wants in an appropriate way. They can end up feeling unfairly treated and becoming genuinely angry. It is therefore important to set and maintain good limits with the behavior that accompanies instrumental anger and not to allow the adopted stance of anger to defeat the parents' determination or undermine the child's best interests. At the same time, although instrumental anger is not connected to specific emotional needs, children who resort often to instrumental anger have a need for understanding and for help in understanding and managing their emotions. They especially need help to learn how they can express their needs and wants in a healthy and appropriate way. They also need help to learn more sophisticated strategies for their social interactions.

EXPERIENCE IT: INSTRUMENTAL ANGER IN ADULTS

Can you think of a situation with your kids where you used instrumental anger? Where you adopted a stance of anger when you did not really feel anger? You might have given a consequence because your partner or your own parents thought you should and not because you believed it was necessary. You might have pretended to be strict and angry because you thought you should be. Or you may have used anger, without actually being angry, to get your child to do what you wanted quickly, like brushing their teeth, getting to bed, or getting out of the house in the morning.

Think about what happened, what you were thinking, and what feeling showed up for you in that situation. How did you learn to use instrumental anger? Did you learn it from someone in your life? How do you feel when you think about your own instrumental anger? If you notice that you feel a bit embarrassed about it, see if you can meet that embarrassment with kindness and understanding. What would you like to change? And when do you think it's okay to use instrumental anger?

EXPERIENCE IT: INSTRUMENTAL ANGER IN CHILDREN

Can you think of a situation where your child used instrumental anger, that is, where they adopted a stance of anger when they didn't really feel anger? If your child occasionally shows instrumental anger, are there other instrumental emotions in the mix? Is she adopting a scared stance or crying crocodile tears?

If you can think of an example, or two, of when your child has shown instrumental anger or other instrumental emotions, take a moment to think about it. How did they learn to use anger in this way? What is your response to your child's instrumental anger? Are you irritated or afraid? Do you set limits, or do you give in? Do you laugh at or make fun of their seemingly fake emotion? What other reactions do you have? What makes you react the way you do? What is it about? What experiences have you had that have led you to have this particular reaction to your child's instrumental anger? Reflect on these questions, and try to come up with some answers before you move on.

What does your child need when they adopt a stance of anger that they may not really feel? What do they need from you? Don't worry if it's hard to come up with answers; you'll get help with this later in the book when we go into more depth about how parents can handle their child's anger in a way that works for parent and child.

Regardless of the type of anger, few things are more challenging than when a child becomes aggressive and threatening, which is the fourth challenging anger scenario. What happens when a child becomes aggressive? Why does it happen? And what is the difference between anger, aggression, and violent behavior? These questions are answered in the next chapter.

CHAPTER 5

CHALLENGE 4: WHEN ANGER GETS AGGRESSIVE

Children who act aggressively and out of control are a huge worry for parents, as well as for teachers and other adults in their lives. Some children act out only at school. Other kids destroy the house and hit their parents while feedback from school says they sit quietly, concentrate, and are well behaved in class. It can be a mystery as to why anger and aggression come out in certain places while the intense emotions and problematic behavior are not apparent elsewhere. Some children resort to physical violence only toward adults. Others lash out only at other kids. Among the parents we have met, the biggest concern when their child acts out is when violence is directed at younger siblings. Having an aggressive big brother or sister can cause serious and lasting harm, physically and emotionally. We have had numerous adults in therapy who were exposed to violence from a sibling when they were young, and it can have a long-lasting and traumatic impact. Some are not able, or willing, to have any contact with the sibling who was violent, even as adults. Others blame their parents for not protecting them. It goes without saying that when a child's anger turns into aggression and out-of-control behavior it is extremely challenging and creates a highly complex family dynamic.

A first important step is to know the difference between anger and aggression. An understanding of the difference is essential to being able to create protective boundaries without damaging the child's capacity to feel healthy anger or weakening their ability to assert themselves. What, then, *is* the difference between anger and aggression, and how can we understand strong aggression in children?

THE IMPORTANT DIFFERENCE BETWEEN ANGER AND AGGRESSION

Anger is emotion. *Aggression* is action. There is a difference between feeling angry on the one hand, and screaming, making threats, or slamming your fists on the table on the other. We can be angry without being aggressive, and we can be aggressive without feeling anger. Violence, which is behavior that can harm others, is the most serious form of aggression.

Note that there are also occasions when an aggressive attitude is appropriate, like on the football field or in a debate, especially if the opponent is themselves aggressive. Another example of appropriate aggression is to protect oneself in a threatening situation. We can therefore have positive aggression that is not harmful or destructive but instead is a resource, in competition or in other important areas of life. However, throughout this book, when we talk about aggression, we are referring to problematic aggression in the form of verbal or physical acting out, and not to the positive type of aggression.

Aggression can take the form of verbal comments or violent acts. A simple definition of *aggression* is the intention to harm someone who does not want to be hurt (Baron & Richardson, 1994). However, we don't necessarily think consciously about wanting to hurt someone when we become aggressive or violent. It can be experienced as a blind rage—the curtain falls, and everything goes dark. Sometimes we call it "seeing red." The behavior is often about eradicating or stopping something or someone that is causing us emotional pain (Ferris & Grisso, 1998). The goal of the aggressive behavior is to stop the painful feeling or to achieve some other similar goal (Meloy, 1988). In other words, aggression can be an attempt to solve a problem. Even when we see aggression as unacceptable and harmful, it's important to recognize that it is motivated by a need for protection—and that it works. Thus, although the aggression is problematic, the motivation can be healthy in that it is an attempt to meet an unmet need. Keeping this in mind can help parents enormously when they face the very problematic reality of their child's aggressive behavior. It also guides parents to start finding a solution, by trying to identify the child's unmet need.

Aggression and violence most often arise from secondary anger that cloaks underlying feelings of vulnerability. Cloaking anger, which protects us against those underlying painful feelings, can be so intense that those experiencing it may resort to aggressive acts. It's important to remember that cloaking anger is genuinely felt anger, in the same way self-assertive anger is. The difference is that cloaking anger is about protecting oneself from other emotions that are too difficult to handle, rather than it being about standing up for oneself.

The second most common source of aggression is instrumental anger. Some people use violence to impose their will or get what they want. One reason why someone might be aggressive when they are adopting an angry stance is to get a point across when no other emotional persuasion seems to work. Think of a child who is very upset over a long period of time, but no one meets their emotional need. One day the child might pick up a cup and throw it on the floor, not because they are angry but just to be seen and heard.

We can also use aggressive behavior and violence to defend ourselves. Aggression can be a behavior that actually arises from healthy, self-assertive anger. When one child hits a child of the same age, the child who is hit might fight back in self-defense. Defending oneself physically can be important in social interactions between children, in spite of our own varying opinions as adults on whether or not kids should fight back. A child who asserts themselves physically will be more likely to avoid further physical attacks. We have heard many stories from adults who were bullied as children and who say that the bullying stopped when they fought back. There are also stories like this about domestic violence: that the violence from the mother or father ends when the child gets bigger and is able to assert himself physically and fight back. The problem is that even if retaliation can put an end to bullying and violence, if the child is in an ongoing and toxic situation where they have to fight back repeatedly, where it's not just occasional schoolyard fisticuffs, it can be the beginning of a violent life path.

Some children are aggressive because the aggression has been helpful, or even necessary, in the past. At some point, however, it no longer works. On the contrary, the aggression that previously protected the child begins to create new problems that need to be solved.

REASONS WHY A CHILD BECOMES AGGRESSIVE

The reasons why children become aggressive are a mix of temperament and what they have learned from experiences in their past. They often have challenges that they aren't able to solve, and they have a brain and emotional system that are not fully developed, and so they aren't yet equipped to handle their emotions on their own. Children also become aggressive because they've learned that it works, because they need aggression to protect themselves, or because the brain tells them to get angry time and time again and they don't know how to stop or not act out.

Children get aggressive for the same reasons as adults. Sometimes the aggression is due to painful emotions that the child needs to protect themself from. An example is a child who loses a board game, and feels very dejected and possibly ashamed, and so diverts the feeling by throwing the game against the wall. Other times, there are needs that the child is unable to express or that are overlooked or not listened to, such that the child's important emotional needs are not met. This might be a child who feels different and not a part of the family, without anyone in the family noticing or helping. For some kids, aggression can be an attempt to solve an underlying emotional problem and to be seen, heard, understood, and met in regard to something important.

A child can also become aggressive when someone treats them unfairly, insults them, or tramples over their boundaries, but the child doesn't know how to express the anger in a healthy, self-assertive way. However, the most common situation that triggers aggression in children, adolescents, and even in adult children still under their parents' roof is when parents set limits and expectations and the child wants to do something they aren't allowed to do, or won't do something that they have to do. This is usually when the sparks fly. The classic example of when anger boils over into aggression is when an adult looks their child in the eye and says: "If you don't . . . then . . ." When a child acts out aggressively in this type of situation it is most likely because there are vulnerable feelings underneath the anger and aggression.

Here is an example: A child is unable to sit still and concentrate at school because the family cat died a few days ago. The teacher is increasingly strict in setting limits and eventually says, in a stern voice: "Look at me when I'm talking to you! If you can't sit still in your chair, then you have to go and sit by yourself in another room." The child storms out of the class and hides in the washroom. The child and the teacher are concerned about two different things: The child is sad and needs comfort, whereas the teacher wants the child to sit still and learn.

There are other explanations as to why children can appear to be more impulsive in their aggression and violence than adults. A child's brain and emotional competence are not yet fully developed. Aggressive children, adolescents, and young adults in their early 20s usually become less aggressive as they grow and mature into older adults. Aggression fades with the years. Aggression can then increase again when we get older and our cognitive functions are reduced again. If you have a child who is particularly aggressive, you want ways to deal with the aggression in the moment that will lead to a better outcome for all. We find that parents feel far more empowered and effective in dealing with their child's aggression when they can respond with clear limits and expectations conveyed with understanding and inquisitiveness rather than give lectures and consequences that are punitive and rigid.

Some people, adults and kids, have a neurological condition or developmental disorder that makes them inclined to become frustrated more quickly. Some of these children may never manage to learn advanced ways to express their wants and needs. Nevertheless, many of the same triggers will lead them to act out: having limits and expectations imposed, longing for closeness, feeling humiliated, or feeling frustrated over not being understood. Everything in this book is just as relevant for children with developmental disorders and congenital cognitive challenges as it is for children without.

Another common reason why children are aggressive is because they learned it from their older siblings or from their parents. Children don't do what we tell them to do. They do what we do. Take a breath as you jump into this next section. Remember that we see you, the parent, as the one equipped to help your child learn to live with their anger as a normal and even healthy human emotion. Give yourself a break right here and now. Ask yourself, "Were my parents good anger coaches?" No disrespect intended to our parents, but often the answer is that they were not! Most of us who are parents did not ourselves have parents who were good anger coaches. Let's go easy on ourselves as we dive into understanding our own maybe less-than-ideal way of dealing with our own anger, which we came by honestly from not having someone to help us with our feelings and our aggression. If we don't get too hard on ourselves, that will make us way more able to figure out what we can do to support our children in their angry feelings and to defend ourselves in the face of their angry explosions.

AGGRESSION AND VIOLENCE IN THE FAMILY

Have you ever seen a look of shock in your child when you showed or expressed anger? Have you seen fear in their face? Have they told you that your angry face was scaring them? Have you seen humiliation in their face when you've criticized them? Have you taken in their reaction when you've pulled away and gone silent with simmering frustration? Have you hit your child? A slap in the face? A smack on the leg? Grabbed them by the hair? Shaken them? Held them a little too tightly on the arm?

You are not alone. It goes without saying that violence is totally unacceptable, and threats and rage can harm a child's development. However, it's normal that when it comes to anger, things will at some points go absolutely wrong. It's even understandable that for some families, things can even go very wrong. Anger is tough, and tough to understand. We can't always make sense of why we get angry, make threats, or raise a hand. But we can say that when it happens, it happens for a reason, and this reason is often connected to the activation of an emotion that we don't like or accept. Aggression is our brain's attempt to have us avoid that painful feeling. The problem is that the aggression has a harmful outcome. There are very few exceptions to this.

If you are someone who has treated your child in a way that you now know is not okay, it is likely connected, whether you are aware of it or not, to a feeling in you—a sense of hopelessness, intense fear, deep shame, an extreme feeling of loneliness, or profound despair. Maybe you were scared, intimidated, or humiliated as a child. Maybe you had poor role models, and you weren't given help to cope with your difficult emotions as a child. Perhaps you were left alone, abandoned, or never recognized and respected for being who you are.

You had a need to protect yourself. Maybe anger and aggression were your best protection against painful emotions. Now that you're a parent who often feels furious, maybe it's because that little child that was you, who was hurt and who didn't get their emotional needs met, is still a part of you.

Many parents who meet with us say they have no problem with anger when it comes to colleagues or friends. It's only at home—when a partner or child challenges, criticizes, or dismisses them—that it becomes a challenge. Then things go off the rails. It is of course in our closest relationships and with those we love the most that we need to feel closeness, love, respect, acknowledgment, and a sense of belonging. When those are threatened, old wounds open up and stir memories, which then trigger old protective strategies. Those strategies can lead to us hurting those we love the most.

The profound regret, guilt, and shame we feel later, when we take our anger out on our kids, can turn into unhealthy self-criticism and even self-hatred. We have to defend you as parents here. The aggression came out originally in the past because it was behavior that paid off. It was behavior that protected you against physical threats or that protected you from an internal breakdown. You came by it honestly. It doesn't have to define you or determine the future of your family. Remember: It's not what happens, it's what happens next.

As a final note on this topic, there are some people who have certain neurological conditions that lead to aggressive and impulsive behavior and some who are not able to feel empathy. For these people, anger and aggression work differently than for the rest of us, and this is not what this book deals with. What we are referring to is the case for most of us, where if we show aggression, it is because we learned to use aggression to protect ourselves from feeling other painful emotions that we weren't taught to handle. This makes anger an extra challenge for those who have had especially painful experiences earlier in life. When shame and guilt are activated in new situations, the old shame, loneliness, or fear is also activated. Just know that if you've been made to feel that you were bad or unlovable, then where you are is understandable, and it doesn't have to define where you'll end up.

EXPERIENCE IT: AGGRESSION AND VIOLENCE IN ADULTS

Think of a time with your child when you were verbally or physically threatening and when you came close to or crossed a line that doesn't feel okay when you look back on it. What did you say? What did you do?

Try first to understand what happened. What triggered your anger? What did you feel in that brief instant before you got angry? Can you slow the scene down in your memory and find the moment you went from not being angry to feeling anger or rage? Close your eyes and try recall the feelings.

Emotions don't just arrive out of the blue and for no reason, even though it can feel that way. There is always a logical explanation, even if it's hard to figure out at first glance. Did you feel the person was dismissing or disrespecting you? Rejecting you? Walking away from you? Did you feel criticized? Were you scared or worried? Were you tired or hungry? Were you disappointed?

Embarrassed? Feel into it and allow your body to help inform you. Were you already having a bad day? Or was it a good day that suddenly took a bad turn? What did you need in the situation? What was your need? And what did you, deep down, really require the most? Did the situation connect to an old, unmet need? Or was the situation more related to challenges, problems, and worries that are current? Take some time to sit with these questions and try to find some answers.

While you are recalling the scene, imagine your child at the time. What's happening for them when you make an angry face, hiss, withdraw, shout, scream, threaten, or grab or hit them? What do you see in your child's face? What do you see and sense in their body? What is your child doing? What emotions are visible from the outside?

Now imagine that you are your child. Imagine that you can actually switch places in the scene so that you have your child's perspective. Feel what your child is experiencing. If this is hard to imagine, try sitting or standing the way your child was in the situation. Try to imitate their facial expression. Try to feel what it's like in your child's tummy and chest, where the feelings sit. What is stirring on the inside? What is your child feeling? Anger? Fear? Sadness? Loneliness? Shame? Guilt? Contempt, or even hate? If your child is angry, what's underneath the anger? Try to discover whether there are other feelings you haven't yet noticed. If you take the time to feel deeply into this (you might have to try several times), you will come up with something, because you know your child.

Still imagining that you are your child, what do you need? Take time to formulate what this need is. Write it down if you like. What does your child need from you emotionally? Do they also need help to solve a problem?

As yourself, the responsible adult, what do you feel towards your child right now? What would you like to say or do?

EXPERIENCE IT: AGGRESSION AND VIOLENCE IN CHILDREN

Think of a time when your child was verbally or physically threatening you or one of their siblings or someone else. What did your child say? What did your child do? Close your eyes and play the scene out in your mind.

After you have gone over the scene, imagine seeing your child. What is happening for them? How does their face look? Their body? Is there more than just the rage that you can see from the outside? Do they have trembling lips or tears in their eyes that show they have other feelings inside?

Now imagine that you are your child. Imagine that you can actually switch places in the scene so that you have your child's perspective. Feel what your child is experiencing. If this is hard to imagine, try sitting or standing the way your child was in the situation. Try to imitate their facial expression. Try to feel what it's like in your child's tummy and chest, where the feelings sit. What is stirring on the inside? What is your child feeling? Anger? Fear? Sadness? Loneliness? Shame? Guilt? Contempt, or even hate? Is there something underneath the anger, or is it self-assertive anger being expressed in an appropriate way? If it's cloaking anger, what feelings is the anger cloaking? Try to discover whether there are other feelings you haven't yet noticed. If you take the time to feel deeply into this this (you might have to try several times), you will come up with something. Once you are able to identify your child's vulnerable emotions, then continue with the exercise.

Imagining yourself as your child, what do you need? Take time to formulate the need, and even write it down, if that helps. What does your child need from you emotionally? What do your child's feelings need? What limits does their behavior require? Do they also need help to solve a problem?

Now return to being yourself. How do your child's rage and acting out affect you? What did you feel in the situation? Were you afraid? Angry? Worried? Sad? Defeated? Did your child's behavior awaken old memories and feelings in you? Think about this before you go on.

Ask yourself, the responsible adult with the information you have now gathered about your child, what do you feel toward your child in the present moment? What would you like to say or do?

Giving parents the support they need to look behind aggression and violence in this way can open a path to changing behaviors. Perhaps the tools in this book can help you and your family. You can start today to reduce the number of aggressive acts toward your child. By doing this, you are also helping to ensure that your children don't carry the aggression forward into the next generation. It's never too late to teach your children something new. It's not what has happened or what you or they have said or done. It's what happens next.

The most important thing as a parent is not whether you can identify exactly which type of anger your child has, where it comes from, or what underlies it. What's important is to build an awareness that anger and aggressive behavior in kids can have many causes. It can be rooted in emotions and needs that we, as parents, can learn to handle. You don't need to understand your child's anger 100% in order to help them with it. The next section of this book is all about how to respond when your child is angry.

II

RESPONDING TO YOUR CHILD'S ANGER

INTRODUCTION: RESPONDING TO YOUR CHILD'S ANGER

Validating a child's anger when we understand why they're angry is one thing, but what if we think the anger is unreasonable, incomprehensible, or malicious? Most parents are afraid of raising kids who aren't kind and well behaved. We worry that if we validate their angry feelings, we'll actually be telling them that aggressive behavior is acceptable. But contrary to what these parents may fear, when we let our kids know that it's okay to express anger, we actually avoid situations where we have to work hard to get them to calm down, change their behavior, or remember the good values we've taught them. When we show our children that anger is a valid feeling, it makes it easier for them to figure out whether other emotions are lingering under their anger or whether anger is in fact the main thing they're feeling, in which case they need to speak up and stand up for themselves. The result will be that the angry child has a chance first to settle down and then to solve their own problems more easily. When we show that we understand why our child is angry, through our words and actions, we validate the child's feelings of anger. There is definitely an art to validating anger that comes with aggressive behavior and anger that we don't understand. The first chapter of Part II, Chapter 6, shows you how to validate your child's anger.

When we validate our child's anger, it's easier for them to see the situation from a distance and to take someone else's perspective. In most cases, a validated child will come to their own solution. But what do we do when we validate the emotion but our child doesn't get any better at being able to solve their own challenges? Chapter 7 explains how to continue validating your child's anger while helping them problem solve.

Many things can go wrong when we respond to our child's anger. Thus, Chapter 8 helps you troubleshoot common problems with validation, and Chapter 9 helps you handle your own emotions in the midst of your child's intense anger. Sometimes we respond defensively or in a rushed way, and sometimes we make plain old judgment errors that can hurt our kid. No one is perfect! Chapter 10 helps you repair any ruptures in your relationship with your child using a thoughtful, heartfelt apology.

CHAPTER 6

THE ART OF VALIDATING ANGER

To validate means *to acknowledge.* Acknowledging that your child is angry is very different from suggesting that you understand your child's anger. You've probably already experienced it—saying "I understand how you feel" can make them angrier and make them throw back at you "You don't understand anything!" We suggest instead that parents show they understand by being more specific about what it is they see the child experiencing. To validate means to put words to anger that is present in the moment and to acknowledge in words what it is that makes the anger valid. Validation also involves acknowledging the experience as well as the feeling (Dolhanty et al., 2022). For example, we can add something about how lousy it must feel to get in trouble, as well as acknowledging that they feel angry. In this chapter, we review the basics of validating your child's anger.

DOS AND DON'TS OF VALIDATING ANGER

Your angry 6-year-old hits you because you said "No" to ice cream, and they scream "I hate you! You're so mean! Go away!" What is your immediate feeling? What is the first thing you want to say? Some of us might answer by saying things like "You don't mean that," "That's not true," "I don't believe that," "We love each other," or "You can't be angry just because you didn't get ice cream." These are examples of what we call *positive invalidation*. The impact is to say that the angry feeling is not valid, but when we say things that are kind and caring and therefore "positive" first, it's as though we think that makes it less invalidating than if we were critical. The goal has real care and concern behind it: We're trying to help our children not feel angry anymore. We deny or downplay the difficult feelings, thinking that will help to make it better. And doesn't it make sense that a parent would react this way? As much for our child's sake as for our own, we don't want there to be any suggestion that they really hate us because we denied them ice cream. Positive invalidation is a common response to children's anger, especially at times when we aren't angry or emotionally activated in the situation ourselves. But even if caring is the goal of positive invalidation, denying and downplaying anger never makes it feel better or go away. The child is left feeling that you don't get it, that they said something wrong, and that they're not allowed to be angry. "There's no need to be angry—we love each other and you're a good boy." The message is—your anger isn't valid, and anger is inconsistent with being a good boy.

At other times, our child being unreasonable and difficult does trigger our own anger, or other feelings, such as embarrassment at the child's behavior. We might respond with: "Don't talk to me that way!" "Hitting is not okay!" "There's nothing to get angry about!" "Just because you can't have what you want is no reason to be rude." We call this *negative invalidation*. We're still invalidating—there's nothing to be angry about, so being angry is not understandable or justified. But this time, instead of trying to soften and soothe their anger with what we see as positive alternatives, we communicate the invalidation with a negative or critical message: "There's nothing to be angry about—you're behaving badly, and I'm displeased." The message is—your anger isn't valid, and being angry is wrong or bad.

We also end up resorting to "value lessons" or lectures when our child is behaving unreasonably and acting out. We tell them the rule, for example, that they aren't allowed to hit or lash out. We tell them this as though they didn't already know our rules and values, as though they don't have good values of their own, and as though the middle of an emotional storm is a good learning opportunity moment! No one who is emotionally activated has access to their reason. Kids don't hit or kick because of a lack of knowledge about what behavior is acceptable. In fact, they can feel insulted that we don't know that in the moment—that we're so worried that they won't learn their lesson that we feel compelled to say it again anyway—"Hitting is not nice." Lectures about values, rules, and morals just make negative invalidation feel worse and add fuel to the fire of kids' anger.

Sometimes we send a "negative" message even when we do validate our kids' anger. This can happen when we're having a bad day or are stressed or exhausted. "I get it, you're angry—and you're ruining the day for everyone." "Of course you get angry at that because you never take 'No' for an answer." "I see that you're angry—what else is new?" "Okay, so that bugged you and now you're angry and you're no fun to be with. Is that what you want?" We call this *negative validation*. We convey that the anger is a valid feeling, but we say it in a way that's negative and critical. The message is—your anger is valid, and it makes you a pain to be with. Negative validation can feel a bit like we're being brought down to the kid's level and fighting back. But let's not be too hard on ourselves! We all end up there sometimes. It's just that we don't have a good feeling afterwards and we can see on our kids' faces that neither do they—and it doesn't help us to help them get better at feeling and dealing with their anger.

Empathic validation, in contrast, could sound something like: "You know what, it's no wonder you get angry when I say you can't have ice cream because it's your favorite, and you were counting on it. And it's hard to hear 'No.'" The message is—the feeling of anger is valid, plain and simple, in this moment. We don't address the behavior or restate the limit we set. We wait for the child's response, and only then do we take the next step.

Three elements are crucial for validation to be empathic:

- that as adults, we're able to put ourselves in the child's place, imagine how they feel, and have empathy for them;
- that we help the child put their feelings into words by guessing out loud and by expressing empathy through validation; and
- that the validation is heard and taken in by the child in a way that is useful for them.

It's not enough to feel empathy for the child without expressing it. It's not sufficient to express empathy by actively validating the child's feelings if the validation doesn't reach the child and resonate. This is not to say that it's not worth trying, even if you fail. But these three elements must be included for the validation to work. If you see that the validation has not worked, it may be worth reflecting on where things went wrong. Then you can gather important information on how to adjust the validation for the next time, to increase the chance that you really reach your child.

SEPARATE THE FEELING FROM THE BEHAVIOR

If we validate the feeling of anger and there was a behavior involved, such as hitting or being verbally aggressive toward us or a sibling, validation can help the child stop the problematic behavior or comply with the expectation. Validation increases cooperation. If they stop the behavior, that's a sign that the validation was helpful. It's okay if they still have feelings about it! Part of helping kids get better at feeling is not "shoulding" on their feelings. We don't want to confuse the behavior and the feeling and imply that they not only have to stop hitting their sibling, but they also have to put on a happy face at the same time.

If the child accepts the limit but still shows signs of feeling angry, we can simply validate the feeling again. "I can see you're still angry. That's understandable. I really appreciate you not hitting her anymore, even though you still feel angry." Or, if it's getting off a video game: "I can see you're still angry. I get it. You thought you had until 10 and I made you get off earlier and do homework. It's okay to be mad when we make you stop what you like doing and do stuff you don't like." We can't say enough about how much this simple step of validating their feelings after they've complied with a limit or expectation can help. We've seen parents work hard to get better at setting limits, and then, when their child is still angry, they think their limit-setting wasn't done right or wasn't successful. But don't assume that. Let your child have their feelings about how lousy it is to have to stop something they like to do or to start doing something they don't like. It's much less complicated to have feelings and behaviors not mushed together.

If the child's anger calms down and they accept the limit-setting, it may appear that the situation has been resolved. But if your child gets quiet and looks down, it may be that they feel guilty for having lashed out. Again, you can then validate the guilt: "I know you know you're not allowed to hit, so I wonder if you're maybe feeling a bit badly or upset now?"

If your child feels sad after you validate their anger, be aware that the sadness may be about something that the child was upset about before they got angry You can then validate the sadness, too.

If the child is not only still angry but also still hitting and kicking, and the validation did not work, the child's activation may have become so high that they can't take in what is being said. Then it can be validating just to stay in the room, sitting quietly. Later in this chapter we discuss in more depth how to handle acting out physically, but the first step is just to hang in there with your child. This itself can be validating. If you walk away from a relatively young child who is acting out, the child may perceive that you can't take it, that it's too much, or that it's frightening for you, which in turn can have a negative effect on the child's self-image.

One last important point is that it's never too late in the situation to start validation. Even if you started by getting angry, setting a limit, or trying to cheer up your child—and the situation didn't move in the direction you hoped—you can always still turn the situation around by validating. You have not lost the opportunity to validate just because it wasn't your first response. You can change strategies at any time.

THE TONE OF YOUR VOICE AND THE LOOK ON YOUR FACE

When validating anger, it's important to be aware of how we use our voice and facial expressions. If your teenager is furious and you say, "Of course you're angry," in a quiet voice and with a gentle expression on your face, it can provoke an even more enraged response. Anger needs to be validated powerfully. This is not to say that you should respond to their anger with anger. But you do need to speak with a firm and clear voice that matches and thereby reflects and validates the power of anger. An empowered stance makes the validation feel more genuine. It indicates that we are in the emotion with them and that we really get and accept it. People often confuse empathy with using a gentle tone. True empathy means that we are able to step into the other person's experience. In other words, true empathic validation is a validation that resonates with the child so that the child can benefit from it and become more receptive to your care. If the validation does not reach the child, then we've missed the mark and need to try again. Empathic validation of anger requires a powerful voice and a facial expression to match, but it is very different from actually being angry oneself.

For some parents, it's easy to validate anger in a way that matches the power of the child's anger. For other parents, it's really hard, and we have to challenge and push ourselves to be clear in our words and expressions. A hesitant attempt to validate anger can send a signal that you're anxious and don't know how to handle the situation, whereas a powerful validation signifies confidence. If we appear confident, then it will be easier to help the child move through their anger and become more calm. Some parents have to work on conveying this confidence and practice turning up the volume on their speech until they can genuinely and naturally present a clear validation of anger. As one dad put it, in the face of our child's anger we have to convey that we have broad shoulders and can take it.

Carly is 3 years old and does not want to have fish for dinner. First, she says she doesn't want to eat at all; then she says she wants it to be put in the freezer so it gets cold, but she gets a "No" in response to that request. She is so angry that her face turns red and she pees her pants. When her mom takes her upstairs to get her cleaned up, Carly refuses to undress. Mom takes off her pants and underwear. Carly refuses to take off her sweater and pulls it down over her legs as far as she can. Mom tells Carly to lift her sweater up so she can clean her up. Carly shouts and cries furiously in the shower and screams "NO!" Mom starts the validation:

> You wanted your dinner to be cold, but it was warm. You wanted Mommy to put it in the freezer, and I said no. And now I'm telling you to take off your sweater, and you don't want to. You aren't allowed to decide things for yourself, are you? No wonder you feel angry!

Carly listens attentively and with wide eyes as her mom speaks to her. Her crying stops the moment that Mom begins to validate her feelings. Now Carly lifts her sweater, and Mom is able to rinse her off.

REMOVE THE IMPLIED "BUT"

One important aspect of tone of voice is whether you convey an implied "but." People hear very clearly when there is a "but" coming. Our voice goes up at the end of the sentence when we say things that are positive and understanding, things that we know are going to be followed by a "but," and then we say what we actually mean. This is why teenagers often roll their eyes or even stop listening long before we get to the negative part of the sentence. Children hear it as the usual rant we go into when we want them to know that they've done something wrong. When we validate and there is no "but" implied, our tone of voice drops at the end of each sentence or phrase. We speak in a tone that is grounded and conveys conviction and sincerity. We take our time because we are often thinking more deeply as we go. We're carefully choosing the right words, and so there might be more pauses, as though each sentence is final. Think of hearing: "I get it" (tone goes up) . . . (but!) versus "I get it" (tone goes down signaling "I get it—period"). When you nail it in this way, your child is more likely to stop and listen and be interested to hear what you have to say.

However, the "but" is not easy to eradicate:

- "Of course you feel angry when the other kids treat you unfairly . . . but you can't hit them."
- "No wonder you get angry when Peter talks behind your back . . . but it's probably not easy for him because you're so much better than him at football."

- "Everyone feels annoyed when people lie . . . but if you hadn't told me that you'd freak out if I went in your room, then I wouldn't have lied about it."
- "Of course you feel furious when I shout and tell you to get off the computer . . . but being rude is not going to get you more screen time."
- "No wonder you feel upset and angry when the kids won't play with you . . . but I want to play with you!"

We often start by validating, but then it's so tempting to throw in a "but." We then follow it with something that conflicts with our attempt to acknowledge our children's feelings. We start by saying we understand, but our agenda of wanting to reassure them, enforce a rule or set a limit, or teach a lesson, takes over—and the child can feel it coming a mile away. At other times, we begin with warnings about values—for example, that hitting is not allowed—and so this stops the validation before it's even begun. Sometimes we can't help but tell our kids what we are unhappy with, and so the understanding we show at the start of the sentence is almost like an attempt to soften the criticism that we intend to get to eventually. In these instances, we aren't focused on what our child is experiencing but we're kind of using validation to couch the negative message in a way that we tell ourselves will be more acceptable because we dressed it up in validation. Our wish to have our children see the other's perspective takes over and gets in the way of us acknowledging their feelings. In highly stressful situations, we may begin to validate but then end up with threats and aggression. A "but" is often followed by something negative. Note that it can also be a positive invalidation that crushes our attempt to validate. We might start off well but end up downplaying the child's emotions or diverting their attention elsewhere in an attempt to take away any painful feelings.

There are several reasons why we build up a sentence by saying something validating first and then cut the validation off at the knees. Sometimes we mean well and start to validate—we truly want to empathize with our children's pain—but then comes our need to say something positive. We end up in positive invalidation, which means that we have still not acknowledged the emotion. At other times, we're annoyed at our children, and we try to be understanding but can't quite get there. Our worries about our children, and about their behavior, can also lead us to giving warnings and threats. It also isn't the norm to use validation, and we haven't learned how to do it, nor have we experienced others, such as our own parents, speaking to us in a way that is validating.

Thus, validating and then using a "but" that is followed by cheering-up or criticism nullifies the validation. This duty and the responsibility we feel to offer a moral lesson or help our child see the situation from the other's point of view make our message more confusing than clarifying. We start a conversation with conflicting intentions, and then it becomes difficult for the child to understand where we are headed—or, more likely, they can tell exactly where we're headed, and they tune out. Instead, we want to get our agenda clear in our heads before we start so that we can focus on what the child needs now. Do they need care, validation, problem solving, limits, information, or an apology?

REPLACE "BUT" WITH "BECAUSE"

To help us deal with this tendency to say "but," we swap the word "but" with "because." Using "because" instead of "but" can help us be successful with our validations. If we hear ourselves saying "but," we can go back and use "because" or "when" instead. The word "because" helps us to convey that we understand the child's feelings and we think that those feelings are valid:

- "Of course you feel angry when the other kids treat you unfairly, because it hurts."
- "No wonder you get angry when Peter talks behind your back; that's not what good friends do."
- "Everyone feels annoyed when people lie, so no wonder you were mad when I lied to you."
- "Of course you feel furious when I shout at you and tell you to get off the computer, because you're having a great time, and I ruin it by shouting."
- "No wonder you feel upset and angry when the kids won't play with you, because it's no fun to play by yourself."

The point is that when we begin to validate, the validation has the greatest impact if we do it wholeheartedly. Teaching a child good values comes indirectly through validation. If more is needed, we can teach values at a later time, when the child is calm and receptive to learning. Children's brains are not receptive to insights, teachings, and messages when they are very emotional. The same goes for boundaries. Children need boundaries, but in some instances we need to focus on the validation and work on boundaries later. The need for boundaries is also lessened when we use validation because children then have less need to argue and are less inclined to misbehave. This is also the case when it comes to attending to the child's emotional needs. Sometimes a child is receptive to comfort, acknowledgment, or protection right away, but other times we have to go through the validation to get to a place where the child can receive the comfort and reassurance.

As you read this, you can use the concrete examples of how we word things when validating, so that it's easier to get started. As you progress, you can find your own ways to express yourself that suit you and your child.

RETELL THE STORY OF WHAT HAPPENED

A good way of validating young children is to retell the story of what happened—and include the feelings. Sometimes it's helpful to state the reasons for the anger before we put words to the feeling itself, even if the classic form for validation is to name the feeling first and then follow with all the "whys." Experience shows that it is sometimes easier to capture a child's attention by retelling the story before we put the feeling into words. Many adults have likely had the experience of a child yelling "I am not angry!" when we say that we can see they're mad. In this case, starting with the reasons for the anger before actually putting words to the emotion itself can be a smart move when we want to validate a child who does not like it when we tell them how they're feeling.

Sander, 9 years old, has divorced parents and lives half the time with each of them. The boy is at his father's house, and they're watching TV together on the couch. Sander tells his dad that he feels squished and wants more space. He feels annoyed at his dad. Sander then asks if he can have a Coke, and his dad says he can. Sander asks his dad to get it for him, but his dad says he can go to the kitchen and get it himself. Sander is suddenly furious and shouts at his dad.

> *Sander:* You get it for me! If you don't, I'll smash your face in!
>
> *Dad (shocked and confused, and now angry that Sander has shouted at him):* Why are you behaving like this? I'm being nice letting you have a Coke, and then you scream at me because I won't get it for you?!
>
> [Sander runs up to his room and slams the door. Dad follows him and opens the bedroom door.]

Dos and Don'ts of Validation

√ DO empathically validate the feeling before addressing the behavior ("It's so frustrating when you're really into your game and I come along and say it's time to do homework").

√ DO separate the feeling from the behavior ("Having a little brother can be super annoying. No matter how annoying he is, it's not okay to hit him").

√ DO use tone of voice and facial expressions to convey empathy (e.g., to match the energy of anger, use a strong tone, and a facial expression that says, "I get it!", not one that says "Aw—I'm sorry"; e.g., with sadness, use a face and tone that suit the particular child so that the one who seeks comfort gets comfort and the one who is feeling ashamed of the feeling can feel understood via a passing gesture rather than feel called out with a big display of what they would experience as pity).

√ DO retell the story of what happened ("You waited so patiently for it to be your turn. And you had to wait a long time. Then when it was your turn, it was time to get ready for bed. That feels so unfair").

✗ DON'T give positive invalidation (When they're annoyed at their sister . . . Don't say: "Just think of all the ways that having a sister is fun").

✗ DON'T give negative invalidation (When they fail their driving test . . . Don't say: "That test is easy. Your sister passed the first time she took it. You must have really messed up to make them flunk you").

✗ DON'T give negative validation (When they suffer a romantic breakup . . . Don't say "Get used to it. The kind of love you're looking for just doesn't exist. It's better to know that now rather than keep getting your heart broken").

✗ DON'T immediately lecture about values, rules, and morals (Don't say "You've got to learn to share better if you want to make friends" or "Why is it that every time I ask you to do something you roll your eyes?" or "If you had worked harder at it you would have gotten the result you wanted").

✗ DON'T negate your validation by saying "but" (Don't say "I know right now this feels like a really big deal. But in time you'll see it really isn't that important").

> *Sander:* Get out of my room!
>
> *Dad (validating the boy's anger from the doorway):* You are really angry at me for something, and I am not sure what it is, but you must have a good reason for being so mad. It's not like you to get so angry when we're watching a movie and having a nice time. I'm not sure what's going on, but I guess that something must have happened earlier today. Maybe I said or did something that upset you. Or maybe something else happened that I don't know about. Whatever it is, I really want to hear about it. I know there is a good reason that you're angry.

Sander starts crying and says that he doesn't want to go to his mom's house on Monday because she is so strict and is always mad at him, and he misses his dad when he's there. Dad goes over to his son and comforts him. They have a good chat about how he misses him and what is bothering him at his mom's. After the chat, the boy feels better about going to his mom's house.

VALIDATING ANGER THROUGH A CLOSED DOOR

Lots of parents give up on validating when their child goes to their room and closes the door or lies on the bed and pulls their duvet up over their head. It takes practice to get used to the fact that emotional guidance can also be given through a closed door, or when a child has hidden their face in their hoodie or under a baseball cap, or through a text. When children are angry and push us away, the pushing away is often a misleading signal because what they really need is for us to continue to be present and try to reach them. The most common reason for a child to want distance when they're angry is because we've treated them unfairly or haven't respected a boundary, or they need to mark their own boundary by creating distance. It can be hard to distinguish between assertive anger and cloaking anger, but there are two things in particular to reflect on when this situation arises. The first is to think back on the day to see whether you, or someone else, has trampled on the child's boundaries, or if the child has had some kind of negative experience. The second is to assess the type of anger. Is it an accusatory rage? Or is the child showing clearly that they are angry and why? Cloaking anger is often accusatory and hard to understand, whereas assertive anger makes sense based on what the child is experiencing, and the child is able to speak about their experiences and needs.

WHEN THE ANGER IS DIRECTED AT OTHERS

Ahmed, age 12, has gone home a few hours before the school day is actually over. The school calls his father to let him know that his son has left. Ahmed's dad goes home and finds his son in bed with his iPad. In a stern voice, his dad asks why in the world he has come home from school and tells Ahmed that he has to go back right away. Ahmed gets angry. He says he hates school and doesn't want to go back. They're all idiots. Dad validates what he hears.

> *Dad:* No wonder you don't like school when you're not happy there. Of course you're angry if the other kids aren't being nice.
> *Ahmed:* Karl and Mohammed took my eraser.
> *Dad:* That's not okay. Of course you feel angry when they take your things!
> *Ahmed:* Well, they took it because I took Karl's pencil first, but it was two against one.

> *Dad:* Two against one isn't fair. [He lowers his voice.] So, you were angry and maybe you felt a bit left out?
>
> *Ahmed:* Yeah, I feel left out lots of times.
>
> *Dad:* Yeah, when you have a group of three best friends then it's easy to feel left out when two are on one side.
>
> *Ahmed:* Can you drive me back to school? I wanna give Karl his pencil back.

It can feel challenging to validate that a child has painful emotions connected to other people or environments, such as school. We may be afraid that if we validate those painful emotions connected to friends, their other parent, siblings, school, or teachers, then we are choosing sides in a conflict. We worry that this might make a difficult relationship even worse or create a bigger problem. On the other hand, if we don't validate a child's painful feelings connected to someone else, the child can feel like we're taking the other person's side and not listening to them. They might scream and lash out even more in order to be acknowledged. It's a balancing act to validate feelings without judging whether others have said or done something wrong.

Sometimes it's more important that we trust our child's experience and validate their emotions than it is to have an objective understanding of the situation. We can communicate that our loyalty lies with our child without downplaying someone else's feelings or experiences. If our child isn't able to navigate a difficult relationship, see someone else's perspective, or come up with a solution to a problem, then we can step in after we've validated. We can help them see the situation from a broader perspective and then suggest solutions—just not at the same time as validating. It's only once a child feels seen and heard, and has had their feelings taken seriously, that we can move into problem solving and offer help in a way that they're able to receive. It can also be the case that someone has actually mistreated the child, and so we need to support the child in the situation, including in conflicts with authority figures such as teachers or principals. However, supporting the child in the conflict situation does not mean that we are speaking negatively about, dismissing, or blaming the other person. The most important thing is to put into words how it must feel for the child to be treated badly or unfairly.

WHEN THE ANGER IS DIRECTED AT YOU

Suzanne, age 17, discovers that someone has been in her room and has read her journal. She storms into the living room and furiously accuses her mother. Her mom says that she has been so worried about her drinking and drug use that she felt she had to look at her journal. Suzanne is enraged and throws every swear word she can think of at her mom. The mom realizes that she has really crossed the line and validates the anger:

> *Mom:* You know what, you have every right to be angry at me. It was really disrespectful of me to read your journal. Those are your private thoughts. I completely understand that you wouldn't want me to read them. I could have told you that I was worried about you and asked you if you've been drinking or taking drugs. Instead, I acted like I didn't trust you. Of course you're furious at me for that. I didn't respect your boundaries at all.
> *Suzanne:* Yeah, don't do it again!

Some parents notice that it's easier to validate a child's anger when it's directed at someone else; we feel much more vulnerable and threatened when we have to validate anger that is directed at us. It's especially hard to validate their assertive anger when we have not respected a boundary or treated our child badly in some way. It's not enough simply to see the situation from our child's perspective and put words to how it must have felt for them. We also have to admit our mistake or bad decision. On the other hand, there are some situations that absolutely require the parents to breach the child's privacy, such as when there is a risk of self-harm. Our own feelings may then get in the way, and we may either not validate at all, or do it half-heartedly. When it's necessary to breach privacy it's always possible to repair things later. We can still acknowledge and wholeheartedly validate how awful it was that, for example, we read their journal. The most important thing is that we stay curious about our own emotions and about what prevents us from wanting to validate and stay aware of our own fears or shame and the impact they have on the important work of being our child's emotional guides.

VALIDATING ANGER, NOT AGGRESSION

A little sister (age 1) is having a cuddle on her mom's lap, and her big sister (age 4) feels jealous. The big sister reacts by biting her little sister. Many parents, when they learn about validation and start using it, still find it very difficult to validate a child's feeling when the child is misbehaving. And it's understandable why this is so challenging. It's as though validating the child's feelings is like saying that biting or hitting is okay. We worry that if we don't teach them properly, kids who act out at home will also have problems at school and with friends. Before we know it, we're also worrying about their future. Will they function well in society? Abuse alcohol and drugs? Be alone and lonely? Even end up in prison? Our problem is that we want so desperately for our children to have good lives. We worry so much that we end up raising them thinking about who they should be in 10 or 20 years, rather than what they are experiencing in the moment and how they'll feel in the next 5 minutes or for the rest of the day. When we are so focused on our children's long-term development, and what they need to learn to become well-adjusted people many years from now, we often miss what the child needs right here and now. Ironically, it is what happens here and now that will support their development into well-adjusted adults.

Right here and now, the 4-year-old who bites her sister needs supportive limits to stop the harmful behavior because it isn't good for her or her sister. What is the most effective way to stop the biting that will also help with the behavior for the rest of day? We need to help the 4-year-old with the feelings that result in her biting.

The best way to teach this is through validation. The adult might say,

> It didn't feel nice that your sister was getting all the cuddles, did it? You wanted some cuddle time, too. You saw that she was getting all the cuddles and that felt unfair. No wonder you felt angry, and maybe also a bit sad.

When the 4-year-old feels seen and understood, she will begin to understand that feelings are important and that they teach her about her own needs. The next time she feels jealous, instead of biting she might be able to say "I want cuddles, too." It's also fine to set a limit and say "No biting." But the limit-setting needs to be done after the validation, when the child is less emotionally activated. In this example, it could go like this:

> No biting. I get it that it's hard not to bite when you're angry at your sister when you see her getting so many cuddles, and it doesn't feel fair. But biting is never okay. Got it? Come—let's have a hug.

We thus validate the anger; we don't validate the behavior. We don't say, "It's no wonder you bit your sister when you felt angry and sad. It's hard to see her getting all the cuddles." An effective validation keeps the feelings in focus: "It's no wonder you felt angry and sad, because it's hard to see your sister getting all the cuddles." When we keep the feelings in focus, it's also easier for us to validate because it's usually the behavior that we can't accept. Validating the feelings is not the same as accepting or approving of the behavior. We can validate the feelings and set limits for the behavior.

COMFORTING THE VICTIM

Let's pause to address a key concern from the above example: The little sister who was bitten also needs to be comforted! There is no hard-and-fast answer as to which child should be validated first and at which point to insert the limit. It depends on the situation, how serious the bite was, and the type and intensity of the reaction from each child. You need to use the information in the situation to determine if you need first to deal with avoiding another bite, or if the younger sister needs comforting before you validate the older one's anger. It's important not to spend too long speaking to one child before turning your attention to the other. It's also helpful to explain to one child that they just have to wait a sec.

When the problematic situation is over, and the 4-year-old's emotions have leveled out—for example, later in the evening—then Mom can talk to her about how difficult it can be to have a little sister who needs so much attention. This gives the 4-year-old a chance to express more of her feelings about this massive change in her little world. If necessary, Mom can find yet another time to talk about how bites hurt and help the 4-year-old find other ways to deal with feeling jealous. It might also help if Mom and daughter agree on their own special cuddle time so that they are ahead of the game when it comes to the older sister's need for cuddles and for time with Mom apart from her little sister.

VALIDATE THE FEELING, SET LIMITS ON THE BEHAVIOR

Although emotions may be hard to understand or accept, they are always valid. Children feel what they feel, and we don't get anywhere by saying that their feelings are wrong. Feelings can cloak other feelings, or they can be old and come from the past, but they show up whether we like it or not; they sit in our bodies, and they are real. We are not helping our child when we deny anger, try to talk the anger away, try to set limits to stop the anger, or simply tell them that anger is not allowed. When we are able to communicate that our child's anger is valid, no matter what, when, where, why, or at whom, then we are teaching our children to listen to their emotions and to take themselves seriously. We end up with wiser kids who have a better chance of making good decisions. This applies even if your child has threatened you with a knife, hit you, or pushed your other child down the stairs. Validating feelings of anger is not the same as accepting violence and threats from the child. Validation can be perfectly combined with clear limit-setting and prevention of negative behavior.

For us to rise to the significant challenge of separating feelings and behaviors, and validating feelings while setting limits on behavior, we need first to take a good look at our own fears and worries, and at our own cloaking anger, before we can trust our abilities to validate our child's anger. This is especially true when the child is acting out. Validation can be one of the most effective methods to help a child find strategies for handling painful emotions that do not include aggression, threats, or violence. Let's dare ourselves to try this and to continue to practice it so that we can see the effect that validation has on problematic behavior.

Kenneth, age 9, visits his grandparents on Thursdays. Kenneth struggles with some of his school subjects and has trouble concentrating. When he visits his grandparents on Thursday and his grandma says that it's time to get his books out to do homework, Kenneth refuses. We can relate to his grandma's frustration.

Grandma: Sit down and do your homework now so you can go outside afterward. It will take you half an hour. We're going to do it now. Come here and sit down! You have to try and concentrate. Just write down the answers to these five questions. Concentrate! Stop messing about! Look at me! If you don't stop jumping around, you're not going outside at all!

Kenneth (throws his textbooks at his grandma and hits her): I hate you! I hate homework! I hate school!

Grandma realizes that she has to stop nagging. She stands up and validates with a loud and clear voice.

Grandma: Of course you're angry. Homework is horrible for you. And it's not nice for you when I push you and get impatient.

[Kenneth's facial expression softens, and Grandma can see that her validation is reaching him. She continues].

Grandma: I say that you just have to answer the questions and it will go quickly, but that's not true. It's hard for you to sit still, you don't understand the exercises, and we always spend a long time on homework. I understand that you feel furious at me and at your school. I wonder if it's hard when you see that others have an easier time with schoolwork and your little brother just speeds through his homework while you find it a lot harder.

Kenneth (nodding): Yeah, it's really hard. So, you get why I don't want to do my homework?

Grandma: I understand that you feel angry about having to do something hard, especially when I'm shouting at you. Then you don't get your homework done and you don't get a chance to go outside and play. I'm not sure, but I think that when you can't concentrate it makes you feel like you maybe can't do anything very well, or maybe that you aren't very smart?

Kenneth: Yeah, I feel like I'm bad at everything. I'm the dumbest kid in the whole world.

Grandma: That must really hurt to feel like that.

Kenneth: So then I don't have to do my homework?

Grandma: Well, here's the hard part. The homework has to get done, even if it's horrible.

Kenneth: What if we do one question, and then I get five minutes to play before the next question, and then do that for all of it?

Grandma: That's a great idea. Let's do that.

Although as adults we differentiate between validating emotions and behaviors, the child might very well see it as an acceptance of their behavior when we affirm their feelings. When his grandma understands how hard it is, Kenneth hopes she'll let him skip the homework. This gives us a unique opportunity to teach kids the difference between emotions and behavior. We continue to put words to their feelings and experiences, acknowledge their anger, and help them face and solve the problem rather than avoid it. When the difficult situation passes, and the child is no longer highly activated, we can talk to the child about the unacceptable behavior and examine, in a caring way, what their thoughts or feelings are about the behavior now. If the child feels guilty, we can validate that as healthy remorse and help them move forward from it.

COMPARING YOUR CHILD WITH OTHERS AND GUESSING THE UNDERLYING NEED

You'll notice that in the example of empathic validation, we have Kenneth's grandma compare him with his little brother. You'll see us do that in several examples in this book, where we have parents compare their child's experience with that of siblings or friends, when the child themselves did not make the comparison. You may wonder whether this could encourage a child to compare themselves negatively with others. Whenever possible, we gather as much information from the child as we can so they can use their own words. But children often have a difficult time connecting their feelings with their experiences and are therefore often unclear about what the feeling is. The reality is that children do compare themselves unfavorably with others, and then they feel inadequate. Parents may not dare to bring it up until the child does, fearing that acknowledging it will hurt more. But this avoidance on our part means we risk it taking a long time, maybe years, before the child is able to talk about it and work it through. It's up to us to get over our hesitation or fear, and to say out loud what we know our children are experiencing. The key is to guess what is happening in a way that is questioning and not accusatory. But it's a kind of knowing guess because we've seen our child's struggles. We therefore guess and make suggestions with a sense of "If I were the child" and then explore with them to discover more of exactly what they are feeling or experiencing.

Parents often hesitate to suggest to their child what they might be feeling, believing that if they don't know for sure then they shouldn't speculate. But we've had two observations about this. One is that parents often do know (as though in their bones), or at least have a pretty good idea of, what's up with their child. The second is that even if they get it wrong—partly or wholly wrong—it can still be extremely helpful. It's often a relief for the child to have someone put words to something that they couldn't express for themselves. Also, right and wrong guesses can be especially fruitful. If the parent gets it wrong but offers their version in a way that encourages the child to explore with them, the child can offer a correction that the parent's speculation helped them find.

> *Parent:* It sounds like you might worry that if you stay home to study, you'll regret not going if it turns out to be the best party of the year.
>
> *Teen:* No, you know what it is, Mom? I feel pressure to go, but this exam is super important to me. I worry that if I do go, it won't be worth it if I blow the exam.

You might be thinking that teens would never say this. But never say never. With parents helping them sort out their feelings, kids can surprise us with making good decisions! Also note how different this is from a parent stating "I understand" or "I see you're angry," to which the child will often reply angrily, "You don't understand anything" or "I'm NOT angry."

Now let's give you an example where the parent got it right: Agnes was a mom who worked really hard to learn how to validate her adult daughter's feelings. She had to fight her own instincts to do it. She worried it was like putting words in her daughter's mouth and robbing her of her self-determination. But one weekend, her daughter was so distraught that when Agnes's efforts to reassure her daughter failed, she took the plunge and tried the knowing-guess version of validation. Her daughter loved a good party but was becoming more serious about her schooling and wanting to work towards her career. She didn't have a drinking problem; she was just very social and loved a party. She had just decided to reduce her drinking because of her career motivation. But, as one might, she lost track. She had too many drinks and woke up the next morning realizing she had lost her phone. It was a brand-new phone that was expensive and that she had paid for with her own money that she'd earned. And she loved her new phone. She was beside herself. She was sobbing. Mom was kind and reassuring, saying, "It's okay. It's just a phone. You can have my old phone." But to all of this, her daughter just brushed her off and remained as upset as ever. Mom eventually just kind of slipped away. Once out of her daughter's room, Mom thought again about what she had learned from us about validation. She took a breath and thought, "I can do this," and then went back into her daughter's room.

> *Mom:* Do you know why I think this might be so devastating? I think it's because you made such a commitment to your studies and your career. And that was a really big step, and you felt really good about it. And you felt kind of proud of yourself, I think. And then you worked so hard at it. You've been going out less and making different choices and making a huge effort. And you've been doing great at it. And then you had one slip—just one little slip—and you had to pay such a high price for it. It just feels so unfair.

Neither mom nor daughter were very inclined to talk like this about feelings, but when Mom took a chance and took the plunge, her daughter followed suit—and Mom was astonished, and felt very reinforced, by her daughter's reaction.

> *Daughter:* That's exactly it. That's it, and I didn't even know it, and you figured it out. That's exactly how I feel. That makes me feel so much better to get it. I knew it was just a phone, but I couldn't help feeling it was the end of the world. And I couldn't figure it out, but you did.

This illustrates something we tell parents to remember—that "the thing is never the thing." The phone was not the thing. Another mom told us that this is her mantra: "I just tell myself—'the thing is never the thing.' Then I ask myself what the actual thing might be."

You might be wondering where the line is between a parent validating a feeling their child expresses or shows and speculating about a negative emotion they might be feeling. How will a 9-year-old experience hearing an adult say that they think he feels like everything is hard and that he doesn't feel smart? Parents often worry that introducing a feeling in this way could actually make the child feel it and thereby make them feel worse. But it takes a lot more to make someone feel a painful emotion than just guessing what the child is feeling and why. If the child doesn't relate to the suggestions, they will most likely just correct the adult. If the child says that they agree without it being true, or we suspect this may be the case, then we can try guessing again and validating. If they get angry that we keep getting it wrong, we can even do an apology if need be. There is a much greater risk in putting all the responsibility on the child to put words to their own feelings and experiences than making a wrong guess ourselves. We can end up overlooking a lot of pain, and the child can end up not receiving the help they need.

But, of course, parents don't relish the idea of validating when a child has painful feelings, like feeling stupid or ugly or fat. It makes sense that we feel scared of validating these types of feelings, and it isn't easy to overcome the fear that we will make things worse for our kids by putting words to the feeling we think they have but wish they didn't. But here's the thing: It's often the feelings that we are most scared to validate that our children most need us to validate. They need to understand what they feel, and why they feel that way, so that they can identify the underlying need and take steps to get that need met. The next chapter focuses on what happens next after validation: problem solving.

CHAPTER 7

FROM VALIDATION TO PROBLEM SOLVING

When our children are in pain, having conflicts with friends, being excluded by others, or envious of a younger sibling, it can make us feel that we have to solve their problems. This isn't surprising. Of course, we want to do everything we can to make sure our children are okay, and it's understandable that we want to jump into action when they are in pain. For some of us, being good problem solvers can be very tied up with our own sense of identity, and it might feel like it is one of the best things we have to offer.

The same goes for when our children are angry. We want to get rid of whatever is making them angry, either by setting limits and reprimanding them or by letting them have their way to make them happy. Parents may feel helpless and even despair a bit when they are told to validate before solving problems. It's important to note that we aren't necessarily validating instead of solving the problem. It is the order of things that is the most important. When we validate, the result is often that children solve their own problems.

VALIDATION MAKES FOR BETTER COOPERATION

We can support our children in the solutions they come up with, rather than coming up with the solutions for them. It is good for children to solve their own problems, for a number of reasons. Children, like most people, will have more faith in a strategy working, and be more motivated to continue with problem solving, if they have come up with the idea on their own or even if they've adopted the idea from someone else in a way that lets them take ownership of it. Coming up with solutions is important for the child's development, and it gives them a sense of mastery and pride to be able to solve their own challenges. Every day, our emotions inform us about big and small challenges that need to be solved. We want, as much as possible, for our children to solve their own problems, with lots of good support and cheering on from us.

Mathew, age 10, has a dinosaur named Rextor. It's a big dinosaur that lights up and roars. His little brother, Declan, age 5, played with Rextor and dropped it down behind his bed, and one of the dinosaur's legs broke off. Mathew is furious when he finds out what happened—that Declan went into his room and played with it without asking. Their foster dad sends Declan down to the living room so that he can have a chat with Mathew in a way that validates his feelings.

> *Foster dad:* Oh, boy; it's really annoying when your little brother plays with your things without asking. And of course you feel even more angry when it turns out that he broke your favorite dinosaur.
>
> *Mathew:* I hate Declan! I wish he was never born!
>
> *Foster dad:* Yeah, you feel really furious at him when he takes your stuff. Of course you do.
>
> *Mathew:* It's not the first time he's done that.
>
> *Foster dad:* Yeah, you're right. It has happened before. You have every right to be angry. And this time it was your favorite dinosaur. It's awful!

Mathew (lets out a big breath): Declan is only five, so he
doesn't really understand what he's supposed
to do. (Pauses) Do we have any super glue?
Foster dad: We do. (Goes to find it.)

Mathew glues the dinosaur's leg back on and says that he'll
change his name to Rex Raven, and he explains that Rex Raven
has been in a fight and hurt his foot but that nothing stops the
super-dinosaur!

THE FOUR-STEP PROCESS

When we validate our children's feelings and step into their anger
with them, a natural process occurs that helps them access their
assertive anger and problem solve:

1. When we validate, the child doesn't have to convince us how
   angry they are, or that the anger is justified.
2. This frees their energy up to focus on being assertive.
3. When the child is allowed to feel their assertive anger, it gives
   them information about what they need and gives them direction to find a solution.
4. With validation and a little help from an adult, children often
   come up with their own solutions to the problem.

For example, Kai says something mean to Mari, who responds
by hitting him. If an adult validates Mari's anger by saying, "No
wonder you feel angry when Kai says mean things," then Mari's
assertive anger will inform her that she doesn't like the way Kai
talks to her. She wants it to stop. Instead of hitting him, she can say,
"I don't like it when you say those things to me, and I don't want to
play with you if you do that." Children can also more easily accept

someone else's perspective when their feelings are allowed to be present. In this example, Mari might realize that Kai says mean things because she won't let him decide any rules for their game. She can then apologize to him for that. The best scenario is when we can support our children in doing their own problem solving. It is more important for children to try and solve their own problems, and adjust as they go, than it is for us to present a better solution from the start. A solution is not necessarily better even if it seems wiser or more rational. The best solution is usually the one a child comes up with, or one that they like, because they will be more motivated to try it out and see if it works.

Let's see how the fours steps occurred in this example:

1. Mari doesn't need to spend time and energy convincing her parent that her angry reaction is justified so she can use her energy for problem solving.
2. When Mari's anger has been validated, this allows her healthy, self-assertive anger to come up.
3. Healthy emotion—in this case, self-assertive anger—gives direction for action (i.e., for problem solving).
4. Mari can put her problem solving into action—in fact, into two actions. First, she can firmly set a limit: Don't say mean things. Second, she can apologize for not letting Kai have a say in the rules.

There are times when children can't come up with good solutions on their own and they need lots of help from us. Also, children who experience a lot of anger may come up with solutions that are themselves problematic: "He broke my toy, so I'll break one of his." They think this is fair and that it makes things "even." It's important to continue to validate the child's anger and to work together to come up with a better solution.

WITH CLOAKING ANGER, THERE'S AN EXTRA STEP

When we validate cloaking anger, which protects us from other vulnerable emotions, the journey from anger to problem solving passes through difficult emotions along the way. The following is a story that illustrates the extra step into the vulnerable emotions.

Aisha, age 16, went to a party at her good friend Stella's house. At the party, Aisha saw her other good friend, Amber, steal some $20 bills from Stella's drawer. Amber realized that Aisha saw her and tells Aisha to keep quiet or she'll tell Stella that Aisha said she doesn't like her new pink hair color. In the days following the party, Aisha is in a bad mood and annoyed with everyone in her family. She gets angry at anything and everything. One evening, her dad comes into her room, which she shares with two siblings, and sits down next to her. Her dad acknowledges her anger over the past week, even if she isn't actually mad right now.

> *Dad:* Aisha, you have been so angry this week, and I can tell something is bothering you. No one feels so mad without good reason. I know you've really wanted to have your own room so you can have more privacy . . .
>
> *Aisha (interrupting):* That has nothing to do with it!
>
> *Dad:* Okay, then something else must have happened. Did something bad happen at school?
>
> *Aisha:* No!
>
> *Dad (trying again):* I know it's irritating when I don't understand. Maybe you're angry at me because I've been a bit strict lately?
>
> [Aisha starts to cry. Her dad rubs her back, and she leans her head against his shoulder.]
>
> *Dad:* Oh, honey. I'm sorry I've been so grumpy.

Aisha (laughing through her tears): It has nothing to do with you, Dad. Something stupid happened at the party.

[Aisha tells him what happened.]

Dad (validating): Aisha, sweetie, it's no wonder you feel angry and stressed out. It's a really difficult situation you're in! Of course you're worried that Amber will get mad if you tell, and then you'll end up not being friends with either of them if Amber tells Stella what you said about her hair. You must have been going around in circles thinking about this and worrying what to do. I understand why you've been so angry and out of sorts. It's too hard to hold onto such a big secret.

Aisha: I know what I have to do, but I'm just so scared that Amber is going to get really mad at me.

Dad: I'm sure you are. You're scared you won't be friends anymore and it won't get better.

Aisha: I have to talk to Amber first and see why she did it, and let her know that I have to tell Stella.

Dad: Do you want a ride over to Amber's? We can pick up some of those donuts that Amber likes on the way.

Aisha (smiling and wiping her tears): You want me to bribe her with donuts?

[They laugh, and Aisha says she'll text Amber, and they can decide about the donuts on the way.]

In this story, we see that Aisha and her dad go through five steps to get to problem solving. The extra step is Step 2: going through the vulnerable feeling of fear that lies underneath the anger. The five steps from validation to problem solving are as follows:

1. Aisha doesn't need to spend time and energy convincing her dad that her anger is appropriate, so she can use her energy for problem solving.
2. When Aisha's anger has been validated, the cloaking anger disappears, and she can access her vulnerable and painful feelings, like the fear of losing her friends.
3. Dad attends to those painful feelings with empathy and validation, until the other healthy and reparative feelings, such as self-compassion and assertive anger, emerge.
4. All the new, alive feelings that belong to the present situation give good information and direction, and Aisha is able to come up with her own solution and is more receptive to help and comfort from her dad.
5. Aisha puts the problem solving into action, with the help and support of her dad.

Again, some challenges are so big or complex that they go beyond the child's ability to solve their own problems, and then parents have to take a more active role. Examples of challenges that children cannot solve on their own are bullying, physical and psychological violence, abuse, addiction issues, self-harm, death of a close family member, death of a pet, a best friend moving away, persistent absence from school, and other similar serious issues. In such cases, when the situation is beyond a child's problem-solving abilities it is still important to validate before we solve the problem and to involve the child in the problem solving. If we trample over the kids and force a solution that they haven't helped to come up with, they can have negative feelings toward the solution itself and probably won't see it as good or necessary. It can take time to find a good solution, and we will often make mistakes along the way. We just keep trying.

WHAT DO YOU VALIDATE WHEN ANGER IS HIDING THE "REAL" FEELING?

As we've said, when anger is a cloaking device it covers other vulnerable emotions. This is why it's important to learn how to validate the emotions that lie underneath. The validation is done in the same way as it is for anger, but we often have to change our tone when we are validating vulnerable feelings. In the same way that anger needs to be validated with a voice that is empowered and matches the child's anger, we need to adapt our voice and facial expressions when responding to vulnerable emotions. For example, when a child is sad, we lower our voice and validate with a more gentle and caring tone of voice. Children who are feeling scared should be validated with a steady voice, which isn't as quiet and gentle as with sadness but also not as powerful as when validating anger.

Shame is the trickiest in terms of how to validate it. That's because it can be shaming to have someone identify and draw attention to our shame. Shame is also not as straightforward in letting us know what we need. Shame tells us to hide. But hiding what we're ashamed of—for example, not telling the truth about it—actually increases the shame. What we need when we feel shame is actually, first, a little break. We need a distraction or a reprieve because shame is so aversive, and a spotlight on it intensifies that. "Looking away" can help the person regain their equilibrium. Then, for a more lasting resolution of the feeling, shame actually needs self-compassion more than it needs compassion from others. Basically, what our children need from us, is for us to facilitate and support their own self-compassion to counteract their shame.

One parent reported really "getting" this when their son told them a story from class. The son was 10 years old, a good student and a good athlete, with a good reputation as a leader among his peers. When his class was working on something he was usually good at, and he didn't get the answer right, his pride was hurt. The parent was amazed at how kids often "get" this stuff more intuitively than parents. The son told the parent about a situation during a test that day at school. He realized he hadn't studied a certain section and had no idea how to answer that part of the test. He felt instantly mortified and embarrassed. He put his hand up and asked to be excused to go to the washroom. As he told the parent the story, he said, "Mr. G got it and knew that I just needed a minute, so even though it was a test he let me go." That's all he reported, and yet the relief and appreciation he felt were obvious. The parent was thinking, Who knows if Mr. G actually did "get it" and realized the boy needed a minute to recover from his shame? What was shocking, though, was how clear the boy was on what he needed. With his appreciation of the teacher, he was saying, "What I needed was the opposite of a spotlight on my shame. I needed a minute to get out of there and reset." Therefore, the key to validating shame is not to overstep what the child is offering up for validation— not to do much guessing and to monitor our tone of voice. Too much gentleness can feel patronizing. A tone that is maybe not lighthearted, but a bit offhand or casual, can show that you can relate without making a big deal: "Oh jeesh, I hate it when that happens. You want to just disappear." Then if the child offers more, you can reflect more.

> *Son:* Dad, I felt like such an idiot.
> *Dad:* Oh that's a gross feeling. You just think—"Why did I say that?"

We also distinguish intense shame in the moment that needs the "break" to reset, from a more pervasive underlying shame of feeling "not good enough." Again, we follow the guidelines of response up to the level that the child brings—but it will also be necessary to look beyond cloaking anger and make it possible for the child to express the pervasive shame. Then the parent can use a caring voice and style suitable to very vulnerable emotions: "Yeah; feeling embarrassed about who you are is an awful feeling. It really hurts."

As you work toward validating vulnerable feelings, it can be helpful to read some examples so that it's easier to find the right words. Painful feelings can be uncomfortable to validate because we worry about making our child feel more scared, or sad, or ashamed. It can be helpful to read some stories, feel your own reactions, and then try it out to find your own evidence that it will go okay. What follows are examples for each painful emotion.

Validating Underlying Sadness

Sandra, age 13, is acting really angry and snapping at everyone for no reason. Her mother validates her anger and then guesses that Sandra is actually feeling sad. Her guinea pig, Marshall, has cancer and has to be put down at the vet's office tomorrow.

> *Mom:* I'm just wondering if you actually feel more sad than angry, because Marshall is sick and has to be put down tomorrow?
> (Mom tries to hug Sandra, but she pushes her away. Mom gives her a little more space. Sandra's bottom lip begins to tremble, and her eyes fill with tears. She sits down.)
> *Sandra:* Does he have to die? Can't the vet help him?
> *Mom:* The cancer has spread all over his body, so the vet can't get it all out. It's so sad that there's nothing we can do to help him. You must be so sad, and

you must be dreading tomorrow. I know you're going to really miss him.

Sandra begins to cry, and the tears pour down her cheeks. Mom sits down and hugs her, and Sandra accepts the hug. They sit like that for half an hour, as Mom holds her daughter tightly, wiping away her tears. Every now and again, Mom says something to continue validating her daughter's feelings.

> *Mom:* It's really sad that Marshall is going to die, isn't it? It really hurts to think about.
>
> *Sandra:* Can Marshall sleep in my room tonight? It doesn't matter if I don't sleep well. It's his last night.
>
> *Mom:* Of course he can.

Validating Underlying Fear

The parents tell Steven, age 7, that he'll be alone with his big brother, Thomas, age 12, while his parents go out shopping for a couple of hours. Steven spends the whole morning trying to pick fights with his brother, which he succeeds in doing. He tells his parents that they can't stay home alone since they are fighting so much. Steven's dad acknowledges his son's anger and guesses that Steven is also afraid.

> *Dad:* Steven, I'm wondering if you've been so angry and getting into fights today because you don't want to stay home alone with Thomas. I'm wondering if you're a bit scared of being alone with him because of that time a month ago when he hit you and threatened you.
>
> *Steven (stiffening):* Six times.

Dad: Huh?

Steven: He has hit me six times before, and it always happens when we're alone.

Dad: I didn't know that was happening so often. No wonder you don't want to stay alone with him. Of course you're scared when he treats you like that.

Steven (softly): He said he'd beat me up if I told you or Mom.

Dad: Oh, wow. Well then, I can see how impossible it was for you to tell us and how hard it's been. You must have been really worried and scared, and I can see that you're scared now.

[Dad sits down and hugs Steven, and Steven climbs onto his lap and tells his dad that he's scared of his brother. Dad strokes his son's back.]

Dad: You don't have to be alone with Thomas. We'll figure something out. Maybe you can go to Espen's house, if you want, or come shopping with us. And I'm going to talk to Thomas.

Steven: No! You can't say anything to him! Then he'll kill me!

Dad: I get it. Thomas might try to get revenge if I speak to him. And then it will be even worse next time you're alone with him. You might be worried that he'll really hurt you badly.

Steven (crying): Yeah, I'm scared he's going to really beat me up.

Dad (holding Steven tightly): This has been really hard. Being so scared! It must be awful that your brother, who's supposed to look after you, gets angry and beats you up. And how awful not to feel safe in your own house. We've really let you down.

Steven: I'm not as scared now.

Dad: I am going to look after you, and Mommy will too. You don't have to be alone with Thomas.

Steven: But do you have to talk to Thomas?

Dad: Yeah, because I need to find out why he gets so angry with you, so that we can stop it.

Steven: Maybe he doesn't feel happy.

Dad: Maybe.

Steven: Okay, you can talk to him, but I don't want to be home alone with him.

Dad: You won't be.

Validating Underlying Shame

Valerie, age 13, is furious at her dad because he says she's not allowed to go to her friend's house until her room is tidy.

Dad: Why do you always have to be so difficult!? Come on!

Valerie: Why are you always so mean to me?! You don't even like me! You love Nadia more than me. You don't even care about me!

[Dad calms himself and realizes he needs to try some validation.]

Dad: You know what, you have every reason to be mad at me. That was a really silly and hurtful thing for me to say.

[Valerie's anger disappears right away. She looks down and is quiet. Dad uses a gentle voice and steps a little closer to Valerie. He guesses that underneath her anger, she is feeling shame.]

Dad: I'm wondering if that makes you feel like you're not good enough.

[Valerie nods in agreement with what her dad says, without looking at him.]

Dad: Maybe you sometimes feel like we don't get you or we think you're bad?

Valerie (slumped, with her head hanging down): Bad. I feel like I'm bad. And like there's something wrong with me.

Dad: Because I shout at you a lot and tell you that I'm not happy with you. No wonder you're afraid I think you're bad, or that I don't love you or even like you. You can see that Nadia and I are more alike and that we don't argue very often, and I think I even hug her more. So, it's not surprising that you end up feeling like you're bad.

[Valerie listens and is obviously interested to hear more. She quickly looks up at her dad before staring down at the floor again.]

Dad: It must be hard that I'm always getting after you, and telling you to do the same things over and over, which must make you think that I don't trust that you'll do things unless I nag. And I am probably stricter with you than with Nadia, and that's really not fair at all. It's no wonder you feel like you're not good enough, because I make you feel that way.

Valerie (looking up at her dad): Yeah, exactly. I know that I'm more like Mom, so we click better, but I also want you to like me.

Dad: Of course you do! And I do! I love you. And I am so proud of everything you've done with your dance

group. I think I don't say it because I tell myself
that then you'll just be interested in dancing,
and not do your schoolwork. But I know that's
ridiculous that I hold back and don't tell you
how much I love your energy and strength. And
maybe it doesn't even help that I'm saying it now
because I've said the opposite so many times.

Valerie (smiling): It kind of helps.

[Both of them chuckle.]

Valerie (jokingly): So, I guess I don't need to tidy my
room then!

Dad: Nice try.

Valerie: Okay, I'll do it since you asked me.

[She hops up and goes to tidy her room.]

EXPERIENCE IT: VALIDATE YOUR CHILD'S FEELINGS

Think of a situation when your child was angry and you weren't
sure what to do, or you ended up handling the situation poorly.
Imagine that you are in your child's shoes, as though you are your
child in the situation. Take a moment to see how it feels in your chest
and stomach. What's happening inside your child? Is it assertive
anger? Or are there other more vulnerable feelings under the cloaking anger? When you have a sense of what your child is feeling, get
a pen and paper (or your phone) and practice validating the feelings
that you discovered. Start with the anger, and then move on to the
vulnerable feelings afterward, if there are other feelings underneath
the anger.

Validating anger:

1. "No wonder you feel angry, because . . ."
2. See if you can come up with three points after "because."

Validating vulnerable feelings:

1. "I wonder if you're also feeling scared/sad/disappointed/embarrassed/stupid, because . . ."
2. See if you can come up with three points after "because."

Try validation the next time a similar difficult situation occurs. You can start validation at any point. Even if the situation has escalated and you're feeling angry, or you've criticized or dismissed or tried to reassure your child, it is never too late to stop and switch over to validation.

VALIDATE THE GOOD STUFF, TOO!

Joy, pride, curiosity, and eagerness also need validation. Having adults acknowledge not only the painful but also the pleasant emotions is an essential part of children developing emotion competence. Children also need help when the good feelings take over and turn into restless "ants in the pants," or when the child becomes overexcited. For example, when we validate pride and curiosity, it strengthens those emotions. They will last longer, and the child will experience that it is okay, and even good, to be proud or curious. It is intuitive and easy to validate pride when a child is between 1 and 3 years old. We clap our hands with them when they build a wobbly little castle in the sand, and praise them when they show us how "big" they are. We do less of this as kids get older. It's as though we forget that celebrating the emotions that feel good is just as important to the child's well-being as having them navigate the painful ones. Once kids can talk, we overestimate their ability to put words to and manage all of their feelings, including the good ones. Next is a story about Isabella and an example of validating pride.

Isabella, age 13, comes home and tells her mom that she's had a fight at school today with her best friend, Maria. They were chatting with a group of girls and talking about their periods. Maria said, as a joke to look tough, that Isabella hadn't started her period yet, even though it wasn't true. Isabella says to her mom,

> I was so mad at her but I didn't want to say anything. But afterward, I grabbed her jacket and I said, "Next time you talk to someone about my period, we're not gonna be friends anymore. I didn't like it! It wasn't funny." And I'm really happy I said that because I'm usually so scared of hurting someone's feelings, and so I'm not very good at speaking up when I'm angry, but this time I did. I'm really proud.

Her mom responds, "Well done! You have every reason to be proud! That can be really hard to do. I'm proud of you, too! I'm proud that you stood up for yourself and said something."

Validating pride works best when the child has the feeling first rather than when we say we are proud of them when the child isn't actually in touch with that feeling. It's easier to feel your own pride when it's there, compared with feeling someone else's pride in you when the feeling is not activated. This is especially important for children who don't feel good enough, because our attempts to transfer our pride over to them can end up reinforcing their shame instead, as though they're in need of us to build them up.

Birthday parties and special holidays or events are classic times when kids' good feelings can escalate and become too much. They can become impossibly restless and unable to concentrate, sit still, or stop moving. Their excitement and joyfulness can become overwhelming and lead to conflict and can "ruin" the family holiday for everyone. It can end with the parents frustrated and the child upset and embarrassed. These kids will need help to settle down, and validation can help. We once spoke to a mother in counseling who had a wonderful way of validating overexcitement at Christmas:

> You're so excited for Santa to come and bring your presents that it looks like you have ants in your pants. It's hard to sit still and it feels like this night is going to last 100 years. It's really hard to wait because you're so excited and looking forward to opening presents.

Her experience was that her son became much calmer after validation. After half an hour, he started getting worked up again, and then calmed down with another round of validation. In this way, they avoided conflict and had a much nicer Christmas Eve.

GREAT, I VALIDATED . . . WHAT'S NEXT? MEETING OUR CHILDREN'S EMOTIONAL NEEDS

Once emotions have been validated, we can help our children solve problems and offer them the comfort and care they need. What emotional needs does the child have, and how do we know what we should offer, and when?

As we mentioned in Chapter 1, all basic emotions have an associated emotional need. Angry children need limits and need to stand up for themselves or find a way to remove an obstacle that stands in the way of an important goal. Scared children need protection, safety, or reassurance. Children who feel ashamed need a respite from the intensity of shame, acknowledgment and normalization, self-compassion, and support to mend a damaged sense of self. They need assurance that they are still a worthy member of the family, the class, or their friend group. Children who are sad need closeness and comfort.

Our emotional needs are always connected to our primary emotions, not to our cloaking emotions. If your child is assertively angry because you crossed their boundaries, got in the way of an important goal, or treated them differently from a sibling, then the child needs you to accept their anger and show them respect. If your child is angry at another child, then they might need support from you so they can stand up for themselves, speak up, or set a limit. If your child has cloaking anger and is protecting themselves against underlying vulnerable feelings, then your child's emotional need is connected to one or more vulnerable feelings and not to the anger. In this case, the anger is a misleading signal. It's important to guess what is actually bothering your child, and which emotion they are trying to hide, so you can figure out what type of care they need. Sometimes we meet an emotional need without clear problem solving, and other times we might think we have found a solution to a problem but end up not meeting their emotional need. Problem solving and meeting your child's emotional needs are often two sides of the same coin and can happen simultaneously. In the next section, you will find some examples that illustrate how problem solving is sometimes a part of meeting the child's needs.

Meeting the Unmet Need When There's Underlying Sadness

It's not uncommon for grief to hide underneath cloaking anger. Sadness needs closeness and comfort; not comfort that tries to cover the pain but, rather, comfort in the form of "I am here with you, and I can handle your grief." Once we've allowed them to share their grief and we've validated it, then some cheering up or distraction can be a good thing. But it's important to pay attention to the order and timing. A fresh, new sadness can be validated as follows:

> Mmm, yeah, it's so hard that your best friend is moving away. You guys are so close and spend so much time together. Maybe you're scared that you won't be friends anymore and that you won't see him again, or that you're just going to miss him so much. It's so sad that he has to move.

The child nods and cries. Mom responds, "Let's just sit here and feel sad together. It's important to grieve when a friend moves."

Old sadness is often connected to feelings of loneliness. Children can be lonely if they are alone a lot. They can also feel lonely even if they do have others to be with but are alone a lot with their painful feelings. It can feel as though the people around us are distant or miles away. There are lots of reasons why kids can end up feeling this way. Some common ones are a parent having a mental or physical illness or addiction, or the loss of a parent. It can also happen if parents or other adults or a group of friends don't pay much attention to the child's feelings or to how they are actually doing.

Old grief or loneliness can also be validated:

> *Mom:* It's no wonder you feel lonely because Dad and I have been so focused on the new house, and on your little sister and our jobs, that we haven't really talked to you properly for a while. Maybe you're even a bit scared that we forgot about you, or maybe you haven't really felt like a part of the family. It is so painful to feel alone in the world.
>
> *Child (crying):* That's exactly how I feel. I feel totally alone, and I have ever since Mary was born.
>
> *Mom:* I am so sorry that I haven't been here for you. I will change that, starting right now. I don't want you to be alone, and I really want to have time with you. Maybe we can find something that just the two of us do together regularly. And I'm going to ask you more often how you are.

Meeting the Unmet Need When There's Underlying Fear

If a child is scared because they are experiencing, or have experienced, something frightening or dangerous, then they need an adult to stop whatever is dangerous, help them out of the frightening situation, and make sure that they aren't exposed to that same danger again.

If your child is scared of something that isn't actually dangerous, such as the dark, or sleeping alone, they still have a need for protection and reassurance that everything will be okay. Problem solving can be an important part of this type of care. It might be that leaving a light on or a door open is enough to help the child fall asleep.

If you have a child who is carrying some old fears—fears that come from memories of a time when they were very scared and had good reason to be—then the child has an old unmet need for security. It is important to validate the old fear and say that it's no wonder the fear is still there. An example of validating a 13-year-old who has an old fear would be to say:

> Of course you were scared when your sister was always hitting you. It was very scary. And we didn't know how serious it was and we didn't help you to feel safe. We didn't stop her. You were afraid, and we didn't make sure you were safe. So, that's why you still feel scared when people come up to you suddenly or raise their voices, especially when it's your sister.

We try to meet the old unmet need with the validation. We also make it okay for the child to feel the fear while we are there and can offer reassurance.

When we validate old fears, the child has the opportunity to be in the fear until new and different feelings show up that change the fear.

- Assertive anger: "I am actually really mad at Stella for scaring me like that. And I'm mad at you for doing nothing."
- Self-compassion: "What happened was so terrifying. No wonder I ended up being afraid of so many things."

- Grief: "I didn't really get a chance to be a kid. I missed so much because I was so scared. I couldn't even go on sleepovers or school trips."

Assertive anger, self-compassion, and grief are good ways to deal with old fear because you can't feel fear in the same moment that you feel anger, self-compassion, or sadness. When you give the memory of being scared more emotions than just the fear, the memory becomes less scary. For example, a child might say, "I know she doesn't hit anymore, and she doesn't want to hurt me, but I've been scared anyway. But I think I'm not as scared now. I think I'm actually mad at her."

Old fears can be lessened, or even disappear completely, when the appropriate feelings of assertive anger, grief, and self-compassion are combined with an adult trying to meet the old unmet needs for protection and security. We can then reassure the child that the danger is over and that we will protect them if something dangerous happens in the future.

Meeting the Unmet Need When There's Underlying Shame

Reprimanding a child serves no purpose when they are already ashamed of having done something wrong. The child knows what they've done. They learned that from you. They learned from your "No," which they heard every few minutes from the time they were 18 months old, that they weren't allowed to hit, bite, push, steal, say mean things, or throw things. When a child feels shame for doing something wrong, they need help to get out of that place of shame and be invited back into their social sphere. The child needs acknowledgment and normalization and often needs an invitation to resume relational contact and feel once again like a valued member of the group.

Let's look at an example. Four-year-old Vanessa is not allowed to watch TV, and she is angry. She looks angrily at her mom and at things in the room and then notices her mom's computer.

> *Vanessa:* If you won't let me watch TV, then I'll smash your computer.
>
> *Mom:* What are you talking about, Vanessa?
> [Vanessa slumps over a little bit and looks at the floor as her bottom lip starts to tremble.]
>
> *Mom:* Oh, dear, saying that makes you feel yucky, doesn't it? You know you aren't allowed to smash Mommy's computer, and I know you would never do that.
> [Vanessa stands motionless. Mom motions for Vanessa to come over to the sofa and she lifts her up on her lap. Vanessa continues to avoid her gaze.]
>
> *Mom:* Come and sit here. We all say things we don't mean sometimes. Mommy and Daddy do that sometimes, and your sister too. We all say or do silly things sometimes.
>
> *Vanessa (sniffs):* Everyone says dumb things sometimes.
>
> *Mom:* Yeah and when we do, we get that yucky feeling in our tummies that lets us know. I'm not mad at you. Can you look at me?
>
> *Vanessa:* Yes. [Looks up at her mom.] Everyone says dumb things sometimes.
>
> *Mom (in a kind voice):* Yes, we do.

It is definitely more challenging when children don't show a clear response of feeling remorse but instead laugh, make a joke, or shrug. Remember that this doesn't mean a child isn't feeling remorse or that they're unaware of what they've done. Using humor is just a way to protect themselves from the awful feeling of shame. Sometimes it's possible to guess that shame or feelings of self-blame lie underneath the humor or the shrug, in which case you can validate those feelings. It can have a positive effect even if the child doesn't seem to take it in. Of course, it's harder to validate shame that is covered by other emotions because we can get triggered and feel angry and worried for our kids when they don't show remorse, making us think they don't understand right from wrong.

When children are ashamed, their bodies slouch, they hang their heads, and they avoid eye contact. It can be hard to get out of the "shame bubble," even when things start to feel better inside. This is why children need help to lift their gaze and physically reconnect to the outside world. Sometimes they manage to have only a quick look at an adult, but if they are met with a friendly face, that can be enough to help. Asking children to look at us so we can help them out of their shame is totally different from when we ask them to look at us when we are angry and we want them to listen. In that situation, asking a child to look at you can be hard for the child and even cause them to act out more.

If your child is ashamed because of feeling ugly, gross, fat, mean, boring, or stupid, and not because they've done something wrong, those feelings still need validation. Such "old shame" is possibly the most difficult feeling to validate because we are afraid of confirming that it's true that they are fat or stupid. When we find a feeling hard to validate, then our fear of getting in touch with that emotion can prevent us from meeting the child's emotional need. In the next sections, we provide some examples of how a child's old shame can be validated.

Peter Feels Stupid

Peter, age 12, often makes comments at home about feeling dumb when he answers a question wrong at school or when he struggles with an assignment. He also has a hard time getting his home-work done. He puts it off and makes excuses even though he always feels better once he sits down to do it. Today is no exception, and Peter's dad can see that Peter looks a little down when he picks him up from school. Peter doesn't say anything when he gets in the car. When they get home, they carry the groceries into the kitchen:

> *Dad:* You're so quiet. Did something happen?
> [Peter says that they were given a big writing project.]
> *Peter:* I don't even know what I'm going to write about. I don't have smart ideas like everyone else. I feel so stupid.
> [His big brother pipes up and says: "I remember that project. We had the same one. It was totally fun!"]
> *Dad:* Yeah, it sounds like a very fun project. You'll have no problem!
> *Peter (shouting angrily):* You don't get it. You're completely clueless. It's not going to be "fun." It's going to be the worst.
> *Dad:* Don't talk to me like that! You're certainly not going to get anywhere with that attitude. Listen, I get that you're not feeling great about this assignment, but you have the whole week to do it. I'm sure you'll come up with something to write about.
> *Peter:* You don't get it. You never get it, and you never help.
> [Peter's big brother decides to steer clear and leaves the kitchen.]

Peter's dad tries to understand how Peter is feeling, and he begins to validate the shame that Peter describes when he says he feels stupid. Dad knows he is in dangerous waters here, and he isn't exactly sure what to say, but he dives in anyway:

> *Dad:* No wonder you feel stupid because . . . you have a big brother who likes to tease you and tells you that you're stupid. Maybe you start to think it's true.
>
> *Peter (listening to his dad and nodding):* I just feel so dumb. I can't do anything.
>
> *Dad:* It's hard to come up with good ideas when you feel like that. And then you probably tell yourself that you're not good at anything, instead of reminding yourself that you always end up doing okay. And it doesn't help when I tell you that you're smart and I have faith that you'll get the project done and do a really good job, when you're telling yourself that it isn't true.
>
> *Peter:* So you think I can do it?
>
> *Dad (looking at Peter with a firm and steady gaze):* Absolutely! You are so creative!
>
> *Peter:* Can you help me think of a good idea?
>
> *Dad:* Sure I can!

If a child accepts the validation and is allowed to feel the shame with you, then they may also be more open to receiving care. Be prepared for them to need a bit of time before they're ready. You may need to test the waters and offer more validation and understanding before the child is ready for care and help. Some parents might think "But my child freaks out every time I try to validate and show understanding. He just screams that I don't understand. Do

I just keep validating?" It's often the case that validation requires several rounds, so yes, more validation can definitely work. At the very least, we can validate how frustrating it is for the child to feel like we don't get it and can't help them put words to their feelings. If the child is so angry that he can't even hear what you're saying, the best thing may be just to be quiet but still present. Eventually you can try to calm him down by offering some physical contact. If the child is still so angry that he acts out, you need to set a limit for the behavior while also allowing the feelings to be present.

When the child feels shame, the need for acknowledgment and normalization could be addressed by the father in this way:

> There are probably lots of boys who feel like they're in the shadows of their older brothers. It's impossible to be as smart as someone who's four years older than you, even if you are just as smart as him. Which you are. I am so proud of you. You are so thoughtful and nice to your friends, and you keep on working really hard at school and with your homework.

STAN FEELS STUPID

Stan, age 12, has dyslexia and also struggles with math. He is doing his math homework and feeling more and more angry. He shouts, "I can't do this! I'm too stupid!" Mom validates the cloaking anger first and then validates the feelings of shame that lie underneath:

> It makes sense that you feel stupid because you see the other kids in the class doing their math so easily when you have to work so hard at it. It's so unfair that you struggle with math when that's the exact subject that your friends really like. You feel like you're not good enough when you compare yourself to them, and that must really hurt. It doesn't even help that you are really good at English, when you're sitting in math class and feeling lost.

If the child accepts the validation and is in the feeling of shame with you, you can then try to help to improve his self-image:

> There are lots of people who are bad at math who have done well in life. You might not want to study math and science, but you have such a good ear for languages. Do you think you can look at me?

He looks up at his mom.

> *Mom:* I am so proud of you, and there are so many things you are good at that are just as important as math. Languages, like I said, but you are also so good at drawing.
>
> *Child (looking up and smiling):* And I make the best guacamole in the world.
>
> *Mom:* True! The guacamole!

Susan Feels Ugly and Gross

Susan, age 13, can't find anything to wear in the morning. She gets so angry and frustrated that she screams loud enough for the whole house to hear. Her dad validates her anger, and her eyes tear up. Susan says she doesn't have any clothes that fit, and she says she looks fat and ugly anyway. Her dad validates her feelings of shame about her body:

> *Dad:* It's painful to feel unhappy about how you look. And it's no wonder that it's hard to feel happy about it when there is so much focus on appearance and pressure to be thin. Nobody can live up to the ideals of beauty we see on social media or on TV. It's really horrible not to like yourself. It's painful.

> *Susan:* I'm not really so unhappy. I dunno. I just suddenly felt so ugly. Maybe those jeans I had on are just too small, and so I felt fatter than I actually am.
>
> *Dad:* It's really rough not to feel good. If it's any consolation, I think you are absolutely beautiful.
>
> *Susan:* It's a very, very small consolation, Dad, but it helps to talk about it. I feel better now.

CARA FEELS UGLY AND GROSS

Cara, age 14, has cerebral palsy and uses a wheelchair. She has had a tough day at school because some of the kids in the grade above her made some nasty comments about her. When she gets home, her stepfather is the only one there. When she sees him, she starts to cry. She says that she hates her body and that she will never leave the house again.

> *Cara (shouting):* I'm so disgusting and ugly that no one even wants to look at me!
>
> [Her stepdad validates the shame she is feeling about her body.]
>
> *Stepdad:* It makes sense that you'd feel lousy. It's hard to be different. And kids don't handle that well. They make comments, and I know they've even said you're ugly and you sound weird. Those kinds of comments really sink in. It's so unfair that people don't see all the things you're good at. And I know it also doesn't help that I think you're beautiful, because you need to feel good about yourself, and it's so painful when you don't.
>
> *Cara:* I'm actually so angry at all the idiots who don't realize that even if I have CP, I'm just a normal kid. I can't do anything about how I look or sound.

> *Stepdad:* Right?! Exactly! They're a bunch of fools. I'm so glad that you came into my life. People who don't see how full of life you are and who don't see your great sense of humor are just blind idiots.
> [They look at each other, and then start laughing and crying together.]

As parents, we sometimes validate as best we can, or even totally perfectly, and yet we can't get to the emotions behind the anger. Instead, the conflict escalates when we try to get closer to our child's feelings. What do we do when validation does not work? The next chapter will help you troubleshoot the most common problem scenarios.

CHAPTER 8

TROUBLESHOOTING WHILE VALIDATING

After working with emotion focused skills training for parents for many years, we have discovered that some parents are afraid to validate their children's painful emotions, fearing they will actually create or reinforce those feelings. We've also seen that validation doesn't always work and that, in some very specific situations, the validation can actually make a situation worse for the child. To be successful with validation, it's important to know the potential pitfalls and common challenges that can occur before, during, and after validation.

WHAT IF I GUESS THE WRONG UNDERLYING EMOTION?

If you decide to try validation, there is no doubt that things will go wrong—many times. Mistaking which emotion needs to be acknowledged, and not figuring out why the child is feeling the emotions they're feeling, are going to be a part of your validation journey. We want you to hear this: It is fine to fail. What follows is an example of validation going wrong when the adult mistakes which feeling is underneath the anger.

Jamal, age 7, has been very angry all week, becoming annoyed at anything and everything. This time he's having a fit because he doesn't want to have a bath. His mom recognizes that he's angry, but she also sees that there must be something else, more hurtful, underneath.

> *Mom:* Of course you feel angry when I say you have to have a bath and you wanted to watch more TV, but I'm wondering if you're actually also sad about something.
>
> *Jamal (screaming):* I'm not sad! I just want to watch TV! I AM NOT sad!!
>
> *Mom:* I made a mistake. You aren't sad. I got it wrong. It must be so annoying when I don't understand what's going on.
>
> *Jamal (quiets down):* Yeah, you don't understand.
>
> *Mom:* It's frustrating when even your mom doesn't understand, so no wonder you feel angry.
>
> *Jamal:* I'm scared to go to bed. There are vampires in my closet. That's what Abdul said.
>
> *Mom:* Well, then, of course you're scared. That's super scary.

For most children, it's much easier to hear an emotion word from us and see if it resonates with what's going on inside their bodies, or to get a suggestion from us about what might be the cause of the emotion, than it is to come up with an answer to a question like "What are you feeling? What happened?" Young children find it hard to explain what they are feeling, and even older children can have painful feelings without knowing why. Kids often don't dare to say what they're actually feeling. It's easier for a child to get a suggestion, and check whether it fits, than to have to come up with an answer to a question. This is especially true when the child is highly emotionally activated.

Many parents are afraid that guessing or suggesting what the child is feeling will be invasive. They worry that it will be like putting words in the child's mouth and telling them how they feel. There are two important things to consider here. First, validation is a dialogue, not a monologue. We validate and give the child time to respond. If necessary, we build on the validation with a few "because" statements, or we validate more than one emotion, or we correct a validation that didn't land—all depending on what is going on for the child. In situations where there are complicated emotions, the validation turns into a bit of detective work in which there is a conversation between the parent and the child, with the parent leading the discussion. Second, to believe that validation works, and to make it work, you have to jump in and try it. Many parents are surprised at how effective validation is. The children don't find it annoying or disruptive. Instead, they find it helpful and empathic. They feel like we are really trying to understand them, and that we're curious and want to help, even if we get it wrong.

WHAT IF MY CHILD REALLY DOESN'T LIKE WHEN I GUESS THEIR EMOTION?

A small minority of children do not respond well to standard validation, or at least they don't respond to validation of all the various emotions. Some children don't like to be defined, and it is important to them that they come up with their own words. Young children who are in the midst of an intense development phase are particularly averse to being forever defined by their parents.

If you have a child who does not like standard validation, it can be helpful to validate in a more questioning way. Allow your child to choose from several suggestions and to redefine the emotion words and use their own words, even if the words are exactly the same as what you suggested.

Mom: Maybe you feel a bit lonely?

Child: No, I'm not lonely, but I don't have anyone to play with.

Mom: So, you're all alone when you're at school?

Child: Not all alone. There are other kids, but I don't have any friends.

Mom: It must really hurt not to have friends. It's no wonder you feel sad, or feel dumb, or maybe you feel a bit nervous about not having friends?

Child: I feel dumb and like a loser. No one likes me because I'm weird.

Mom: It's no wonder you feel dumb and like a loser when you're scared that no one likes you. It's really too bad that no one at school is similar to you and likes what you like.

Child: Yeah, it's really stupid. I wish I went to a bigger school with more kids. Then there'd probably be someone who was just as weird as me.

Mom: Yeah, it would be good to have a best friend, and it must be really hard that you don't.

Child: Well, luckily, I'm good at school and I like my classes, and I think the teachers like me because I always do what they say really fast.

WHAT IF OTHER PEOPLE ARE AROUND?

There are other ways to mess up a validation, aside from making a wrong guess about a feeling or the reason for the feeling. We can also mess up the timing. As we've said before, it is important that the validation comes before the solution and limit-setting. We often need to wait for a vulnerable feeling to show up before we consider the validation of cloaking anger to be complete. We also need to wait for the right time. A validation that happens at the wrong place and the wrong time, when other people are present who the child doesn't want to appear vulnerable with, can fail miserably and make the situation worse for the child.

Two families of four have been on a cabin holiday together. It's early in the morning, and one family is leaving. Four-year-old Carly has been given a nice drawing from her older cousin. She has been carrying it around all morning. On the way out, everyone has to walk down a hill to where the car is parked. Carly trips her twin sister, Vanessa, who falls down the hill. Vanessa starts to cry, and Carly laughs.

> *Carly:* Vanessa's crying! Vanessa's a baby!
> [Moments later, Carly trips and ends up in the mud with her drawing. Carly gets up and looks very upset.]
> *Mom:* Oh no, it's so sad that your drawing, that you like so much, is covered in mud.
> *Carly:* I'm not sad!
> *Mom:* Of course you're angry. It hurts to fall, but I wonder if you're also a bit sad because your drawing is ruined.
> *Carly (starting to cry, speaking through her tears):* I'm just sad because you're making me sad!
> [A bit later, she is still crying and angry.]
> *Carly:* Why do you always have to make me sad?

In this example, it looks like the mom validated well and that she gets one of the emotions we imagine Carly must be feeling: sadness. However, the validation does not end well. The key issue is that Mom has not read the whole situation, and she doesn't realize that her daughter feels ashamed when her sadness is validated in front of her sister, aunt and uncle, and cousins. The validation contributes to Carly's feelings of embarrassment. This is partly because just before she fell and started crying she had made fun of her sister for doing the same. But this is also an example of when calling attention to and shining a spotlight on shame makes it more shaming. Mom's attempt at validation actually highlights Carly's shame in front of her whole family. This includes her older cousin who she looks up to and in front of whom she wants to feel proud. This is a perfect illustration of how an attempt to validate shame, without careful consideration of timing and of how shame operates, can make the painful feelings even worse. We need to be aware of whether it's okay to validate vulnerable feelings when others are around, or whether we should wait until later, or whether we could even let the whole situation go without any validation. This would be a case where "looking away" from shame may be the best validation of the child's feelings and the best way to meet their need. It is a balancing act for parents, and timing is one of the important elements.

WHAT IF MY CHILD GETS ANNOYED?

If the validation keeps going awry and your child gets annoyed or feels like you don't understand anything, then you can validate how frustrating it is that you keep making mistakes and don't understand. Then you can apologize. Even the worst validation fails can provide an opportunity for repairing the relationship, which in turn can strengthen the bond between you and your child. If you later realize that you've validated the wrong emotion or been overly insistent in your suggestions, or you've messed up the timing, you can still bring it up with your child, apologize, and say something about how that must feel for him or her. Trying to validate and guess what is going on for your child, even if you occasionally fail, is still the opposite of avoiding the painful feelings. Just to make the balancing act even more tricky, there are also times when the best way to validate the child is—to say nothing! This is especially true for parents who "over-validate." These kids need us to validate, with our silence, their feeling that they can handle the emotion without us making a big deal.

WHAT IF I HAVE NO IDEA WHY MY CHILD IS ANGRY?

We often don't know why our children feel the way they do. But it can still help to validate. In fact, as parents we know more than we think, whether we realize it or not, and that's because we do know our children well. We just need to allow ourselves to take in what we see in the child. It also helps to have some tips to get started. For example, we can start with the phrase "Of course you're angry because. . . ." Then we can try to understand how our child is doing by imagining ourselves in our child's shoes, as if we are the child. This gives us a surprising amount of useful information. But sometimes, even when we do the work of imagining ourselves as our child, we can still draw a blank. The following are two examples of how you can validate when you have no idea why your child is angry.

A 12-year-old boy comes home angry and slams the door. His mom talks to him that evening.

> *Mom:* I don't know what's up, but I do know when you're angry like this, it's because something bad has happened. You're allowed to be angry, and there is always a reason for it when we feel like this. Maybe you also aren't sure why, or maybe you don't feel like telling me about it. And I don't blame you because I'm not always so good at helping you when you're having a hard time.

> *The 12-year-old (in a calm and sad voice):* I just want to be alone, Mom.
>
> *Mom:* Okay; I'm here if you need me, and I'll check in again in a couple hours.
>
> *Twelve-year-old:* Okay.

A 4-year-old and his big sister are playing with LEGO, and he is suddenly very angry at her. He screams and throws some of the blocks at his sister and then picks up the whole thing they've been building and smashes it. His mom has no idea what has gone on. When Mom walks in, the older sister says that he was suddenly so angry but that nothing had happened.

> *Mom:* Oh, you're really angry. Something must have happened. Maybe something wasn't how you wanted it, or there was something you couldn't do.
>
> *Four-year-old (shouting):* NO! I'm not angry!
>
> *Mom:* Okay, you aren't angry, but something happened. Maybe you feel sad.
>
> *Four-year-old (looking down):* I'm sad.
>
> *Mom:* Sweetie, I don't know what happened but, hmm, I can see you're sad. That's okay. We can figure it out together.
>
> *Four-year-old (looking embarrassed):* I peed my pants.
>
> *Mom:* Oh, okay, then of course you feel upset and you were trying to keep it hidden. Maybe you were worried I'd be angry?
>
> *Four-year-old:* Yeah.

We don't always succeed in figuring out where the emotions come from. Often it's unclear for both the adult and the child.

Validation can still be a valuable tool because it's not about finding the reason or cause but about accepting the emotions. The "because" is important only when it helps to make clear that we truly understand and acknowledge the child and their feelings. The cause is not always important in itself. The following is an example of how validation can work well, even if it's hard to know what the painful feeling is about.

Nadia, age 14, is lying in her bed, and her mom comes to say goodnight. Nadia is reading and quickly puts the book away when her mom walks in. Mom sees that Nadia has new cuts on the inside of her arm. Mom looks at Nadia's arm and says: "Honey, I know you've been feeling rotten lately." Nadia quickly pulls her arm away and hides it under her duvet.

> *Mom:* It's no wonder that makes you angry. I came in here and saw something that you wanted to hide from me.
>
> *Nadia:* Yeah, obviously. Oh my god!
>
> *Mom:* Maybe you're afraid that you'll get in trouble?
>
> *Nadia:* No, I don't think I'll get in trouble.
>
> *Mom:* Okay, but there is something that upsets you about me knowing that you're in pain and struggling.
>
> *Nadia:* It's just embarrassing.
>
> *Mom:* I understand.
>
> [Mom sits on the edge of the bed, and they are quiet for awhile.]
>
> *Mom:* It must be awful to feel this bad. There's something I've been thinking about. Dad and I have been arguing a lot lately, and I'm wondering if you're worried that we're going to split up.
>
> *Nadia:* Mom, you guys will never split up. You're totally dependent on each other. I know you really want

to know why I don't feel good, but I don't know why. Nothing bad happened, and everything is fine here at home. Nobody's attacked me or anything, and I have lots of friends. I just don't feel good. I just feel sad. It's like I have this ache in here (points toward her chest).

Mom: Yeah, okay; it's painful in here, and she points toward her own chest.

Nadia: Yeah.

Mom: It must be really painful to feel so sad and not know why. Maybe it feels a bit confusing?

Nadia: It's actually just painful. I think you're the one who's more confused.

Mom (smiling): You're probably right.

Nadia: Can you just lie beside me for a bit? But no talking?

Mom: Of course.

[Mom lies down and puts her arm around Nadia. They lie together for awhile.]

Nadia (suddenly crying out): Oh my god! It hurts so much! I can't handle it, Mom!

Mom (holding Nadia tightly): I know, honey. It is so painful. Of course it hurts when you feel all torn up inside. We'll get through this together.

WHAT IF I GIVE TOO MUCH VALIDATION?

There can definitely be too much of a good thing when it comes to validation. The idea is not to validate every one of our child's feelings all the time. In fact, research shows that children who constantly have their emotional needs met can also end up having a problematic relationship with their own emotions (Beebe & Lachmann, 2013). Children need to learn how to handle their emotional challenges on their own some of the time in order to develop emotional competence. If parents are too involved in their children's needs, day in and day out, the children can end up struggling with feelings. It can feel invasive, and the child may end up in a state of learned helplessness or may rebel and not want any care from the parents.

Validating too much may seem like an unlikely problem for most of us to have. Very few of us have the capacity or motivation (or the time) to cover all our children's emotional needs. We are busy with other things and with our own tasks and pursuits. And, quite frankly, we are not typically that tuned in to everything our child needs. The issue is more that some of us tune in excessively to our child's emotional ups and downs and feel an urge to intervene too frequently. We've all heard of the "helicopter parent" who hovers anxiously over their child's safety. What we are referring to here is referred to as the "snowplow parent"—parents who try to clear all emotional obstacles out of our child's path. You might recognize yourself in this if you find validating "easy" (while many parents find it challenging) and yet your child (especially teen or adult) seems more frustrated than appreciative of your validation efforts. This is what we mean when we say that for the kids of these parents, the best validation—the most effective way to show that you "get" what they're feeling and experiencing—is to button your lip and say nothing. These kids are not in danger of you neglecting their emotions and needs. One parent reported that they really got this when their teenager said to them: "Mom. Neglect me. Please." There is also research showing that it's good for parents to make mistakes and not always meet their children's emotional needs, and that although ideally we would repair those mistakes, its best if we repair only about half, which means we have a nice big margin of error (Jaffe et al., 2001; Tronick, 2007).

Being connected to our children's emotional needs at absolutely every moment means that the children don't learn to handle their emotions and needs, or how to resolve conflicts. They also don't learn that relationships can survive conflict and still be good. These children can find their parents invasive and the excessive "help" in the form of too much validation shaming. It's as though the parent sees the child as inadequate to deal with normal challenges without Mommy or Daddy jumping to the rescue. It can feel like their parents see them as weak, needy, and unskilled. This type of parent will think they're being helpful and be surprised and even hurt at their child's intense anger and seeming ingratitude for all the parents do.

If your child is functioning adequately and doing mostly okay, then once you've learned validation you don't need to overthink whether to validate or not. You can trust that your parenting intuition, combined with your new validation skills, will guide you through big and small challenges. It's always good to learn more about emotions and to use that knowledge when practicing how to care for your children. But for the most part, your inner parenting wisdom will suffice. At some point, though, parents will come up against something more difficult that needs more specific attention. Then validation can be an even more important tool. The more your child struggles, the more specific attention they need and the more important it is to have skills that will help you meet the child's emotional needs.

All this knowledge about feelings is very important for parents who want to understand their children better, just in the same way that knowledge about flossing and brushing our teeth has helped our children to have fewer cavities than past generations. However, the specific skill of validation is most important when the child has strong emotions that are difficult to understand, or when they have very painful emotions. Validating a feeling is not the same as meeting emotional needs or solving a problem. We often go right to problem solving or meeting needs instead of validating. Then we hit a wall. It's like kids have an instinctive response when parents go straight to problem solving. Whether passively or more assertively, they will shut us out. When the child is not receptive to the problem solving, and rejects the adult's care, comfort, acknowledgment, and reassurance, then validation is especially useful. It can be the foot in the door and get you to a place where you can help your child navigate the challenge successfully. Validation is a useful tool when the child has mental, developmental, or behavioral challenges, but it is also useful to use on the big everyday emotions, such as when a child experiences extreme unfairness; is rejected by friends; has a big fight with a sibling; refuses to follow rules and respect limits; or experiences crises such as their parent's divorce, death of a loved one, or a major loss or defeat.

Although some parents are too close to their children, it is more common that they are not close enough. This means that many of us have something to gain from understanding and affirming our children's feelings a little more often than we do. Keep working on your awareness as you read, and try these things out. Keep noticing what "lands" with your child. Be aware of misleading signals, such as when kids who want us closer try to push us away and when kids who need more space let us come close because they fear hurting us if they push us away. This is how you'll find your unique way with validation, whether your kid is angry because you validate too much or, more typically, because they need you to validate more.

WHAT IF THERE ARE TWO KIDS WITH VERY DIFFERENT FEELINGS TO VALIDATE?

It can be a real challenge when siblings are fighting, or when two friends argue and the gloves come off. What do we do when there are two children who need validation? The first thing to do is to make a quick assessment of the situation. Can you validate the children's feelings while they are both there, or should you validate them separately? There are no hard-and-fast rules about what is right, but there are a few important questions to ask yourself: Do the children have a secure relationship with each other, or is it a relationship with a lot of insecurity or an uneven distribution of power? How serious was the incident, and how affected are the children? If the children are equal, have a secure relationship, and the incident is not very serious, then it is usually fine to validate the children together, including the vulnerable feelings. If the relationship has an uneven balance of power, or a serious conflict has arisen where one child has seriously upset or hurt the other, it is best to validate them separately. There are also many different factors that come into play that could make one choice better than the other. We need to trust our gut feelings and intuition—and the more we practice, the more we can get there.

If we choose to validate the children together, we take turns acknowledging one's feelings and experiences, then the other's. It's important not to speak too long to one child before shifting your focus to the other so that neither of them feel overlooked. It's fine to go back and forth, understanding and acknowledging each one. What follows are two examples that show this back-and-forth in seeing and understanding two children's feelings at the same time.

Twins Anton and Luka, age 4, are playing in the sandbox. Anton is dominating the game and controlling Luka and the game. It ends with Luka hitting Anton, and both start to cry and scream at each other.

> *Dad (validating Anton first):* Oh, Anton, I see you're upset that Luka hit you.
> *Anton (crying):* Yeah, it really hurt.

Dad: Of course it did. [*Turns to Luka.*] And you, Luka,
didn't get to choose the game, and so no wonder
you felt angry.

Luka: Anton always gets to choose. I never choose.
Anton decides everything in the whole game!

Dad: It's not nice when you don't get to decide the
game. [*Turns to Anton.*] And when Luka got
angry, you still didn't want him to decide on the
game.

Anton: No.

Dad (turning back to Luka): And so then you felt even
more angry, Luka. [*Turns to both of them.*] So
now you're both frustrated.

If you choose to validate the children separately, you can
validate in the usual way. But it's a good idea to tell them that
you're going to talk to both of them and then let them know
who you'll talk to first. If the children are different ages, it can be
smart to speak to the younger child first. At other times, you may
need to take other things into account. It can be a good idea to
talk first with the child who has a harder time handling their feelings, or the child who has been more affected. If there are other
adults or older children in the house, it may be good for the child
who's waiting to be with someone else, but sometimes the child
simply has to wait alone. It's good to say something comforting
to the child who has to wait and let them know approximately
how long it will be before you're back. Also, it goes without
saying that if one child is being physically aggressive toward the
other, the parent must set the limit and stop the hitting before
any validation occurs. In Chapter 12, we discuss in more detail
how to set limits with aggressive behavior while validating angry
feelings.

WHAT IF MY CHILD RESISTS FEELING PAINFUL EMOTIONS?

Some children get very angry when we validate vulnerable emotions because they don't want to feel them. It can be difficult for them to accept the validation of vulnerable feelings that they're trying to avoid, precisely because it hurts when we do focus on them. But it's still important to validate. Children need the experience of having their emotional needs met. They can learn that feelings aren't dangerous and that diving into the emotions instead of trying to avoid them will ultimately make things better. This will also increase their own skills and competence with emotion.

There are a number of reasons why children try to avoid painful feelings. It can be due to a combination of their innate temperament and personality. Parents will recognize if they have a child who they've always thought of as "too sensitive." These kids by nature are simply more "porous." They pick up subtle messages that go right over the heads of other kids and even over the heads of adults. Small changes in emotion in the air are powerful signals that they experience with great intensity. We can see that this can be easy to validate once we get it: "No wonder you're angry when we argue. We tell you it's just a disagreement, but for you it's loud and nasty." Some kids have also experienced that it's overwhelming or dangerous to show vulnerable feelings. We suggest that, with these kids, it's important not to push during validation, but it's also important not to give up. Some children are open to anger being acknowledged, even if they don't like to feel the vulnerable emotions. If you try to guess that the child is experiencing a vulnerable emotion and you are met with anger, it's also good to acknowledge how irritating it must feel that you want talk about painful feelings that the child doesn't want to feel. And then you can validate that: "Of course you don't want to feel it. It hurts." This can help the child be aware that they're avoiding painful emotions, and feel validated that they want to avoid them, but also know that the feelings are there regardless. This will increase the likelihood that, over time, painful feelings may be safer to feel. It's easier to talk about painful feelings and to get help handling them when they don't seem so threatening.

It's good to be close to your child and have quality time together and regularly ask how things are going, even if they don't want to talk about difficult emotions. Your child will know that you'll be there when they are ready to share.

CHAPTER 9

BUT I'M NOT A ROBOT: PARENTS HAVE FEELINGS, TOO

When children express intense anger, parents can experience their own intense anger, deep despair, hopelessness, profound shame, or intense fear, which can overpower their motivation to be the best for, and help, their children. Drowning in these feelings, many of us end up resigning ourselves to the situation and almost abdicating our role as parent. We can end up rejecting or dismissing our child in big and small ways: "When you act like that, I don't want to be around you." We might put the task of caring for our children on to others—the other parent, grandparents, or another support system: "Can you fix her?" Some of us become desperate and use strategies we learned from our own childhoods, which we know don't help in adulthood, but in the absence of anything else we end up threatening, hitting, or criticizing our angry child. All of this is in a desperate attempt to change the child's behavior so they conform to social norms. "If you can't behave, we'll have to call child services, and they'll have to deal with you!" "You are so rude and badly behaved that no one wants to be with you." "I wish you had never been born." All of this also comes from our own emotional wounds, unresolved from the past and therefore triggered by our kids' emotional style and then passed along, without our awareness, for them to carry.

As they say in the safety announcement when you fly: In the event of an emergency, put your oxygen mask on first, and only then put one on your child. As parents, that's what we need. We need oxygen if we're to be available to our child. In this chapter, we explain how to put your own oxygen mask on—that is, how to handle those times when you are overwhelmed by your own emotions, which makes it hard to respond effectively to your children's anger.

FEELING TRAPS

When our own emotions get in the way of helping the child, and we use old learned strategies that don't work, or are not good for the child, we end up falling into what we in emotion focused skills training call a *feeling trap*. This is when our own old, painful emotions get in the way of meeting our child's emotional needs. When we are caught in a feeling trap, it doesn't help that we've learned about validation, apologies, or the healthy setting of limits. We are incapable of validating, apologizing, or adjusting boundaries, even if it's what the child needs.

To understand the feeling trap, think of the example of a war veteran who struggles with posttraumatic stress. If someone comes into their yard, a reasonable and appropriate reaction would be to assess the situation and respond according to the level of threat, which may be high, low, or nonexistent. It might be a child selling Girl Scout cookies, a neighbor coming to ask a favor, or a beloved friend or relative coming to visit. There is also some chance, though maybe remote, that it is a stranger or enemy meaning harm to the individual and their family. The range of reasonable emotional reactions goes from inquisitiveness to curiosity to pleasure to caution to alarm and defense. And which of those the individual feels will guide their actions; remember that every emotion has a need associated with it, and an action to get that need met. If the homeowner

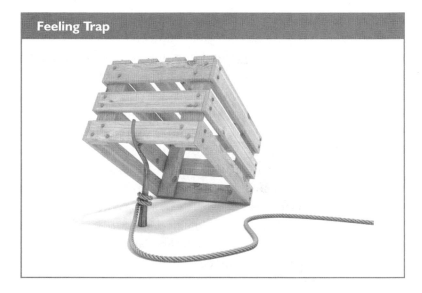

Feeling Trap

feels curiosity, they might ask the visitor a question; if they feel plea-sure, they might offer a handshake or a hug. If, however, the indi-vidual suffers from posttraumatic stress, the mere presence of the visitor may trigger an "intruder alert" in the homeowner's brain. With no capacity to see the visitor impartially or accurately, the veteran is transported automatically and instantly into an attack-or-be-attacked stance. In the context of battle, this is not only the appropriate reaction, it is the reaction that protects and saves lives. In the postwar context, however, it can result in tragedy.

It is therefore not the particular emotion that makes a feeling trap. It is the automatic, hijacking nature of it; the lack of aware-ness of being hijacked; and the actions that it leads to—protective in the past, destructive in the present. For example, we could say it's normal and appropriate to feel angry when your child steals money out of your wallet or when your teen states that they intend to destroy your relationship with your new partner. Such healthy, assertive anger can help you in establishing and maintaining health boundaries. This is not a feeling trap. If, however, you "see red," go from 0 to 60 in a second, and shout insulting or personal criticisms or hit them, this is more of a feeling trap. When the anger prevents you from being able to validate your child's feelings, set healthy limits, or repair the situation afterward, then it's a feeling trap.

All parents stumble into feeling traps all the time. If we are able to feel compassion for ourselves when we are up to our ears in a feeling trap, it actually makes it easier to regain focus on the child. The brilliant psychologist Carl Rogers taught us the *paradox of change*: "Only when we accept the way things are can we have any hope of changing." Therefore, don't feel bad for being caught in a feeling trap. If you can accept it and feel it and be curious about it, it may resolve enough in the moment for you to regain your parenting skills. And if not, there will always be a second chance later to take responsibility for what it must be like for your child when you are acting bonkers.

MAGNETS AND TRIGGERS

Some feeling traps are less problematic than others. Imagine a day when you're putting the kids to bed, and you just aren't in the mood and don't have the energy to validate or set good limits. You're exhausted and worn out, and all you want to do is flop on the couch and watch TV. You might convey or say to the kids, with little patience, "It would be in your best interest to cooperate." If you and your child have a strong relationship and there is nothing particular that has happened, you can take shortcuts every now and then and relax with a clear conscience.

This is a completely normal feeling that you don't need to work on. But what if you're exhausted and worn out every day, and every bedtime becomes a battleground? Then you might use your awareness to see that this is a feeling trap and figure out how to get yourself some oxygen so that things can go more smoothly. What if the evening shortcuts we sometimes take to get to the sofa and TV as soon as possible turn into long detours? If our child has an important need that we consistently don't meet, when we sink down instead onto the couch, it can become a larger problem for your child over time.

When feeling traps become problematic and your child's struggles are still present or have gotten worse, or there is increased conflict in the relationship between you and your child, or the relationship has a cold distance, then you need to take another look at working on your feeling traps. How can you get some oxygen? The best way to start is to increase your empathy for yourself and your past, because there are always valid reasons why our feelings exist, even if they seem irrational and bring a lot of pain to you and your children. Our self-compassion often increases when we recognize our own vulnerability, which often has to do with our childhood and upbringing, or traumatic events that we've experienced along the way. We might have experienced bullying, abuse, or neglect, or had too much time where we were left alone. We might have been overlooked, treated unfairly, overly criticized, prevented from being ourselves, or subjected to social shaming. We might have had overly strict or overly permissive parents, or parents who were not strong enough to handle the difficulties of life or to handle big emotions—ours or their own. As adults, we might have experienced intense loss or despair. We are more easily triggered by stuff that touches these old wounds and unmet needs. Those wounds are like magnets that attract specific experiences, information, or feelings, and when they get triggered—for example, by our kids, who seem to have a knack for exactly that—then those old wounds feel new.

There are two basic types of magnets, and we all tend to have more of one type then the other. Depending on your magnet, elements of your child's behavior will trigger you, and certain emotions will send you into a feeling trap. Your innate temperament, your innate abilities, and your personal experiences function as a finely woven and intertwined whole. You were born with some inclinations and sensibilities, and you have experienced moments in your life, big and small, that taught you and reinforced you in how you relate to your magnet. These all contribute to the kind of magnet you're likely to have.

The two magnet types are strongly connected to people's two basic needs.

1. *Identity*: the need to find one's role in the big herd. We refer to this as "who I am."
2. *Attachment*: the need to be closely connected to others and have a sense of being a "we." We refer to this as "who I'm with."

We all have both needs. We all need to know who we are as an individual. And we all need to be protected by, and belong to, the herd and our loved ones. Most of us, however, find that one of the two is more of a magnet that can get triggered more easily, and that throws us into a feeling trap. We refer to this as being "built" more around either "who I am" or "who I'm with."

What is your inner magnet? Some of us have no fear of loss or abandonment in our close relationships (which would threaten our attachment), but our inner magnet gets activated in response to anything that could be perceived as criticism (which threatens our identity). Those people are built more around "who I am." Others of us are terrified by a sense of impending abandonment or loss of connection and our inner magnet sends out a panic message instantly, whereas criticism doesn't have the same weight at all. Those people are built more around "who I'm with." The things that activate our magnets are called *triggers*.

MAGNETS AND TRIGGERS FOR PEOPLE BUILT AROUND "WHO I AM"

Some of us come into this world with an enormous urge to explore independence, mastery, and freedom, and we place a very high value on these things. One of the most important things for people built around "who I am" is to figure out their place in the world, whether it's on the other side of the globe or in a culture different from their own. It's important for them to know that they make an impact, that they contribute to the community, and that they are recognized as important members of the herd. Their biggest fear is being criticized, disrespected, losing their esteem, or being rejected by the community as worthless. People built around "who I am" may have a competitive instinct and will always try to perform well. They may seek to be the best and achieve status in what they do. They are largely driven by enthusiasm and curiosity, and they have a clear need to feel proud, which is strongly linked to their sense of identity. Shame lurks in the shadows and tends to play a significant role. The shame of not being good enough. The shame of being fat, ugly, boring, stupid, or bad. People with the strongest identity magnets react to triggers of criticism, disrespect, and the restriction of their autonomy or freedom or their opportunity to explore.

These features extend into our roles as parents. When we are built around "who I am," then feeling criticized, ignored, or disrespected can trigger our identity magnet and add to our feelings of not being good enough. This can lead to a strong inner critic who pushes us down even when others no longer do so. When we become parents, we can be triggered when our children are critical or disrespectful. We can also be triggered by needs that our children have that we don't fully understand or feel unable to meet. We might be triggered by a child who is clingy and anxious, who needs a lot of physical contact and always wants to be close to someone, and who doesn't dare to explore or try new things alone. We just don't get it, and we may keep urging the child toward autonomy, unable to validate their more pressing need for connection or reassurance. Parents built around "who I am" may be quite happy in their own company; they can love their family fully but not necessarily miss them when they are not present. They rarely have the feeling that they are "losing" their family if they haven't seen them for awhile, and they will assume that they love each other just as much even if they are not together all the time.

MAGNETS AND TRIGGERS FOR PEOPLE BUILT AROUND "WHO I'M WITH"

Some of us are born into this world with an enormous urge to be close to another person. We highly value relational security and the closeness of social bonds. One of the most important things for people built around "who I'm with" is to find their safe place and safe people in the world and to be able to feel that they are two people with a common "we." It is important for them to know that they are helping to nurture close relationships and that they are being protected and loved back. Their biggest fear is being abandoned, being alone in the sense of feeling they have no one to turn to or lean on, and losing loved ones. People built around "who I am" will often make a great effort to make others feel good. They want to create a safe and good home and will prioritize time with family. Others built this way will not want to risk connecting with anyone for fear of being rejected, and so they will choose a life of isolation and loneliness. They may reject others first, out of a fear that the other will reject them. The person built around "who I am" is largely driven by a sense of security and belonging in a small group, such as a close group of friends, their family, and close colleagues. A small number of people built this way are also afraid of being exposed to dangers that they have experienced earlier, and they are scared of dying or being injured if they are alone.

People who have a strong attachment magnet, meaning that being close to another person is the most central need, react strongly to any threats of abandonment and lack of contact with others. This also applies in their role as parents. When we are born with a strong attachment magnet, challenges such as abandonment and experiences of loneliness and loss related to illness and death, will heighten the reactivity of the attachment magnet. We may fear that others will not stay close or that love will not last. We often develop a strong inner voice who scares us and threatens that we will lose those we love, even when there is no danger of this happening. As parents, we can be triggered when our children push us away, but we can also be triggered by our kids having needs that we can't relate to and don't understand. We can get triggered if our children have a greater urge to explore than to stay close, who need more freedom and time for themselves than we think they should have, and who may leave home early and move far away. Parents with an attachment magnet are happy at home and in close community with others. They feel best and are most productive when someone has their back.

People with an attachment magnet get a better feeling from the sense of harmony of sharing an experience with loved ones than from the autonomy gained from doing something on their own. They take for granted that everyone is happy as long as they are together and feel safe and good. Parents with an attachment magnet may be anxious, for themselves and for their children, or they may overfunction and try to rescue their loved ones. It's hard for them to see that their own unmet needs for secure attachment, and to have been rescued when they were young, are not necessarily present for their kids.

Children can be affected differently by the same situation, depending on whether they have a strong identity magnet or a strong attachment magnet. If you have two children built differently in this regard, who both hear their parents shouting at each other and at them, then the one with the attachment magnet may be mostly afraid that the parents will divorce, and they may feel lonely or scared. The child with the identity magnet may, to a greater extent, feel that they're not good enough and that it's their fault that their parents fight so much because they are too demanding, and so this child is left with feelings of shame and guilt.

Your magnets and triggers affect what it is about your life situation, and your relationship with your child, that sends you into a feeling trap. In addition, your child's magnets and triggers will affect which of your behaviors they react to most strongly. Awareness of your own magnets and triggers, and those of your child, can act as a guide when you fall into a feeling trap. This awareness can help you feel more self-compassion and more empathy for your child. Your partner or coparent will benefit from it as well.

Even if your need for identity is strongest, you can still have a child who first and foremost triggers your attachment needs. In other words, even if you are usually very put out by not getting enough time alone, or by being criticized or not shown the respect you deserve, you may still be afraid of losing the connection with your child if he or she is often very angry and dismissive toward you. Our need to be close to our loved ones, and our need for acknowledgment and respect, can be triggered differently in different relationships. For example, we may seek closeness and security in one relationship and acknowledgment and alone time in another. This will also affect our needs and our behavior in the relationship with our children and with our partner and coparent. However, it's typical to have one fundamental need that is more dominant than the other in all of our relationships.

EXERCISE: IDENTIFY YOUR MAGNETS AND TRIGGERS

We all have an identity, and we all have attachments to others. But which of the two is a more powerful magnet in you? Which is the one that gets triggered and evokes painful feelings in you? The following are some helpful questions to ask yourself regarding where you get triggered.

1. **How sure are you of your ability to help your child?**
   Motivation is about the confidence we have in our ability to make a difference and the expectation we have for mastery. Fear, guilt, shame, and our inability to identify and handle our emotions reduces our confidence in mastery and ability (Miller & Rollnick, 2012). On a scale of 1 (*very unsure/no ability*) to 10 (*very sure/very able*), how sure are you of your ability to help your child?

2. **What are your feeling magnets?**
   Which of the following scenarios do you react to the most? Check one.
   - When attachment is challenged (being abandoned, feeling not a part of things)
   - When identity is challenged (not being respected, being criticized)

3. **What triggers your magnets?**
   Which of the following scenarios activate you the most? Check one.
   - When my child triggers my fear of being abandoned (is rebellious, aggressive, bossy, dismissive, quiet)
   - When my child triggers my fear of not being good enough (is needy, clingy, passive, helpless, critical, rude)

4. **How do your magnets and triggers mix with those of your family?**
   - What are your family members' magnets and triggers? How strong is the identity or attachment magnet to them, and what types of behavior or situations trigger these magnets?
   - Do you have the same magnets and triggers as your child?
   - Is it easier or harder for you to relate to family members who are the most like you?
   - What about to those who are the most different?

EXERCISE: IDENTIFY HOW YOU'RE BUILT

Which side BEST describes you? Check the box to indicate your choice for each row:

☐ Say sorry	☐ Don't say sorry
☐ Do not set high expectations of myself and others	☐ Set high expectations of myself and others
☐ Leave decisions to others	☐ Take responsibility for decisions
☐ Seek closeness	☐ Seek distance
☐ Need closeness and security	☐ Need acknowledgment and respect
☐ Not critical	☐ Critical
☐ Dependent	☐ Independent
☐ Come to the rescue of others	☐ Trust others to help themselves
☐ Easily offer comfort	☐ Rarely offer comfort

☐ Don't like to be alone	☐ Like to be alone
☐ Unsure of what to do	☐ Know what to do
☐ Scared of losing loved ones	☐ Not scared of losing loved ones
☐ Cry	☐ Don't cry
☐ Anxious when alone	☐ Feel safe when alone
☐ Can't set limits	☐ Have an easy time setting limits
☐ Feel lonely after a fight	☐ Don't feel good enough after a fight
☐ Feel weaker when angry	☐ Feel stronger when angry
☐ Do things for others	☐ Let others do things for themselves
☐ Happiest at home	☐ Happiest when discovering new places
☐ Need and seek protection from others	☐ Can protect myself

If you checked mostly items on the right side, then it's likely that you're built around "who I am." If you checked mostly items on the left side, then it is likely that you're built around "who I'm with."

A STORY ABOUT A TRIGGER, A MAGNET, AND A FEELING TRAP

Paul has a 6-year-old son who isn't particularly interested in eating and is suddenly having outbursts of anger that are hard to understand. All of the food he gets is "gross," unless it's a hot dog, and even if he gets a hot dog for dinner, he will still only eat a bit of one. It is a trigger for Paul that his son won't even taste other foods or eat more than a couple of mouthfuls, and Paul tends to snap and get very angry in these situations. Paul then presses his son to finish whatever is on his plate. On two occasions, Paul has ended up throwing the leftover food and the plate in the garbage bin and shouting: "Don't you get it? If you don't eat, you will always be skinny and weak!" Paul always feels really guilty afterward and promises himself that he won't get mad like that again. But then the next mealtime comes.

Paul had a generally good upbringing, with secure and caring parents. He was never bullied and didn't experience any big traumas. When we begin to take a deeper look at his family of origin and start to explore how they dealt with emotions, Paul realizes that feelings were generally accepted by his mother as long as they weren't difficult feelings about *her*. If he got angry at her, she would start to cry. When he thinks about it, he remembers that he was always very careful not to upset her and to be sure he paid enough attention to her.

His father avoided sharing feelings, especially the vulnerable ones. Paul doesn't remember ever seeing his father cry. He remembers his father being kind if he was crying, but his father would always say, "Come on; let's go hunting," and that's what they did every time Paul cried. His dad was tall and strong, with a booming voice, and he was a very skillful hunter. Paul never felt like he could live up to his dad's expectations or abilities when it came to hunting, sports, or school. His dad never said he was disappointed in Paul, and perhaps he never was, but it was a feeling Paul got just by comparing himself with his dad. Paul asked his dad once if he had ever cried, and if he had cried when he was a kid. His dad laughed and said, "I assume I cried when I was a baby, but I'm not the crying type." His dad was not an angry man, but he was very direct and instructive, and if Paul or his siblings did something wrong he would be stern in his reproach. Paul remembers that once in awhile he felt scared. When Paul thinks about it, joy and anger were the two emotions his dad showed the most. Shame, sadness, and fear were absent, at least from the outside.

Let's think about how this might have led Paul to develop a magnet for issues relating to identity. In the face of his father's strength, he felt weak. This was reinforced when any gestures of strength toward his mother, such as a healthy expression of self-assertive anger, ended in her being "hurt." Her reaction would dampen these efforts of his to be strong and assertive and leave him feeling weak and inadequate. As is often the case, an incident in his teens came along to seal the deal and reinforce his sense of inadequacy: A girlfriend broke up with him and told him he wasn't a very "manly man." Paul became unsure of himself and felt like he wasn't smart enough or strong enough—and this is how he still feels, even if not quite as much as he used to.

If we could peek into Paul's emotional world we would see that when his skinny little boy doesn't want to eat (and it doesn't help to try and cheer him up, or play, or give him "fun" food, etc.), the situation triggers Paul's identity magnet, and he feels shame. Shame that he's not up to the task of being a dad, and shame to have a skinny little weak son. He is scared that his son will be like he was and not feel good enough or manly enough if he stays small and skinny. Paul is also worried that his son is not getting enough nutrition and that it will affect his ability to concentrate at school or could lead to him being bullied because of his size. He is able to manage his concerns about his son's food intake by getting some advice about vitamins from a nurse. But he cannot manage the shame. When the shame appears, the rage follows soon after. Paul is ashamed of not being big or strong enough. Shame is one of the hardest feelings to tolerate, and when it shows up he is strongly motivated not to feel it. And so he gets angry instead. The anger comes as a reaction to the shame and protects him from having to feel it. In this sense, we say that anger is the soldier of shame. It shows up to protect the self from the corrosive effect of shame.

It makes sense that Paul is more motivated to feel anger than shame. Anger gives power and strength, and so it is an acceptable feeling for him. He turns to the same strategy every time he gets angry. He shouts at his son and threatens him with what will happen if he doesn't eat. It's as if he'll pound the seriousness of it all into his son, and the boy will want to eat just by seeing how angry his dad is. Of course, Paul knows very well that when his son feels scared he is even less likely to eat, and yet he can't manage to change his strategy. Paul has learned about validation and has practiced how to validate his son's feelings, around and outside of mealtimes. However, he is still unable to change his approach to addressing his son's behavior at meals. It's as though his logical mind wants to, but his feelings won't let him. What is keeping Paul stuck in the feeling trap?

THE BRAIN BOSS

When we get stuck in a feeling trap, an inner dialogue—or, rather, a monologue—takes place. Our inner voice tells us what might go wrong if we validate our child's anger or underlying vulnerable feelings, tighten or loosen the boundaries, or take responsibility for the challenging situation that arises when our child becomes angry and acts out. The voice tries to convince us that we have to stick to old strategies. The old strategies differ for each of us. But the essence of the command from the inner voice is to continue to do the "same old, same old." For example, to continue to be strict, yell, punish, or threaten with serious consequences (the way Paul does). Or to continue to be passive, accommodating, and victimlike, and hurt (like Paul's mother). Or to pull away, shut down, and be absent. The inner voice coaches us to hold tight to the idea that it is the child's fault and that it is they who must learn to behave. Or it tells us that we need to be careful about setting clearer limits, to take a step back when the anger builds, or to avoid talking about the difficult situation and just hope it passes.

When we fall into a feeling trap, our thoughts take the form of an inner commentator who instructs and scares us or makes us ashamed by saying things like

- "She will never have a best friend when she is so angry and hits kids."
- "She can't participate in after-school activities if she can't behave."
- "It's embarrassing to have to apologize to the other parents after the conflicts."
- "You have to be strict; otherwise, you're a bad parent."
- "This behavior must have consequences! You have to punish her—cut back on screen time! If you don't, she won't understand the seriousness."
- "Do not validate her anger. It's dangerous. Then you're saying that the behavior is acceptable and she'll never learn. She has to take her punishment when she's been threatening and mean."
- "Definitely don't take responsibility for her anger and say 'Sorry.' That will mean she won and you lost. She has to take responsibility for her actions."

We call this inner voice that scares, shames, and commands us the *Brain Boss*. In some of us, the Brain Boss offers mostly fear propaganda, whereas in others it tries to make us feel like we're incompetent as parents. The Brain Boss evolves in us over the years, from being a healthy version of an inner critic and protector (who makes sure that we see ourselves from the outside, to feel other people's eyes on us, and to be aware of dangers, so that we behave in line with norms and rules and avoid dangerous situations), to being too strict or too scary. For many of us, our own parents, bullies, or a bad boyfriend or girlfriend who criticized or intimidated us have become internalized as our own inner voice. For others, it has evolved in opposition to excessive or overly generalized praise, or it has been driven by high demands and the urge to perform at a high level. Parents built around "who I am," who value alone time, independence, and good performance will often have a brain boss who first and foremost criticizes and inflicts shame. Parents who feel that close bonds and being together are the most important things in life will often have a Brain Boss who first and foremost scares, exaggerates fears, and threatens that they will lose their relationship with their child.

If we go in-depth and really listen to what the Brain Boss is saying, and if we could ask why it is so intent on scaring us, inflicting shame on us, and making us stick to old strategies, we will always get the answer that it's trying to protect us from feeling bad feelings. These feelings are echoes from the past when we felt wrong, unworthy, lonely, or unlovable. This protection becomes a vicious cycle. In the past, it would actually help us avoid the emotion. We might have behaved so well that we never got in trouble, or been so careful that nothing dangerous ever happened. This makes the Brain Boss double down. It makes us feel that this works. So, don't change the strategy.

Let's turn up the volume on the conversation in our head to catch the nuances of what it's saying. The Brain Boss in the example above might continue like this:

> She will never learn to behave if you aren't strict, and she'll think she can make demands and shout about whatever she wants. Everyone can see that you have no control, and you don't know how to raise your own child. If you don't get her in line quickly, you'll have no credibility as someone who works with children. Everyone will think you're incompetent. They're

laughing at you behind your back and talking about how you have no control, just like everyone laughed at you when you were little. You're going to feel totally worthless and ridiculed, and you never want to have that feeling again. That is the feeling I'm protecting you from. So, no matter what, don't take that chance. Don't let go of your strategy of being strict. Keep being strict and trying to discipline her.

The Brain Boss's greatest intention is to protect you from painful feelings. It's like a football coach on the sidelines. It tries to motivate you to use a particular strategy to get what you want in a difficult situation. The problem is that, in that moment, the Brain Boss's goal is to protect you against your own painful feelings rather than help your child with theirs. The Brain Boss also keeps you in the feeling trap and makes it difficult for you to get out. Perhaps you need to stand up to your Brain Boss and let it know that it's not helpful when it comes between you and your child, because then it's just like you're scoring on your own goal.

Changing strategies when facing your angry child can be scary because it shakes your safety net to the core. You are suddenly vulnerable and unprotected. You've put your old strategy aside. But you have no evidence yet whether using the strategies in this book of validation, apology, and revising your limit-setting will work. And yet what we have found in our work with parents is that the thing that is most difficult for us to change is the thing the child needs from us the most. It is tremendously difficult to take the first steps and change your behavior with your child. But we believe you can, and we know you will.

EXERCISE: IDENTIFY YOUR BRAIN BOSS

Think of an actual situation that was difficult between you and your child: a situation that you don't think you handled particularly well, and where you didn't want, or weren't able, to validate your child's anger or their underlying vulnerable feelings, such as shame, fear, or sadness. If you can't think of a particular situation, then think of an emotion that your child has had that you think you should have tried to guess and validate, but every fiber of your being wouldn't allow it. For example, it could be your child's cloaking anger, or your child's self-assertive anger toward you, or when your child felt mean (shame), fat and ugly (shame), dumb (shame), or when your child felt totally alone (sadness/fear), or had social angst (fear/shame), or was in grief (sadness), or when your child has been attacked or harassed (fear/shame), or some other feeling that you think is difficult to validate.

Now write down what your Brain Boss says to you when you are stuck in a feeling trap with your child. Write as if you are the Brain Boss who is speaking directly to you, the parent.

1. What does the Brain Boss say to you to convince you not to validate your child's feeling? "Don't validate . . . because . . ."
2. Scare yourself—what will happen to your child if you validate the feeling?
3. Convince yourself that the strategy you are using in the situation is the best, even if it means avoiding your child's feelings, overlooking or overreacting to bad behavior, criticizing or dismissing your child, or blaming your child for their bad behavior or for their painful feelings.
4. Scare yourself—tell yourself what it will be like for you if you validate the feeling and it goes badly.
5. Tell yourself specifically what feelings you will experience if you validate your child's feeling and it goes badly.
6. Remind yourself of a time you felt that feeling, as a child or young person, and remind yourself how awful it was. Tell yourself that you never want to have that feeling again.

7. Write "It's more important to avoid feeling the painful emotions (from the past) than it is to help (write your child's name) and to validate their feelings."
8. So, continue with the old strategies (specify the same old strategy your Brain Boss tells you to keep using, e.g., keep nagging).

If you want to go even deeper with this exercise, try this:

1. Sit down and place another chair in front of you. Imagine your child sitting in that other chair. Take the time to really picture your child.
2. Look at your "child in the chair" and speak as though you are talking directly to your child. Announce to your child that you're not going to validate their feelings and that you're going to continue (specify the same old strategies, e.g., "I'm going to keep yelling"). End with "It's more important for me to avoid feeling the painful feelings (from my childhood) than it is to help you and validate your feelings."
3. Change seats and sit in the "child's chair." Imagine that you are your child, and see how it feels to hear this. What feelings arise in you, as the child, and what do you need from your parent? Can you speak directly to the other chair as though you are your child speaking to their parent?
4. Go back to where you were first sitting. As a parent, what would you like to say to your child?

CLIMBING YOUR WAY OUT OF A FEELING TRAP

It's painful to admit it when we fall into and get stuck in the same feeling trap over and over. It can be embarrassing and upsetting, and it can make us feel angry at ourselves. And then, of course, the

Brain Boss also arrives on the scene to tell us how incompetent we are. The good news, which can give us hope, is that it is possible to escape the trap and concentrate fully on our child. We have seen this happen countless times. Parents become fierce warriors when they realize that there is a barrier preventing them from getting to their children and being able to help them with their pain. We can do so much more than we think when our motivation to help our child is allowed more space.

Take a Break to Reconnect With Your Emotions

We can get out of some feeling traps quickly if we're aware of what's happening and we're able to reconnect with our emotions. When we have awareness, we can reflect on the situation with curiosity. We can reflect on both our own and our child's experience. Some of us can do these reflections on our own and maybe write our thoughts down, but for most of us it's easier to sort through our emotions by talking to someone. When you journal or talk to another person about the situation, try to be an emotional detective and determine both your own and your child's feelings. Keep in mind that any conjectures or guesses we make about our child need to be tentative. We need to test them out. It is the child who knows the answers to their own emotional life, but you are the best at guessing what those emotions might be.

Not all feeling traps are so easy to escape. We have to work a little harder at some and a lot harder at others. But it's important to note that you don't have to have all your emotional issues figured out before you can help your child with theirs. You can be a good parent even if your self-esteem is not the best and you have some old unresolved relationship issues or trauma. You just need enough contact with your own feelings to access what is going on for you, and what your and your child's needs are. Then it becomes easier to stop, stand up to the Brain Boss and actively choose the motivation to help your child. When the situation becomes too challenging, or when what you try fails, you can take a step back and try again with a new approach. Even when we stay stuck in the feeling trap throughout the whole conflict, or for a whole day or week, we can still come back to it afterward and clean up the mess. Sometimes we need that distance to be able to get in touch with our own emotions and figure out what we need. We need to get some oxygen. Then we can get to our child.

Next time you find yourself in a situation where you are not able to be the parent you want to be, start by taking a few breaths. Take a moment to feel what's going on inside you. Try to feel what's going on for your child. Then start again. You can always, at any time—even in the midst of a conflict—pivot and start again, and then you can try to validate or apologize or set stricter or looser limits.

Do Self-Care to Avoid Traps

The most important thing you can do to avoid falling into a feeling trap is to take care of yourself, because you need to be wearing your own oxygen mask in order to help your child in an emergency. To function well is different for each of us, so it's important to listen to your needs.

If, for example, you are the kind of person who is very stressed by loud noises, you have to say no to your child being able to have toys that make a lot of noise, like a drum kit, no matter how much they might want them. If you are a person who needs time to yourself in order to function well, then you need to create a routine that allows you to have this time on a regular basis. If being with good friends or getting some exercise is the best thing for charging your battery, then it is important for your child that you prioritize these things. If you know that you always feel a bit stressed and annoyed when you get home from work until dinnertime, then explain this to your child and let them know it isn't a great idea to ask for things they want during that time. And if you aren't getting enough sleep, you need to go to bed earlier for awhile, or try to get some time off from the family's morning responsibilities. We are simply much better parents when our basic needs have been met.

We can hear you thinking "Right!" and "As if!" and "When did I last get to sleep in or have alone time?!" We get it. The life of a parent is not a life of balance. But we're encouraging you to think of your needs in a new light with a clear conscience (as opposed to guilt) in relation to your kids. Have you heard the expression "The best gift we can give our children is our own happiness?" Think of your own parents. If they were happy, wasn't that a gift? If not, didn't you wish—when you look back on your childhood—that they could have been? We want you to think of taking care of yourself (and meeting even a few of your most crucial needs) not as taking time away from your kids but as a gift to them. It could take the form of the phrase "It would be in your best interest . . . ," for example, "It would be in your best interest to give me 5 minutes before bombarding me when I walk in the door" or "It would be in your best interest to get yourselves to bed quickly tonight." Be creative. "Alone time" might be hiding in your closet for 20 minutes with a flashlight and a good book. Or no book and a glass of wine. Or no flashlight or book or wine, and instead a pillow and blanket so you can take a flash nap.

All of this depends, of course, on things like the age and needs of your child and the availability of other adults to step in while you slip away. When we say "put your needs first," we mean "after you ensure the basic care and safety of your child." Do what you can to help them by helping yourself feel less stressed.

Some parents have had very difficult upbringings or have experienced traumatic events. This may mean they simply need more sleep and more alone time in order to function. The best thing you can do is confront those old unresolved and unprocessed relationships and feelings. Try to reconcile yourself with them, grieve what you lost, and grieve what you missed in terms of not getting your needs met. Some parents will need to go to therapy for this, but many others will be able to work with these old wounds by getting help and support from loved ones. Be aware also that working through trauma can take time. It can feel like a lot of work. You may need to tell people—your partner, coparent, and others—that you need to do this important work and that you may need them to step in and help. Allow yourself this time to resolve old feelings from the past. You deserve it, and your child will thank you for it.

CHAPTER 10

THE MAGIC OF APOLOGY

Children who act out verbally or physically create big and small wounds in their relationships with others. They may hurt or intimidate others in a way that makes people withdraw. Parents who act out verbally or physically also create big and small wounds—and these wounds, or injuries, are in their relationships with their children. We want to heal these relational wounds so that the bond doesn't weaken or break. Apology is the magic healing tool.

How much healing can really come from an apology? And what is the best way to teach our children to say sorry when they hurt others or do something wrong? Parents can repair both old and new wounds in their relationships with their children. We can apologize for the everyday mishaps, and we can apologize for the pain resulting from old unmet needs in our child. In this chapter, we deal with how we can repair damaged relationships, between ourselves and our child and between our child and their siblings and friends. Taking responsibility, as wise and responsible parents, and repairing big and small injuries in the relationship with our children, leads to reconciliation and forgiveness. To those of you who are weighed down by guilt for unfortunate things you've done or for having hurt or injured your child: It is never too early or too late to do something different and better.

With angry parents and angry kids, we are adamant that the way to navigate the labyrinth of injury and forgiveness is to have the parents do the work of healing and repairing. Hold on to your hat as you feel yourself being hijacked straight into a feeling trap when you hear that. Let's use our feeling-trap–awareness technique: Turn the volume up on what your Brain Boss tells you when you hear that it's *you* who should apologize—no matter what your young child, teen, or adult child has said or done. Whoa! Right? Why should *I* apologize? Hear it as a command from your Brain Boss:

> Don't apologize. It's them who should apologize. They . . . disobeyed you repeatedly. Screamed at you. Swore at you. Lied to you. Stole from you. Broke your heart. What they did was unforgivable. It is them who should apologize.

WHY SHOULD I BE THE ONE TO APOLOGIZE?

If you search "children" and "apology" online, you will find endless references that all instruct us to make our children apologize. Children must apologize. You'll even find lots of references that suggest that if a child is angry and acting out with peers, you must make them apologize in order to "teach them empathy." Now we ask you—how do children learn? The wisdom is old, tried, and true: Children learn by watching and experiencing what their parents do. Children do what we do, not what we say they should do. This is the first rationale for having parents (vs. children) lead the way with apology. Children will only learn apology by having their parents apologize. The child having the experience of receiving an apology reinforces this learning. To receive a heartfelt, authentic, and skilled apology is healing and freeing. And just to give you something to make you think it could be worth it, it is healing and freeing for the one who does the apologizing as well.

The second rationale for us as parents taking the lead and apologizing has simply to do with age and brain development. We know that at any age, strong negative emotion causes the reasoning brain to go offline. Think of how much more derailing this is when the brain is not fully developed, and specifically when it lacks reasoning capacity and is trigger happy and impulsive. If your house were on fire, which neighbor would you run to for help? The preverbal clumsy little toddler in the house on your left? The senior with dementia and a broken hip on the right? Or the 30-year-old with the strong body and healthy mind across the street? No contest. This rationale tells us: Why send a child in to do an adult's job? Get the fully developed brain to do the job of apologizing. Period.

If we accept that we are the ones for the job, and that children learn by watching what we do, both by us modeling and by them experiencing the benefits of apology, then your children will learn to apologize. You will be amazed. We are amazed at how often we have heard it—parents apologizing to their kids and the kids following suit. It's very important to emphasize that we're not asking for an apology in return. It's not: "I apologized. Now it's your turn." We will talk about why that will never work. But when you get the apology right—when you "nail it"—you will get the evidence that they learned their lesson. They will learn it a thousand times better than if we scold and guilt them to "Apologize!" How this goes depends on the age of the child. Parents of young children may report hearing their child apologize to a younger sibling using the same wording for the apology that the parent used. They may overhear their teen apologize similarly to a friend. And when the child is an adult, the parent will often get the sweet experience of their adult child taking appropriate responsibility for their own actions and apologizing in return. We have to emphasize that this is not the same as when a parent is apologizing to a child of any age, and the child refutes the apology by apologizing themselves, or when the child is acting out of fear of reprimand (fearing shame, for people with an identity magnet; see Chapter 9) or fear of loss of connection (fearing abandonment, for people with an attachment magnet) and desperately insists they are sorry and will never do it again. Instead, the apology of the mature son or daughter conveys that the parent's apology was accurate and that there was an injury. It conveys gratitude to the parent for apologizing. And it opens the door for the son or daughter to return spontaneously with awareness of their own behavior. It might sound something like "I know I wasn't the easiest," or "I know I was a piece of work," or "I didn't make things easy on you, I know."

RADICAL RESPONSIBILITY

An important part of repair work in relationships with children is our ability and willingness to take radical responsibility for our children's feelings, behavior, and relationships. The parent–child relationship is not equal in terms of power, responsibility, or influence. In equal relationships, different rules of engagement apply in terms of sharing blame and responsibility. In the parent–child relationship, it makes most sense and has the best outcome if the parents take radical responsibility. This means they take responsibility for what goes wrong, even if what happened was beyond the parents' control. This is also very empowering for the parents. When we take radical responsibility for our children, including for their anger and their aggressive behavior, we put ourselves in a position to be able to act and have an impact on the outcome rather than remain passive, helpless onlookers.

Radical responsibility includes adopting the attitude that when their children get into jams, it's the parents' job to make things right. When our kids start fights at school, we take responsibility for making sure that they understand how their feelings led to bad choices, and we take charge and do what we have to do to make things right. When our children hit us, it's our responsibility to stop them with healthy, effective limit-setting. When they explode in anger at the dinner table, seemingly out of nowhere, we take responsibility for maybe having overlooked important signals and needs prior to the outburst. When our anger at our kids is unhelpful and unkind, regardless of whether we are just tired and stressed or we have a valid reason to be angry, we apologize afterward for our strong reaction. Radical responsibility does not mean that we say sorry for everything all the time, or that we should feel guilty for every up and down. Radical responsibility means that we take responsibility when something unfortunate happens in our relationship with our child, and when our children end up with such big difficulties with others that they aren't able to handle it themselves. We can let our kids sort out an argument without us intervening if they can, and step in if they can't. It is not the child's mistake if they aren't able to sort things out. We want to help with the heavy lifting in managing their anger and thereby unburden them of the unhelpful regret, self-blame, and shame they might otherwise feel after they've freaked out.

Another way to take radical responsibility is to help when sibling arguments get out of hand, or when our child gets in a big fight with a friend that lasts several days. As a rule, children need more help than we tend to give them in their interactions with each other, and they have important needs that we tend to overlook when the conflicts get bigger or when they occur repeatedly. Thus, radical responsibility is more than simply saying "I'm sorry." We can go back and attend to needs that we realize we've overlooked: "You know what, I actually saw that you were sad today, but I didn't take the time to ask you how you were doing. But I'd really like to hear now, if you'd be willing to tell me."

We can also actively address something that we know is difficult for the child, even if the child hasn't come to us about it yet. "It's three weeks until you have to talk to the judge about how it is living half-time with me and half with Dad. I'm guessing you're dreading that a bit." We can also show that we're taking responsibility every day, through many small actions, comments, and nonverbal cues. In addition, we have a parenting skill that may make us feel vulnerable and can be challenging but that is very important for us to use when our children are really struggling: We take radical responsibility for repairing damaged relationships by saying "I'm sorry."

Saying sorry has many positive effects. Apologizing has an effect on both the person who is apologizing and the person receiving the apology, including one or more of the following:

- *Experience.* It feels good when someone takes responsibility and genuinely apologizes. Even if it doesn't feel good in the moment—for example, if the receiver is angry or full of strong emotions—it almost always feels good afterward.
- *Modeling.* When we say we're sorry, our children learn that conflicts and relationship issues are manageable even if they're scary, and that even after a fight people can be friends again. Children also learn how to say sorry just by experiencing how their parents do it.
- *Kindness.* When we apologize, our children learn to be kind to themselves when they mess up and make mistakes. They learn not to fear disagreement and conflict, and they gain confidence that they can mend broken relationships. This happens when we apologize rather than stew in guilt about the mistakes we've made as parents. Our kids learn not to avoid conflict by always caving to others, nor to steamroll over others' rights and opinions, but to express themselves and know how to make repairs if an injury occurs. Healthy remorse and apology are far better than unhealthy guilt, shame, and self-criticism.

- *Openness*. Apologizing leads to more openness about things that are painful or difficult. Taking responsibility, saying sorry, and talking about difficult situations that come up help children see that they're allowed to talk about mistakes that have happened.
- *Trust*. When we take radical responsibility and apologize, we show our children that we can handle difficult situations and painful emotions. When our children see that we can tolerate emotional pain, and we can see what is painful for them and take responsibility for it, they learn to trust us more. They can feel safe coming to us and trust that we will be understanding, whether they bring successes, setbacks, or mistakes.
- *Emotional competence*. Children who learn that it's possible to heal wounds and resolve conflicts can be better at handling their own feelings and the feelings of others. Emotions simply become less scary, and there is less need to avoid challenging feelings and situations. When parents take radical responsibility, it also increases their emotional competence and their own ability to tolerate emotions.
- *Guilt*. Taking responsibility and making a heartfelt apology can free us of guilt regardless of whether our child forgives us or not. Many parents say they feel like a heavy weight has been lifted from their shoulders after they apologize to their child for an old injury. It feels good to take responsibility. It is the opposite of avoidance, which can make us feel more cowardly or weak. When we take the blame, so to speak, it also reduces our children's feelings of guilt, which is a great bonus. Too often, children think and feel "It's my fault."
- *Symptom reduction*. We have observed that having parents apologize to their child who is struggling with a mental health issue can help reduce symptoms such as cutting, starving, or using substances. Freeing our kids from guilt by having us take

responsibility for ruptures in the relationship means they don't have to turn to such destructive strategies to cope.

- *Reconciliation.* Saying sorry helps with reconciliation and creates the opportunity to let go of hurt feelings that are preventing us from moving forward. Our experience is that children want to forgive their parents. They long for closeness and a good relationship with us. With adult children or teenagers who have left home, reconciliation may require more work over a prolonged period, especially if there were serious violations or abuse. We are all aware that not everything can be forgiven. However, we have observed the same for teens and adults as for young children—that the relationship with parents, even if estranged, will always have an impact. It is our observation that, deep down, all children want to forgive their parents for their mistakes and for the injuries they caused. And deep down, all parents long to be forgiven. So don't assume it isn't possible with older children. In fact, we started this entire approach of having parents take responsibility for healing the relationships with their children with the parents of adult children. So—there is no guarantee that it will work, but no assumption that it won't, either.

A STEPMOM TAKES RADICAL RESPONSIBILITY

Sylvia, age 12, lives with her dad, his new wife, and the child they have together, Maria (age 4). Sylvia's mom died when Sylvia was 5 years old. Two years later, Sylvia's dad married again, and she got a stepmom. Sylvia rejected her stepmom at the start, and her stepmom started to protect herself by distancing herself from Sylvia and by being quick to criticize and dismiss Sylvia. The conflict between the two of them escalated. Sylvia always felt that her little sister was the favorite. Sylvia's stepmom sat her down one day to take radical responsibility and to apologize for not being the stepmom she had wanted to be.

Sylvia's stepmom took the initiative for some much-needed repair work:

Stepmom: Sylvia, I want to apologize to you for never realizing how difficult it was for you to lose your mom. You needed kindness and support when you were in grief and hurting. Instead, I got angry and pulled away.
[Sylvia gets tears in her eyes and listens with interest.]

Stepmom (continuing): It must have been so awful for you to lose your mom when you were only five years old. I'm sure you still miss her tons. And then I came into your life, and everything got turned upside down again. I know that I've been strict with you. No wonder you'd think I don't love you when I yell at you and don't spend a lot of time alone with you. Especially when you see that Maria and I are close.
[Sylvia listens intently.]

Stepmom: I'm not sure, but maybe you felt like you couldn't quite find your place in the new family, and I didn't help. It must have felt so unfair and painful first to lose your mom, and then maybe feeling like you lost your dad a bit too. I'm so sorry that these last seven years have been so difficult for you and that I contributed to that. I'm really sorry, Sylvia.
[Sylvia cries. Her stepmom moves closer to her, puts an arm around Sylvia, and continues.]

Stepmom: I should have known how hard it must have been when I came along. You didn't want me, you wanted your mom. Maybe you even felt that if you did accept me, it would be like replacing your mom, and that would be awful. I should have understood that. And I am sorry about things I've said when we were arguing. I said I'm glad I'm not your mom. No wonder you thought I didn't love you when I said stuff like that. You had every right to be mad. I should not have said that, and I deeply and sincerely regret it. I am going to smarten up. Going forward, I won't be so angry at you or reject you when you get mad at me. I'm sure I will still mess up sometimes, but I will take responsibility for our arguments and make things right between us. I would also really like it if you and I could have more time together, just us two, if you'd like that, and so I will be better about asking you if you want to do something with me.

Sylvia: But do you want to do that?

Stepmom: Yes, I really do. And I understand that you need to see it and not just hear me say the words, but I really mean it. I don't blame you if you don't trust me. I know I have to prove it to you. I really do love you, Sylvia, and I want us to have a close relationship.

Sylvia: So, can we do something this weekend?

This example is about an old wound that has become deeper and more painful over time. In this type of case it's extra important to prepare well, and there is often a need for a longer validation than with new or less serious relational wounds. We will have to work through our own difficult feelings before we can manage to take total responsibility for the pain. A good way to prepare is to write down what you want to say, ask someone to read through and give you feedback and, when you're ready, deliver the apology.

FIVE STEPS FOR AN EFFECTIVE APOLOGY

Before you jump into learning the steps, take a minute to realize that you already know, in your bones, what makes an apology land versus crash and burn. Imagine your neighbor borrows your electric lawnmower and when the cord gets tangled, they have an angry outburst and rip the cord right out of the machine. "I'm sorry I wrecked your lawnmower . . . but I was really frustrated." Um . . . nope, I don't feel very forgiving. Or, "I'm sorry if what I said offended you. . . ." The American comic Larry David has made great fun of this one ". . . but I don't think I said anything offensive." A lot of research has actually been done to tell us what our common sense has always told us about how to apologize. Just follow the five steps listed in the display box.

Five Steps for an Apology

1. Say briefly and precisely what you're apologizing for, with no "ifs" or "buts."
2. Say what it must have been like for them.
3. Say "I'm sorry" unconditionally.
4. Say what you should have done different and what you will do different starting now.
5. Expect and validate any and every reaction.

Say Briefly and Precisely What You're Apologizing For, With No "If's" or "But's"

It's important to own the apology fully and authentically. Don't say "if." For example, don't say: "I'm sorry if you feel like I treated you unfairly" or "I'm sorry if you thought I said that I wasn't happy with you." We say "if" when we know we should apologize, but we don't take responsibility and really mean what we say. It doesn't feel good to be on the receiving end of an apology that has reservations. For an apology to be genuine, you have to take responsibility for the outcome, even if it was not your intention to be hurtful. Resist the urge to water down your responsibility. Replace "I'm sorry if . . ." with "I'm sorry that . . ." "I'm sorry that I treated you unfairly," or "I'm sorry that I said I wasn't happy with you." Then you can add a "because" type statement. "Of course you feel that way when I point out every little mistake you make." Similarly, just like with validation, don't say "but." Don't say, "I'm sorry . . . but you were being really difficult." Don't say, "That must have been hard . . . but it was hard on me, too."

Say What It Must Have Been Like for Them

This is sort of like the "because" part of validation. You're saying what you know or imagine the situation was like for the child. You don't have to get it right. You help to open the vault of their feelings by guessing and relying on your inner parental wisdom and instincts rather than asking them. Say "Of course it felt like I wasn't happy with you when I kept pointing out every little mistake you made. It must've felt like no matter what you did, you couldn't win" Or: "Of course you felt like I was treating you unfairly when I let your brother do something and then wouldn't let you. That must've made you so mad." Or: "You must've felt sad and left out when we all kept talking and we didn't listen to anything you said." Or: "It must've been awful and maybe scary when Mom and I were always fighting. And then when we split up it must've felt like your whole world came crashing down. You didn't know where you'd be living and if you'd have to change schools."

Make Your "I'm Sorry" Unconditional

Don't explain to your child why you made a mistake, even if there are many good reasons for it. If you start explaining, it will seem like you're trying to explain things away or downplay your responsibility and defend what you did. Kids usually know what's up with us and know why it's been hard for us. They don't need to hear it, and they need us not to hide behind explanations. If, on the other hand, your child asks why you've been so angry and acting differently lately, you can assess whether it would be helpful to let them in on some details of the situation, appropriately for their age and without letting it be an excuse for hurting them.

Don't ask for forgiveness. A good apology is genuine and without conditions. To ask for forgiveness is asking for something from your child, and that can make them feel like the apology is intended to make you feel better, rather than being for the child's sake. Children will often react with anger when we say, "Can you forgive me?" They can also become compliant and forgiving, without actually letting go of their anger and disappointment toward their parent. Forgiveness is a process, and some children need the time and space to be angry for awhile before they are ready to forgive. Sadly, there are adult children who never forgive their parents. But we have seen that you can make it far more likely that your children will forgive you if you take responsibility and apologize, with absolutely no investment in whether they forgive you or not.

Say What You Should Have Done Differently and What You Will Do Differently Starting Now

The first part of this, say what you should have done differently, is easier than you think. It is often the case that there was nothing we could have done differently: "I couldn't not get cancer," "I had to go away to work to support the family," "Your brother got sick and I was basically at the hospital with him for a year." But, again, kids get this. This is not a "change the reality" demand. The essence of this part is "I should have found a way." "I let you know I had cancer but then I didn't let you in on how to cope, and you ended up really alone and isolated. I should've made sure you had support." Or: "I should have made sure when I was away that you had what you needed, and when I was home, I should have checked in more and made sure you were doing okay."

On the other hand, the second half of this part—what you will do differently starting now—is harder than you think. It's all too common for someone to apologize and then repeat the offense. Eventually, the apology, even if heartfelt in the moment, becomes empty and meaningless, and the child loses trust. So the simple-to-understand but hard-to-implement rule is this: You can apologize only for something you're willing and able to change. You can't change the fact that your child's brother has an illness that lands him in hospital a lot. What can you change? When you're home, you can make up some of the time with this child. Maybe you can have your coparent or another family member accompany the brother to the hospital sometimes. One mom told us that she knew she wouldn't stop shouting. It's how she was, and she didn't really think it was harming her kids—she knew that when it happened, it was quick and over, and she could live with that. What she apologized to her son for was then not listening to his part. She knew she'd have to work on it. But she believed she could do it. "From now on, I am promising to change this and make sure I don't just yell at you, but I truly listen to what you have to say." Be as specific as possible about what you can change.

Expect and Validate Any and Every Reaction

No matter what your child says when you apologize, you can validate their reaction and their feelings. Sometimes it's necessary to repeat Steps 1 through 3 in the display box. Your child might bring up other things that they've been holding onto, and you can apologize for those too. Or they might not be ready to accept and believe your apology; they might need time and proof that you mean it and really will change before they can accept it.

HOW MUCH PREPARATION IS NEEDED?

Apologizing for old emotional wounds can take a lot of preparation in order to be successful. The main challenge is for us to say sorry without being hijacked by our own feelings and needs. Some parents start to cry just at the thought of apologizing, and they worry that they won't be able to hold their tears back when they sit with their child and take responsibility. A good tip for those who get emotional easily is to write down the apology ahead of time and practice reading it aloud alone or to a good support person. Writing and talking about what we want to say to our child helps to settle our own feelings and helps to hold back the tears. It's okay if we start to cry when we apologize, but there are two things that are important. The first is that we don't want to cry uncontrollably, because then our child might have to become the caregiver or feel that they aren't seen and that this is all about the adult. The other thing that is important to do if we start to get choked up, or if our voice starts to get very shaky, is to comment on it so that the child feels at ease. The adult can say something like "You know how I am, I cry so easily, but I can handle it. I'm crying because what I want to say to you today is so important." Other parents can feel ambivalent about taking responsibility and apologizing for fear that the child will get away with bad behavior and will not learn anything. They're worried that it will make things worse for the child if they bring up painful things from the past, or that they, the parent, may not be ready to take responsibility because of their own painful feelings that emerge. It's very important to be aware of how our own feelings keep us from being brave enough to take radical responsibility and apologize. You can read about this in the chapters in Part I if you haven't already.

In cases of severe or prolonged abuse or violence, it is extremely important that the parents don't continue the abuse or continue to deny their responsibility after they've apologized. In these types of serious cases, it is best for the parent to work on how to take responsibility and apologize with a therapist who has expertise in apology with violence and abuse. The apology often requires months of preparatory work before it can be carried out, because we have to ensure that the child is not subjected to an unsuccessful apology, which can then be felt as yet another violation. If we have done something very serious to our child, then we need to take the apology process very seriously and give it lots of time. It takes time to get to the point where we can take full and complete responsibility and change our behavior. If you have little or no contact with your child, then writing to them might be the only way to take radical responsibility. You can also get help from the therapist to go through and edit the letter. Our children deserve genuine and credible apologies, without any doubt as to who has responsibility for what happened, and it isn't enough for the written apology to be good—the intention and responsibility behind the letter must also be good.

Apologies for fresh emotional cuts and scrapes do not require as much repair work as for more serious and long-lasting wounds.

Small, everyday conflicts and missteps can usually be fixed with a quick, impromptu apology. It can still be helpful to write down and practice the apology if it is about a recurring conflict, but otherwise we can just try to follow the five steps. It also doesn't matter if we forget one of the steps. The most important thing is that the apology is genuine and without any conditions or reservations.

GET READY: OUR CHILDREN'S REACTIONS CAN UNDO THE BEST OF US

Children have many different ways of reacting to the apology. Some kids get angry, others start to cry, some will want to comfort the adult, and some feel seen and understood. It really helps to be prepared for their possible reactions. If we validate whatever reaction they have, and even repeat the apology if needed, then we can the save the day and turn a wobbly beginning into a good outcome. Remember: Be kind to yourself. Taking radical responsibility and apologizing can make us feel vulnerable, and it can be really hard when our child reacts with rage or rejection. If we're not prepared, we can end up defensive or hurt, and our reaction to their reaction can ruin the effort. It's also tempting to fall for it when your child shrugs off the apology and says, "It's fine, Dad. It's no big deal." In the next several sections, we describe various reactions to prepare you for what to expect when you apologize to your child.

The Blast

Get ready to be tempted to take it all back when your apology is repaid with a blast of anger, accusation, and rejection. We've seen two reasons for the blast response. One is that they may need more time for the parent to show that they have changed, with feeling of "too little, too late" or "I'll believe it when I see it." The second is when the parent finally listens and acknowledges the injury the child may feel, "Now that I have your ear, I have a few other things you can apologize for."

The blast is the response you want. It's a sign that the child can stand up for themselves and speak up. If you're prepared for it, you steady your big shoulders and take it on the chin. Validate their anger or their fear that your apology isn't genuine. Respect it if they need more time. Say you're sorry for the other issues they raise.

The Emotional Vault

Our kids have often waited a long time to hear us say sorry, and when we do they may let us know how hurt they are or how long they've been hurting. They may start to cry, not because they feel worse but because we've validated their pain. They get access to their hurt feelings and can express them. It is normal for some children to cry for a long time, and it's healing for the child to be able to cry safely in front of their parents. The most important thing you can do is just be present with your child and validate the sadness. Crying is the child's invitation to closeness, and having a long cry and a hug may be a way to compensate for the closeness they've missed. When we can tolerate their sadness, it confirms for your child that "you are really here, you meant what you said about things being different in the future, you can handle all my tears, and you like and love me." So, hang in there when the emotional vault opens, and get ready to validate any other feelings they've been hiding in there as well, such as fear or shame.

The Care Response

Some children try to take care of their parent when the parent apologizes. They don't want their parents to be sad or for there to be something painful and unresolved in the relationship. The care response is not the child taking in and responding to the apology; it is more the child assigning themselves the duty of solving the difficult situation for the parent. The child's care response may be to say they understand it wasn't easy, they know the parents had too much to deal with, and everything is fine. The child may reassure the parents: "You did the best you could." The child downplays the seriousness of the injury to themselves and cloaks their own emotional needs. It's very tempting for the parent to take the child's reassurances at face value and conclude that things are fine. But this is the response that requires the greatest vigilance from parents.

If your child is trying to take care of you when you say sorry, stay strong and repeat the apology. The essence of this is "I was the parent and you were the child. It was my job not yours." Repeat, and make sure the child hears it: What you did that hurt them was not okay. Some children make repeated attempts to comfort the parent or minimize the injury and their own needs. We may need to repeat the apology and hold tight to our responsibility four or five times before the child feels safe enough that they feel it's okay to take in and accept the apology.

It is not necessarily only children who have adopted a parentified role that show this caring response. Some do it because they are caring and empathic individuals. They are in tune with social nuances and are sensitive to interpersonal dynamics and conflict. Children with this type of personality are still at risk of having their needs overlooked, at home and at school, because they appear to be well functioning and self-sufficient when it comes to meeting their own emotional needs. It is important to work a little harder so that these children can also feel what it is like to be seen and understood, fully and completely, so they can get the benefit of receiving an apology from their parent.

For some children, it is so unusual for their difficult feelings and needs to be the focus that they need time to get used to it and to accept the attention. Change can happen, but maybe only in small steps.

It can be difficult to distinguish between the care response and other responses. When the child genuinely takes in the apology, accepts it, and forgives, very often they will also say something to indicate that things are truly resolved and fine. But the emotion they express is different from the care response. When children take in and accept the apology, they experience it emotionally. They may express heartfelt gratitude and relief from the start, or they start with a self-assertive acknowledgment of their anger or disappointment or sadness at the incident and then move to gratitude, relief, and love. But the child with a caring response comes across as untouched by the injury or the apology, or anxious, or cheerful, seeming more invested in hustling to make the parent happy again rather than acknowledging and letting go of their own pain. At other times, the child may carry guilt and want to say sorry back. This response can also be confused with the care response because the wording can be similar.

Again, it is important to read the child's feelings because children are often visibly burdened by guilt if they say that they are the ones who behaved badly. If that happens, hold on to your apology and accept theirs in the spirit of "Of course you didn't feel good when you did that" and not "That's good because I apologized for my part and it's right for you to apologize for yours." The goal is to unburden them of their guilt, which can otherwise lead to them developing destructive self-criticism.

The Interrupter

A less common response is when children interrupt our apology. They want to avoid talking about the painful experience because it is painful. They interrupt us and don't let us finish talking. This is a real challenge for parents. We know the issue is important and had a negative impact on our child. We know it will be helpful for them to hear the apology. Young children can interrupt the repair work by putting their hand over our mouth or saying "Don't talk!" Older children use more advanced forms of distraction and can change topics or say something funny, or they may be clear that "I do not want to talk about this" and actually walk away.

It can be difficult to separate the interrupter from the children who immediately become angry and don't accept any apology, but interrupting is not the same as an angry response. In this case, it is important first to respect the child's boundaries. There are then two strategies you can use. One is to validate the child's reluctance to talk about difficult things. Painful emotions hurt, and the child may be afraid to feel them. When we validate this reluctance we can get ourselves into a better position to apologize. The other strategy is to try again later. The important thing is not to give up. Some children need many attempts and can feel safer and more secure each time we try to approach and attend to their emotions. Some children are never receptive during the day when they are busy with friends and playing, but they may be more receptive in the evening. Some are the most receptive when they are in a neutral mood, while others are more receptive when they are already a little vulnerable. If we are curious and try to find doorways into our child's feelings and needs, then we will eventually get there. Some children simply need a lot of reassurance and time in order to feel and show emotions.

The "Not Relevant" Response

Another response is when children do not remember the situation we are apologizing for and say the apology is truly not needed. They'll often say that it was still nice to have the parents say they were sorry. For some, it gives them the chance to correct their parents

207

and say what it was that actually did upset them. The not-relevant response differs from the caring response in that they come across as genuinely surprised and puzzled rather than being dismissive or minimizing. Even if we apologize for something our child doesn't remember or wasn't affected by, the gesture itself has a healing effect on them—and on us! Apologizing for something we did has the effect of releasing us from the guilt that we have carried for a long time, even when the child doesn't remember it or says it didn't affect them. By taking radical responsibility, and by apologizing, we forgive ourselves. And because it's true that "the best gift we can give our child is our own happiness," we believe that a wonderful way to do that is to give them our own self-forgiveness. Freeing ourselves with forgiveness relieves them of the burden of our self-blame. Our research shows that self-blame is one of the biggest obstacles that stops a parent from being the parent they want to be and stops them from helping their child in the way the child needs (e.g., Ansar et al., 2021).

No Response

It is not uncommon for some children to seem unresponsive to our apology. Some shrug. Some say nothing. Some continue doing other things or even wander away (which is very different from storming away). Some show a delayed response hours or days later. But don't despair. We've been amazed at the number of stories parents have told us of these kids behaving differently after their nonresponse to the apology. Kids behaving nicer toward a sibling, after the parents apologized and validated the child's feeling that they love the sibling more. Teens who shrug their shoulders in the moment but who suddenly spend more time with their parents and tell them more about their lives later in the day. Children being more interactive and open to parents for a long time afterward. Other children have a strong inner reaction but don't show it. We have heard several stories in which children have later shown that they heard everything that was said but were afraid to start crying or to feel the hurt feelings, and so they said nothing. And some children show they've received the apology by going to play happily. We see this especially in young children. Everything is fine, and when life is fine for young children, they play. No response may be one of the most challenging reactions for us as parents, because we have little information about what is going on in the child. Respect the child's response and remain curious. Maybe later you can ask the child how it was for them when you said you were sorry, or you can guess and validate if you think you have an idea what it's about.

The Narrator

Some children start to open up and "narrate" much more about what's going on in their life after receiving an apology. Narrating can come after an initial lack of response as described earlier, and it can also come after all the other responses: the blast, the emotional vault that opened, or the interruption. Thus, the effect of our apology often shows up in our relationship with the child. Saying sorry contributes to our child wanting to be with us more and to invite us into their life. Both the narrator response and the "no response" can thus be incredibly rewarding when, although they say little or nothing initially, they show the positive impact of receiving your apology with their changed behavior and increased openness and willingness to connect.

The Dream Response

Thank goodness it can also happen that children accept the apology with open arms and think it's fantastic to have us take responsibility, validate, and say we're sorry. Some children cry while they're also happy and grateful. Some don't cry; they look happy and tell us that it was good to hear. Many children who take in and accept the apology will also seek closeness, want a hug, and tell us that they love us. It's okay for us to admit it: The dream response is the one we most want and hope for, and that just feels good. Let's just remind ourselves—there is a lot that is good and helpful in the other responses. It is a declaration of trust in us when our children dare to show us their deep vulnerability, and it is truly great when children stand up for themselves and get angry. Children who show more complex responses may be more challenging mysteries to figure out, but it's going to feel good the day you get it. So stay the course. The most important thing about apologizing is that it be genuine and that we take radical responsibility. The most important thing is not that the children accept and forgive. The more we believe these two statements, the easier it is to stand up and validate the children's response to our apology, no matter what they come up with and how challenging it is for us.

Some adults apologize often—okay, let's admit it, too often. It can then be difficult to know how to repair that—whether to apologize, when, how, and to assess which situations require an apology. If we apologize too often, the child may perceive the adult as insecure in their role, in need of forgiveness, and scrambling to get back into the child's good books. The child will then feel that it's their job to take care of the adult. They can also conclude that apologies are not genuine. This is especially true if we apologize but don't change or stop the thing we apologize for. To remedy this, apologize only when there have been difficult situations beyond ordinary everyday conflicts or for things that, for your child, were specifically hurtful. Apologize if you know that there are old wounds in the relationship that have not healed or if you have had a parenting style over time that has made it difficult for the child emotionally. A hint for you to assess whether you are this parent is: Do you find it "easy" to apologize? That seems like it should be a good thing. But when we have hurt our child, it is more typical to find it hard to acknowledge that to ourselves, and even harder to acknowledge it to our child and apologize. If it's not hard for you, you may be an overapologizer. Here are a few crucial rules of thumb for those of us who overapologize.

- Focus on changing what is hurtful rather than repeating apologies without changing.
- Assess whether you're apologizing to be forgiven and be let off the hook rather than giving the apology unconditionally as a gift to your child.
- Don't apologize "for the weather"; that is, don't go around apologizing left, right, and center for things that you cannot take genuine and accurate responsibility for and that your child knows perfectly well you do not have the power to change.

Sometimes a one-off apology may be enough to heal an injury; other times, children may need the conversation to continue and for the apology to be the start of an important dialogue. The apology can open up conversations that give children the opportunity to become more aware of what they've experienced and of their emotions. They need to feel that they have an open invitation to come back to the topic. It's good to be prepared that there may be immediate reactions, more need to talk, or the child might need some distance to digest the conversation and think about it. As well, several old conflicts can come to the surface, and then it is especially important that the adult live up to their determination to take responsibility by being patient with the child and giving them space.

EXPERIENCE IT: SAYING SORRY

Write down the details of a situation between you and your child where they were hurt or their needs were not met and there is a need for an apology. It could be a one-time event, or it could be an emotional style or caregiving style that you've had for awhile that has not served your child well: if you've avoided emotions or involved your child too much in your own emotions; been too angry, criticized, or rejected your child; or if you've been over-protective or too strict. It could be something you've said or done, or something you haven't said or haven't done. Follow the steps listed next, and write out your answers in as much detail as possible, especially for Step 2.

1. Write down what you're apologizing for.
2. Say what it must have been like for your child. Validate your child's feelings without using the word *but*.
3. Say you're sorry, without explaining why things happened the way they did and without asking for forgiveness.
4. Say what you could have done differently. Say what you will do differently in the future. Acknowledge that it won't go perfectly, and that you're likely to mess up, but that you will take responsibility for fixing things if and when that happens.

Read over what you've written out loud to your partner or coparent, or someone else you trust, and get feedback. Try to imagine your child's response, so that you are as prepared as possible to validate it. Will they be angry? Want to care for you? Will they start to cry, or will they reject the apology in some way?

When you feel like you can really own what you've written, and you can wholeheartedly take responsibility, then go deliver the apology. Validate your child's reaction and, if necessary, repeat the steps.

It is normal to have feelings before and while you are apologizing. You might feel anxious, worried, or ashamed. You might be feeling a lot of sorrow and guilt. You might be doubting whether a parent apologizing to a child is wise, but you've decided to give it a go. Validate your own feelings for a sec, whatever they are. Then put them nicely on a shelf, telling yourself, "A good apology conveys remorse for the other and does not try to bring attention back to the apologizer." Your feelings are all valid. Just tell them you'll get back to them in a bit because in this moment your child needs you.

It can feel like there is a lot at stake. If you feel like you have a lot of resistance to apologizing, or you don't dare, or you don't think you can do it in a genuine way, then reread Chapter 9 and come back to this practice and try again.

SAYING SORRY MEANS GIVING PERMISSION TO TALK ABOUT DIFFICULT SITUATIONS

Nora, age 6, does not like what's for dinner and wants something else. This causes a conflict with her mom. Nora ends up kicking her mother and screaming at her that she hates lasagna. Mom grabs Nora by the arm and drags her to her room. She closes the door and holds it shut. Nora kicks at the door and pulls on the handle and yells at her mother to open the door. Her mom continues to hold the door closed for 20 minutes until Nora, exhausted, gives up trying to get out of her room and sits down behind the door. Mom lets go of the door handle and goes quietly to the living room. At 7:00, Mom goes up to Nora's room and tells her that it's time to get ready for bed. Mom and Nora don't talk about what happened. Three days later, Mom sits down beside Nora.

Mom: I'm sorry for shutting you in your room the other day. It was wrong of me. You must have been scared when I shouted so loud and made you stay alone in your room and wouldn't let you out. When I got so angry it might have felt like I don't like you or love you.

[Nora cries, and Mom puts her arms around her. Nora continues to cry as her mom holds her. She welcomes Mom's comforting closeness.]

Mom (continuing): It must feel like I don't like you when you're angry and that I don't want to be near you. You didn't like the dinner I made, and when you wanted me to make something else for you I shouted, and so no wonder you got angry. I'm really sorry I dragged you by your arm and locked you in your room. I'm so sorry. [Her eyes begin tearing up, and her voice breaks a little bit.] I should have a plan for when you don't like the dinner. I can't expect you to eat food that you don't like, and I even knew that you don't like lasagna. I could have just made you some toast. I shouldn't have dragged you to your room and closed the door. I should have tried to understand why you were so angry and talked to you about it calmly.

Nora: And you didn't even say sorry afterward.

Mom: No, I waited three whole days, so it's no wonder you're angry at me for that, too. I'm sorry I waited so long. It must have been hard for you that we haven't really been close for the last three days. You're totally right. I should have said sorry that day. Families argue, so for sure we'll have other arguments in the future, but I'm going to get better at saying sorry and fixing things on the same day. It is my job to make sure that everything is good between us again. When you get angry and I don't understand why, you start to kick and hit because you don't know what else to do. It is my job to figure it out.

Nora: Next time just don't make lasagna, since I don't like it.

Mom: What if I talk to you before I make our weekly dinner plan, and you can tell me what you like and don't like, because sometimes it changes.

Nora: Yeah, I used to like lasagna but not anymore. Now I like hamburgers, pasta with no sauce, hot dogs, and salmon. But if you make something I don't like, I can still have a little bit of it.

Mom: Yeah, that would be good. Can we make a deal that you'll eat a carrot if I peel it?

Nora: Okay; I like carrots. But you have to peel the carrot before dinner, otherwise you get annoyed if you have to get up and do it after we've already started eating.

Mom (laughing a bit): Yes, that's true, I do get annoyed, so that's a really good idea.

Nora: I have lots of good ideas.

Mom: Yes, you do. And I love you lots and lots, Nora.

Nora: I love you too, Mommy.

The day after Mom apologized, the family is sitting around the dinner table, and Nora has a friend from school over to visit. There are hamburgers for dinner, and everyone is busy eating. Suddenly Nora turns to her friend and says, "Four days ago, my mom dragged me to my room and locked me in because I don't like lasagna."

> [Mom swallows hard.]
> *Nora's friend:* Just because you don't like lasagna?!
> *Mom:* I did something that was really dumb, didn't I? I can't believe I locked you in your room.
> *Nora:* It was also because I was hitting and kicking you, not just because of the lasagna.
> *Mom:* I still shouldn't have locked you in your room.
> *Nora's friend:* One time, my big brother trapped me inside my duvet. He rolled me up in it and then sat on me. I almost couldn't breathe.
> [Nora and her friend start laughing.]

Even though it can be uncomfortable when our children talk to others about our mistakes, it's good for them. And it makes it much easier for us to deal with it when we've taken responsibility and made things right. If Nora's mom had not had the apology chat with Nora, and then Nora had said the same thing in front of her friend, it would be much more likely that her mom would feel ashamed and not have handled the situation as well. She might have gotten angry and defensive, and blamed Nora. She also might have asked Nora not to talk about it or, in the worst case, she might have denied it.

EXPERIENCE IT: RECEIVING AN APOLOGY

This is an exercise that aims to give you an experience of how it feels to receive the apology from your parents that you yearn for and long to hear. We know that certain styles of caregiving and injuries are repeated over many generations. Becoming aware of our own wounds and unmet needs can make us better able to handle our child's anger and the vulnerable feelings that lie beneath their anger. When we have more compassion for the little child in us who was scared, ashamed, or lonely, or who perhaps protected themselves by being angry or acting out, then we will have greater feelings of compassion for our own children.

How would it have been for you if your mother or father had taken radical responsibility and apologized for what they did not give you, but that you needed? Even if you had good parents, you may still have felt like they didn't understand you, or you might have not felt fully accepted by them. Maybe they were sick, or got divorced, or in some way weren't able to care for you adequately.

Think of the apology from your parents that you most long to hear, something that you really wish your mom or dad had taken responsibility and apologized for. It could be a single, painful event. It could be an emotional style or a style of caring for you that they had over time and that was difficult for you. It could be something they said or did many times, or something they never said or did. Were they not able to protect you, acknowledge you, or respect your boundaries? Did they keep you from developing yourself? Did they not accept your feelings or abandon you? Were they preoccupied? Did they criticize you? Were they violent, and did they hurt you? Did they make fun of you? Or did they die so early that you weren't able to fix the hurt? Feel into this. What do you wish your parents would take full responsibility for? What are your old, unmet needs that they didn't see and weren't able to meet?

Perhaps your parents have already apologized. Maybe they never will. Whether you are thinking of an apology that has already happened, that you hope will happen, or that will never happen, this is an important and worthwhile exercise to complete. Throughout the exercise, you will be able to put into words what you needed that you did not get at the time. You will validate yourself as the young child who was scared, ashamed, angry, or sad. And you will feel how the apology affects you. This is about the impact of apology, and it is important to have had that experience to help you apologize to your children.

Write out the apology from your mother or father in the first person ("I") as though you are your mom or dad. Follow the steps listed next and write in as much detail as possible, especially under Steps 2 and 3. Note that this is not a reality test. This is not what your parent is capable of saying or, if they are deceased, what they would have been capable of saying. Write the apology that you long for and yearn to hear from them.

1. As your parent, say what you are apologizing for.
2. Have them say what it must have been like for you (their child) and have them validate you—the situation, what you must have needed, and how it must have felt for you (their child) not to have your emotional needs met.
3. Have them say sorry without explaining why it was the way it was and without asking for forgiveness.
4. Have them say what they should have done differently.

Once you have written out the apology:

1. Read it aloud to someone you trust, having them just listen and respond in whatever way feels spontaneous. Don't pretend to be your parent, and don't pretend the other person is you. Just read it to them.
2. Have the person you trust then read it to you as though they were your mother or father. During and after Steps 1 and 2, notice what feelings come up for you. Do you feel angry? Does the apology feel genuine? Do you feel sad and feel like

you are experiencing the old pain all over again? Is it good? Do you accept the apology and want to forgive? Or do you want to stand up for yourself and set boundaries? Your feelings are valid, no matter what they are. Let your emotions be there for awhile and see if they can provide you with some important information. What did you need back then? What do you need now? If it feels safe to do so, speak to the person you trust about the feelings that have come up.

3. If there is no one with whom you feel safe enough to share the apology aloud, then you can read it aloud to yourself. The best way to do this is to set out two chairs. Sit in one chair and imagine that you as a child, who experienced the pain in the relationship between you and your parents, is sitting in the other chair. If the pain is too intense and you are worried that you might feel overwhelmed, then you can imagine yourself as an adult instead. See if you can get an image of yourself as a child or as you are as an adult. Acting as your mother or father, read the apology to the imaginary child in the other chair. When you are done, sit in the other chair and imagine yourself as a child. Experience how it feels. How does it feel to hear and receive the apology? What feelings come up? See if you are able to be curious and compassionate as the feelings arise. Summarize for yourself what you needed that you did not get. What do you need today?

The outcome of this task doesn't have to be that you forgive your parents. Research shows that just grieving what we did not get from our parents can help us to let go of painful feelings left over from not having our needs met (e.g., Greenberg et al., 2008). Thus, one way to work through old relationship wounds with our parents is with reconciliation and forgiveness, but another way is to grieve what cannot be, and thus be able to let go of the pain despite there being no possibility of mutual reconciliation. In this context, letting go means that you no longer expect or hope that your mother or father will meet your unmet needs and that you will no longer try to have those needs met by them. You have come to terms with the fact that it will not happen. You have processed the painful emotions connected to the needs not being met, and you have grieved the loss.

Sometimes it is also necessary to be assertive and set boundaries with others after we have chosen to let go of unmet needs. There is no definite answer as to when reconciliation is most appropriate or when it is most appropriate to accept what cannot be and let go. It is not necessarily the case that the more serious the violation is— for example, with violence or abuse—the more likely it will be that one can only let go and grieve, or that minor issues will always be reconciled. It is up to each individual person to explore what is possible and decide what feels right. The point of both the reconciliation and the letting go is that we can put an end to our suffering. Moving through life with unresolved painful wounds can mean living with fear, deep shame, bitterness, and anger. If we process the pain we experienced when growing up, then we have an adult perspective on where guilt and responsibility should be appropriately placed, and we can look back on our childhood and on ourselves with compassion, self-assertion, or a new and healthy grief over old painful feelings. As you do this exercise, allow your feelings to guide you in finding the outcome that is best for you.

DO NOT DEMAND AN APOLOGY FROM YOUR CHILD

When our children do something wrong to others, parents often say "Apologize!" Sending our child off to apologize is perhaps the most common and concrete way we try to teach our children to take responsibility for their own actions. But does it work? In our experience, it does not. An apology that we insist on or force someone to make, or that we guilt them into making, is simply not the same animal.

First, it can be uncomfortable for the person who is receiving the forced apology, especially if something serious has taken place. Many parents with children who have been bullied have experienced this. Parents arrive at the door with their child and get them to rattle off an apology. Some of these children laugh with embarrassment as they say sorry. The parents whose child has been bullied want things to be put right, but the child who has been bullied can experience this very disingenuous apology as a new violation—making fun or trivializing what actually happened—and this can add to the burden instead of making things better. It is also usually excruciatingly embarrassing for the victim of the bully, and both kids know that it is doing nothing to improve their social status. It generally does no good for the child who is forced to apologize either. They may be ashamed but not have received help in how to deal with those feelings, and so those feelings of shame are exacerbated by being dragged over to the neighbor's with nothing really being resolved. It is simply not helpful to give or receive an apology that is premature and not genuine. In fact, the experience can be so uncomfortable that the children will not feel like saying sorry the next time they make a mistake because saying sorry is associated with such horrible feelings.

Second, research and experience have repeatedly shown us that children learn best not from what we say they should do (our words) but from what we do ourselves (our actions). Being a good role model and showing that we take responsibility when we make mistakes, or hurt or misunderstand someone, is the best way to teach. Our behavior is what teaches our children, not what we try to teach them with ideas or words. The best teaching we can give our children when it comes to responsibility, empathy for others, and saying sorry, is to give them experiences of how good it feels to be on the receiving end of responsibility, warmth, and empathy themselves. They also get to see how it's done, so they can imitate it later.

Teaching our children by being good role models, and by validating their feelings rather than yelling at them and correcting them, can also teach them to be good at taking responsibility when they hurt others. By validating shame and guilt, the emotions work as they should, without being amplified. We can also help them out of their feelings of guilt by acknowledging, normalizing, and helping them to sort out the emotions. If we shout and threaten, then we are in danger of reinforcing the feelings of shame, without the children being allowed to use the shame or guilt in a helpful way, that is, to guide them to make reparations. The shame becomes an unhelpful emotion that will last over time and contribute to more shame and to self-criticism. The child can develop a feeling of "I am a bad person because I do so many bad things."

A child who has a bad feeling in their gut for having said something mean to another child, and who is validated and wants to say sorry properly, will feel a sense of relief and satisfaction when they apologize. The adult won't have to instruct the child to apologize. The child will want to do it once their own feelings have been validated. If this doesn't happen, and they don't seem to want to apologize on their own, the parent can talk to the child about what can be done so that the two kids can be friends again. When it feels good to say sorry, it increases the chances of two things: (a) that the child feels like saying sorry in the future because it feels right and good and (b) a genuine apology reduces the chance that a child will bully again. Feeling guilt and saying sorry is learned from within. Learning through emotions and experiences has a completely different effect on us than someone trying to instruct us, especially if they also make us feel judged with their disapproval and their moral lesson to "Apologize."

III

SETTING AND ENFORCING LIMITS

INTRODUCTION: SETTING AND ENFORCING LIMITS

It is a huge challenge to establish boundaries and set limits for aggression without shaming your child or conveying that "anger is NOT okay." When children are aggressive, it brings up a ton of emotions for us. It's easy to fall straight into a feeling trap. Even the most level-headed parent can lose their cool, trying to set a reasonable limit with a child who just keeps pushing back—testing us to see how far they can go or if we're able to hold strong. We can end up making hurtful, derogatory, or threatening comments or just giving up and storming (or slinking) away. We can find ourselves, in the face of this angry child, saying things like "If this is the way you're going to be, you can go live with your father. And I don't like YOU, either. You're impossible. You always have to make everything SO hard." It's hard to remember that when our child is scornful and pushes us away, it may be because they're unable to express their needs, or because they're deeply hurt and angry about something we've said or done. Children can provoke us like nothing else can. Some find it hard not to go straight to an aggressive outburst when faced with their furious onslaught; for others, it's hard not to collapse into powerlessness and shame, feeling completely ineffective in our efforts to control these ferocious little (or powerfully angry and big) beings. And we can't see the end; we worry that it will never get better. It's not surprising that setting limits for an aggressive child is one of the most challenging things about being a parent.

The goal of this part of the book is for you to go from feeling stressed during difficult limit-setting situations to feeling compassion for yourself and your child, having a good sense of your internal boundary style and how to use it to protect your well-being, and having a tool to help you set limits with clarity and care. This way, your child can have healthy internal boundaries and become good at setting healthy limits for themselves as well.

In Chapter 11, we will invite you to reconsider the way you think about boundaries and to think about what boundary style you bring to the table when you set limits and enforce rules. Recognizing your boundary style is going to be a big help when you're trying to become more effective at getting your kids to do what you want and need them to do, and to stop them from doing what they shouldn't. We'll also get you to think about how to have rules that support the values you want to have in your family. In Chapter 12, we will go over the specific dos and don'ts of effective limit setting. In Chapter 13, we'll explore the difference between giving consequences and handing out punishment and why it's important to tell them apart. In Chapter 14, we will address how you can create safety even in the face of serious aggression.

CHAPTER 11

ALL ABOUT BOUNDARIES

Until this point you've been learning all about anger. You've learned that there are different types of anger and how to read and understand your own and your child's angry reactions. You've learned about the importance—in fact, the absolute necessity—for all of us, children and parents alike, to accept and express our healthy, self-assertive anger. You've learned how to validate your child's anger so they can get better at feeling it and dealing with it. And you've learned how to make up for mistakes and mishaps with anger in your relationship with your child by learning how to deliver an effective and healing apology.

If you're like every other parent on earth, what you're very keen to hear now is how to deal with the behaviors that come with anger. How do we work effectively with boundaries and limits in a way that lets us stick to our values and that doesn't stomp on our newfound respect for anger—but that also gets our child to stop screaming at us or hitting their siblings and that gets them to do the dishes or their homework, to brush their teeth and get to bed, or to turn off the game and go out and find a job?

We're going to introduce you to a brand-new way of thinking about boundaries and a new way to go about setting limits and enforcing rules. You can then make use of your new emotion skills to understand how you and your kids interact around rules and expectations. You can also increase cooperation and decrease boundary fiascoes and meltdowns.

BOUNDARIES

What do you think of when you hear the word "boundary"? Most people think of something like a line in the sand. A wall. A barrier that we erect. In other words, we tend to think of setting a boundary that lets others know that we don't want them to cross it. With our kids, we also try to set boundaries around them that we want them not to cross. But it's our belief that this way of understanding boundaries is not only inaccurate in terms of how we interact around the expectations and demands we have of each other. We believe that this concept of boundaries also misleads us as parents into thinking that our only power is to change our child by "making" them do something or stop doing something. This goes against everything motivation research teaches us. And, more important, it simply doesn't work. If my only power is to make someone else do something different, then all of my power is in the other person's hands. When kids have all the power and parents feel disempowered, things never tend to go well. When people tell us about boundaries, they always tell us what we should get the kids to do differently. It's a great idea, but again, it leaves all the possibility for change and success in the hands of someone else. The cliché is true: The only one you can change is you—if you want to have control over whether the change happens or not, that is. The only way to change the way things go in your house around rule, limits, and expectations is to get that you, the parent, are the answer.

Thus, a boundary is actually a limit that you place on yourself. What are you willing to do? What are you not willing to do? For example, an important boundary is "I will not tolerate my children hitting each other." By communicating this boundary to your children, and then responding appropriately if your children hit each other, you are the person protecting your boundary. You have the power. Let's jump in and work on the way you understand, communicate, and implement boundaries in your family.

THE TWO-PART BOUNDARY SYSTEM

Let's start by talking about a new way of thinking, one that is much closer to how boundaries actually work. Let's consider how we can restore our power and also empower our kids to develop their own healthy, protective boundaries as they venture out into the playground, the schoolyard, the teen scene, and eventually the big world. The two parts of the system are (a) boundary style and (b) limit-setting. Limit-setting is a way of establishing, communicating, negotiating, and implementing rules, expectations, values, and norms (Dolhanty et al., 2022). Let's start by stating this two-part system very simply: (a) We all come with a boundary style that is pretty much a part of our temperament. (b) We can all learn to be effective at limit-setting, regardless of our individual boundary style. But we need to get an awareness of our style, and its impact on our kids, to use it effectively to set limits.

BOUNDARY STYLE

For a moment, get a picture in your mind of the ways different people in different leadership roles (not just parents) enforce rules. Think of people like bosses, police officers, coaches. Think of teachers. As you think of them, picture the different styles they might have in their way of enforcing rules or exerting their authority. Some might have a quiet but firm and determined style that, although it is quiet, makes us feel compelled to do as they ask. Others might have a quiet style that we experience somehow as wobbly and that does not make us feel confident that they can "get control of the crowd" and does not make us feel compelled to comply. Think of others with a bigger, more forceful style. Again, imagine someone more forceful in their style that makes us feel that we are in the hands of someone who can get the job done, and so we go along with what they say. Then think of another person who is also forceful but who makes us get our back up and makes us not want to go along with what they say but rather to fight back a bit in a "you're not the boss of me" kind of way. In other words, some can be more quiet and gentle and yet wield sufficient power to lead, while another quiet and gentle style does not inspire the confidence in us to follow them. Similarly, some with a more forceful style may make us feel safe and confident that they'll lead us in the right direction, and so we follow, whereas others with a forceful style make us feel like rebelling and fighting back.

We can see that whether we find someone else's boundary style to be effective also depends on our own style and what we respect or admire versus what pushes our buttons (Dolhanty et al., 2022; Treasure et al., 2016). But before we even consider the interaction of their style with our own, let's just continue to consider the different styles people have and how their style can be effective despite it being more or less quiet or forceful. We have all seen this in teachers, our own or our kids' teachers. There are the strict ones, who the kids love and respect because it feels fair and because if they toe the line they get to go play soccer for the last 20 minutes of the day, versus the ones who act strict but who end up doing a lot of shouting and sending students to the office. And on the other side there are the more easygoing teachers, some of whom have a more relaxed classroom, but it works and the kids are productive and happy with a certain allowance for music and group discussion, and the other easygoing teachers, whose classroom is too chaotic for the kids to think and learn and thrive well.

What we want you to realize as you think of all of these types is that we have taught you nothing so far about boundary style, and yet you know what we're talking about. That is what we mean by *boundary style*. We all come naturally with a more strict or closed or rigid style when it comes to what we allow to affect us and how we manage others, or a more open or relaxed or porous style. One is not better than the other. We simply all come with a boundary style. Parents will know that it is partly inborn, as they have seen their kids be different from the get-go in terms how thick-skinned or not they are, what they take in or notice and what affects them or not. And that inborn style then interacts with our experiences growing up, so that the boundary style we end up with as parents partly comes from how we were born and partly from our lived experience.

Let's be clear that we mean no disrespect to the teachers in the examples we just gave, just as we mean none to parents who find their boundary house in a shambles. What we are saying is that when we become aware of our boundary style, we can then use it and tweak it with the way we set limits, so that we protect our own well-being and the well-being of those around us. If I do not tolerate chaos and I learn to set limits and rules to establish more order, I am then not stressed. Others benefit because I am not judging them for breaking the rules and stressing me out. If I naturally tolerate less structure, I can establish limits and rules that are more flexible but still achieve an atmosphere that is productive, not chaotic. When we do this as parents, we can then also take into consideration the natural boundary style of our children. We can adapt our own way of working to respect and support their style as well, helping them to grow up with a healthy, protective boundary system that they can use for their own well-being.

One of the main features of boundary style that we can see in the preceding examples is the degree of porousness. Some of us have a style that is more open or porous; others have one that is more closed or rigid. Healthy boundaries are a balance of these two, flexible and firm. They're like a membrane, protecting us the way our skin does, with a balancing act of what they let in and out. Our skin allows moisture and nutrients in and does not allow in bacteria and free radicals. It allows sweat and toxins out but does not allow our blood and essential bodily fluids out. Our skin thus serves as a helpful barrier that has a very useful filter. Our boundaries function in the same way. We can allow important information to come in, and we can filter out useless and stressful ideas and impulses from others. We can show our emotions to others, or not, and act in a way that makes sense given the situation. Sometimes the boundary between us and others is like a thick wall, protecting us from revealing ourselves to others and from being unduly influenced by others. This can help us to stay calm in the face of a crisis, but it can also mean we don't give much of ourselves, making it hard for others to know where we stand. With such rigid boundaries, we may seem uninvolved and uninterested, as though we don't care.

In contrast, while for some of us boundaries can be very rigid, others of us are at the other end of the scale. Our boundaries are porous almost to the point of seeming nonexistent, leaving us unprotected. Others' feelings and experiences, and everything that happens around us, affect and activate us emotionally. Other people's crises become our crises, and we take criticism in and accept it as truth. Our feelings and anxieties are exposed for all to see. We may overreact, or be invasive and unpleasant to be with, as if everything is about us.

Some of us have closed boundaries only when it comes to other people's ideas, and we aren't swayed by anyone, but we willingly share our own thoughts and feelings and want to influence others. We can then be perceived as cold and calculating when we disregard the boundaries of others. Some of us are easily influenced by external ideas but reveal little to the outside world about how we are affected. In this case, it can be easy for others to disregard our boundaries without us defending ourselves and saying something to stop them.

Between the two extremes, there are various healthy boundary styles. We also have varying degrees of awareness regarding how our boundaries work. The less we are aware of how much we let other people's feelings in, the more we are affected by them. The less we are aware that we do not let other people's feelings and lives touch us, the more insensitive and ruthless we may come across to others.

Our boundaries have a big impact on those around us, especially our children. If we overreact when our child acts out, our emotional reaction lands on our child and communicates to them that it is their emotions that are influencing our behavior and our boundaries. Children may seem to fight to get their way, but in truth they long for us to be at the helm. When they see that we are afraid of them or that we don't know how to handle their angry outbursts, they will take it as permission to ignore the limits we set. And they will ignore them. When children sense that we don't feel empowered to enforce limits we set, they feel compelled to test those limits. They have a powerful internal scale for assessing whether our boundary style is too rigid or too porous. It's as though they know instinctively that they need a flexible balance of clear, firm structure and limits to feel safe on the one hand, with sufficient freedom to explore and power to have a degree of self-determination on the other. They react to excessive rigidity with either rebellion or unhealthy submission and compliance. They react to excessive porousness with either apparent disregard of the rules, disobedience, and disrespect for the parent or with adopting the role of rule enforcer themselves, with the clear implication that the parent is not up to the job. Both of these outcomes can be astronomically difficult for parents, leading to stress and resentment.

We can end up with a wall between us and our children, retreating and making ourselves inaccessible, or coming down hard with harsh verbal or physical reprimands. Our defeated or stern looks and collapsed or hard exterior can then be stressful to our children. They will feel like they can't reach us. They will struggle even more to express their feelings appropriately, resulting in increased outbursts or retreating and helplessness, not even attempting to challenge us or trying to get their needs met.

On the other hand, when we allow ourselves to take in our child's frustration and pain, but not so much that we become overwhelmed, and when we stop their acting out with clear instructions and actions, then our child is more likely to respect the limits and rules we set. When children realize that we have our own healthy internal boundaries, they feel that the relationship is safe and predictable. When we are less stressed and resentful, we are more capable of making room for them to negotiate and to have the chance to win an argument. We're more able to hear their input and be influenced by it. In this way they can learn that their views are important, that they can influence the world around them, and that they have good ideas and important information to contribute. It's good for children to learn that sensible and well-thought-out input can lead to change. At the very least, they will learn to negotiate, a skill they can use in many ways later in life. By having healthy and flexible boundaries ourselves, we teach our children to develop good, protective boundaries for themselves. This is one of the most important things we teach our children. If you get your boundary house in order, the benefits to you and your kids will make all the hard work (that you're doing in this book) worth it.

It is essential for us to learn to have a healthy boundary membrane that protects us and keeps us safe as we move around in the world and so that we can set good limits for our children's negative, aggressive behavior. Get ready. Old feelings and new worries can come up when we work on boundaries, and we can easily end up in a feeling trap. The Brain Boss tries to scare or shame us. Our children's anger and aggression affect us and knock us off course. We then struggle with the challenges of actually setting, communicating, negotiating, and implementing limits, rules, expectations, values, and routines with our children. The result is that we can end up alternating between being too permissive or too strict, creating confusion and insecurity for our kids.

EXPERIENCE IT: EXAMINE YOUR BOUNDARIES

Place yourself on a scale from 1 to 10, from *very porous* (1) to *closed and rigid* (10) when it comes to your boundary style with your children.
Consider these questions:

- How does your boundary style affect you?
- What happens to your voice and your body language when you set limits for your child's behavior?
- How does your child typically react when you set limits?
- Does your child tend to comply with the limits or oppose them?
- If your child follows what you have set, what feelings are activated in them? Are they satisfied, happy, mad, afraid, ashamed, angry?

Take time to think about the answers to these questions before you end your reflection work.
Place yourself on a scale of 1 to 10 of how protective you are with your boundary style in terms of what feelings, thoughts, and stories from other people you will allow in.
Place yourself on a scale of 1 to 10 of how protective you are with your boundary style in terms of what feelings, thoughts, and stories you let out.

KIDS NEED BOUNDARIES, TOO

It's important for kids to learn to establish their own healthy boundaries when they are faced with other people's aggressive behavior. Healthy boundaries protect against physical and psychological attacks. Our boundaries affect how others behave toward us. This does not mean that we are protected against everything, but healthy, protective boundaries send out strong and clear signals to others and reduce the risk of others thinking they can mess with us. They also increase the likelihood that we will be able to stop the aggression of others if it does happen, and they increase the likelihood that we will not allow the behavior of others to affect our self-esteem.

Imagine a group of kids in the schoolyard: Josh, age 14, makes a mean joke at the expense of Mohammed, also age 14. Mohammed responds with a confident voice that is lighthearted but also serious: "Hey! Chill! Don't you know that it's way cooler and actually a sign of intelligence if you make fun of yourself instead of other people?" This type of response, spoken in a clear and powerful voice, makes it difficult to breach Mohammed's self-protective boundaries without risking looking bad. When Mohammed shows self-assertion in this way, he is also emotionally better equipped not to be affected if there is another nasty comment. If, on the other hand, Mohammed had been afraid to say something and had been quiet, or looked down at the ground, or laughed nervously, it is much more likely that Josh would have continued to joke at Mohammed's expense, and he would have likely done it again later. It is also more likely that Mohammed would absorb what had been said and would feel ashamed. In order for Mohammed to get to the point of having healthy boundaries for himself, he needs to recognize how Josh's behavior affects him on the inside. He also needs to have experienced that it helps to stand up for himself and that he doesn't need to be treated that way, that he has a choice. He has learned that he can do something to influence what is going on around him.

It is easier to be affected by the blurred boundaries of others if our own boundaries are blurred. The way we set limits for our children when they act out verbally or physically helps to prepare our kids for how to handle complex situations later in life. How can we best prepare our kids so that they don't attack others, and at the same time ensure that they have good boundaries in the face of aggression, threats, or negative behaviors from other people? And how do we go about setting and implementing effective limits for our children?

OUR VALUES INFLUENCE THE LIMITS AND RULES WE SET

Before getting to limit-setting and how to do it effectively, it's good to reflect a little on the rules, limits, demands, and expectations we want to establish in our home and family. These are, of course, related to our values—the principles and qualities that we each hold as important. Our values are influenced by those of our own parents, and those of our society and culture, both the one we are raising our kids in and the one we ourselves grew up in. In some families, a rule of great importance will be to follow the family's spiritual beliefs and traditions. In another family, a main rule may be around mealtimes and all eating together. Families will differ greatly in the limit they place on physical roughhousing, with some having a strict limit around physical roughness and another not minding that and the family getting a lot of joy and fun out of wrestling in the living room. Some families will have a strict expectation for coming home with high grades, and others will place strict limits on curfew time. Demands vary greatly from family to family as well in the children's responsibility for doing chores or earning their own spending money. Some families have expectations that the children keep their rooms very tidy, while others tolerate mess.

There is no universal right or wrong regarding which limits we each establish for our family. The one absolute is that we need effective limits to prevent or stop harmful aggression and violence. In all other matters, the way we establish and implement limits will depend on many factors, including our culture, religion, laws, past experiences in our family of origin, and our wishes and hopes for our family and home life. It will depend also on our awareness of our magnets and triggers and competing motivations as well as how readily we fall into feeling traps and how skilled we are at climbing back out of them.

Children will learn which values are particularly important in their home. For one family, exploration and growth through play may be the most important, while doing homework is considered less important. This could be a value the parents bring with them from their own upbringing, or it may be important to them despite it being in contrast with the way they were raised. For another family, school, higher education, and professional success might be one of the most important values, while there is less focus on other activities. Another family may place higher value on physical fitness and athletic skill, including competition and achievement; another may value spiritual, religious, cultural, or community involvement. Still another family may value outdoor activities and spending time in nature. Parents who value play or athletics the most may be less strict about home-work and less likely to be disappointed with poor test results. Parents who value school and education the most may set stricter rules and higher expectations related to homework and place limits on other activities that take the focus away from school. We may all agree on children's basic needs when it comes to sleep, diet, and care, but professionals have no place in determining a family's values. Parents choose the values they wish to instill in their children.

WHEN VALUES CLASH WITHIN A FAMILY

Regardless of their value system, every family will face challenges navigating that system with their child. Parents will need to find ways to manage should their child not perform within, or conform to, the family's values and beliefs, or not "fit" within the family's way. Emotional mishaps and injuries, and anger, are inevitable. For example, while we tend to choose life partners who share our same values, some parents will have different values from each other. Different ways of prioritizing what is important in raising your children can present major conflicts. Another example is when parents were brought up in one country and culture but have emigrated and are bringing their children up in another. Clashes are bound to occur between values from the parents' culture of origin and the culture in which their children are living and going to school or working. Children compare limits and values in their family with what they see as the limits and values in other families. If there are major contradictions within the family, or with other families close to the child, the child may react more strongly to the limit-setting.

Values and boundaries also present greater challenges if the parents are divorced. The parents may worry more about the values, or perceived lack of values, in the other parent's home, or worry that their own teaching of values is perceived as not good as, or in line with, the other parent's. When parents live together, they'll have a better idea of the limits that the other parent is setting and what each considers the most important values to be teaching the child. It's not unusual for one parent to feel the need to compensate for what they think is lacking in the other's parenting abilities, and we have more control over what we perceive as their "mistaken priorities" when we are living under the same roof. An important part of good limit-setting is agreeing on which values—and hence which limits, rules, and expectations—are the most essential to work on and which are not so important. Perhaps equally important is recognizing that we are bound to differ, and children learn and benefit from our differences as well. Knowing what it is about your coparent's approach that triggers your magnets and throws you into a feeling trap is a great solution. Limit-setting is hard work. If we can stay aware of our own competing motivations, and direct our limit-setting efforts at meeting our children's needs as well as at maintaining our values, it can lead to the payoff that will make it all worth it.

You can ask yourself, in regard to the recurring conflicts that you have with your child: "If I get my child to comply, what will I achieve? Will the payoff make the effort, no matter how great, worthwhile? Or do I need to choose my battles better?" Depending on the answer, you might hold your ground or reevaluate the limits for that situation. It's also best if everyone involved can have a conversation about this, whether you live together or not, including new partners and stepparents. If everyone is focusing on different values, and if they are not aware of how the values are affecting the children's development and well-being, the child can get caught between two biological parents and two stepparents. It's not necessary for the two homes to have the same values, but the adults need to know and understand which values and limits are important in each home. With this information, it becomes easier to appreciate the various efforts being made and to let go of trying to change the other parent's values.

EXPERIENCE IT: EXAMINE YOUR VALUES

Sit alone or with your partner or coparent. Think about and write a list of your most important values when it comes to your child. Ask yourself which values you consider to be the most important for your child to carry forward into adulthood. Write down the three most important values you wish to instill in your child.

When you're writing the top three, think about how you can communicate these values to your child in a concrete way. What rules and routines are important? Are you doing what you need to do to instill these values in your child? Are you helping and supporting in the right way? Are you living in alignment with your own values? Are you setting limits that encourage those values, without being too rigid or too vague, or saying one thing while pushing the child in the opposite direction? Which limits need adjusting? Make a note of the three most important expectations, rules, or limits that you want to uphold in a healthy and flexible way. Have you set rules or limits that don't support your value goals and that you should discard, or tighten, or loosen? Make a note of these. You have now answered a lot of what is important to think about when setting limits for your child.

Now that you've clarified what you want for your child, it's very important to assess whether your plan is appropriate for your child, specifically, for their temperament, personality, and ability. Sometimes the values we want to instill do not match with the child's needs. In addition to taking a look at your own values and assessing whether the existing limits and expectations are helping to teach your child those values, we need to realize that it is in fact our children who are most aware of what they need. Placing the highest value on education might have to be adjusted if you have a child with serious learning challenges or who has difficulty concentrating—or one who loves art or cooking or working with their hands. Valuing play may need to be reassessed if you have a child who struggles to control their emotions, has aggressive behavior, and who has a great need for structure and follow-up. It's important for adults to see what is important for their children specifically and what needs the children have for limits and rules.

INVOLVE THE CHILD IN CREATING AND ENFORCING A LIMIT

Once you've had some time to reflect, either alone or with your partner or coparent, have a chat with your child about limits and expectations. It is especially important to talk about situations where limit-setting is difficult and where disagreements tend to arise. If you and your child argue every day about when they should get off their screen, it might be time to take a step back and find a new way. You can talk to them about what a tough situation it is, and how it often ends up in shouting, and let them know that you want to hear what they think so you can both work towards resolving it. Be clear that there will be a limit and that you won't allow them to spend their whole life gaming or on the phone. Then discuss how you can negotiate and implement that limit in the best possible way. Some children may say that it's important to be able to finish the round of the game they're playing. They might then need help to plan as screen time nears its end. Other children will want to play their game until the time runs out, in order to maximize playing time, and they don't care if they have to stop in the middle of a round. Some children like to be responsible for keeping track of the time themselves, while others want help with keeping time. The point is that it's much easier to implement a limit when the child is involved in creating it and when it is predictable and clear.

The child can also be part of the discussion regarding how to enforce the limit. It's important to talk about what will happen if they don't follow the agreement and if they refuse to stop playing. Children have a lot of wise things to say, not only about what they like and don't like but also about what motivates them to step up and do better that we adults may not figure out on our own. Involve your child in working together to find the best solutions.

Remember that ultimately you are the one who chooses and sets the limits and that the discussion with your child is about getting input on how to make the limit-setting work in the best way possible. If we propose that our child should participate in deciding, but fundamentally disagree with his or her suggestions for solutions, then we have to take charge, validate our child's feelings in the situation, make new suggestions, and again get input from them. If we get into a situation that drags on for a long time without good solutions in sight, then we might have to be a bit firmer and also show understanding for our child's reactions.

Finally, no matter how children agree on limits, they will still have feelings when the limit is enforced. We find parents can doubt their success when the limit "works" but the child still gets angry. Think about it: None of us like to be stopped from doing what we like or forced to do what we don't like. Use that to validate the feelings when the limit-setting works. "I know you'd rather stay on the game. And you're right—homework sucks, when you'd rather be gaming." Compliance and anger can go together. Enforce the limit. Validate the feeling.

EXPERIENCE IT: YOUR CHILD'S PERSPECTIVE ON VALUES AND LIMITS

Get a chair and put it about 2 feet in front of the chair you are sitting in. Imagine your child sitting in this chair. Tell them what values and limits you consider important. Tell the imaginary child in the chair, as if you are talking to them right now.

Now sit in the other chair and imagine that you are your child who has just heard you conveying your values and limits. How does it feel to hear this as if you are your child? Notice feelings in your stomach and chest. Talk to the imaginary adult sitting in the other chair as if you are the child. Speak as your child directly to yourself, the parent, in the other chair.

What emotions come up? Is there resistance to the values or limits, or do they feel reasonable? Does it feel like you, as your child, can meet the expectations? What do you need? Are the limits flexible? Do you need more containment or more freedom? Is there something you like or dislike when the adult sets limits?

SEPARATING LIMITS AND VALUES

We often confuse setting limits with teaching values when we try to get children to do what we want. We want them to go to bed, or to stop a behavior, such as hitting. We also want them to understand what constitutes right versus wrong and acceptable versus unacceptable. It is difficult to separate limits and values because they are intertwined, but they are not the same. Limits help us teach values, but they are not values in and of themselves. It is through limits, among other things, that we teach our child our values. For example, you might have a limit on bedtime, but this limit is based on the broad value of health and being rested in the morning. But when we yell at a child who has hit their friend and who is already ashamed of what they've done, or when we say that it's important to be kind as we try to get the child to sit calmly enough so we can do up their seatbelt, we are often conveying judgment more than giving information relevant to the situation. Children can feel that we're saying we don't like them, that they're not nice, or that they're not who we want them to be. This is a very different message from one that communicates "Stop this behavior."

Limits are only one way that children learn important values such as courtesy and kindness. Other ways include us being good role models for them and having close conversations with them. But for limit-setting to be effective, it is absolutely essential to separate it from value-setting. Think of setting limits and expectations as being first and foremost about stopping or promoting a behavior. This can lead to good values in the long run. But the more explicit teaching of values happens by talking to kids (during moments when their behavior is not an issue) about good behavior and the consequences of unfortunate behavior, combined with being a role model with healthy and protective internal boundaries. Also keep in mind that it is behavior that needs limits, not emotions. We advocate attempting no character lectures or moral lessons while we are setting a limit.

MY KID KEEPS HITTING OTHERS . . . DOESN'T HE KNOW THAT'S WRONG?

It is worth emphasizing that very few children reach school age without knowing that they are not allowed to hit. That value has been served for breakfast, lunch, and dinner in most homes since the child began to do anything other than sleep. If a child hits, it's rarely because they don't know the rule. Maybe they've witnessed or experienced physical or verbal aggression at home and have learned it. If your child has experienced aggressive behavior in your home, from you, your coparent, or from their siblings, it is more important to forgive yourself and work to put an end to it than it is to talk to your child about how to behave toward others. Children have an inherent sense of justice, and if the rules do not match their lived reality it can lead to painful feelings and negative behavior.

More often, children act aggressively and hit or hurt others because they are angry, including when their anger is cloaking other, more vulnerable feelings, and they lack the skills to manage their anger and express it better. This is why validation is so important. In this case, they don't need a moral lesson. Children from the age of 4 or 5 have a well-developed emotional system. They know right from wrong, and they feel remorse after hitting someone. The emotion of remorse has already informed them that what they did was wrong; we don't have to keep repeating the message. That only turns the healthy remorse into self-critical shame. They need instead for us to be forgiving and to invite them back into the fold. The child's own emotional system thus helps you in raising your child. Through the million times that you have told them "No hitting," they have actually learned that they are not allowed to hit. When children over the age of 3 or 4 bite, it's not because they think that biting is allowed. They bite because they don't

245

know how to express themselves and because they don't have control over their feelings and impulses. They are children who still need a lot of help from the adult to deal with their emotions. Our job, as parents, is to help children become better at expressing themselves and to have better control over their own behavior.

CHAPTER 12

SETTING LIMITS

The second part of the two-part boundary system gets us (finally!) to the challenge of working with the behaviors that come with your child's anger. But guess what? Limit-setting may tackle behaviors, but it is actually all about emotion, too. Your emotion education thus far is going to be what makes you ace the limit-setting part. The guidelines and tips for effective limit-setting are strikingly emotion based. They address how to validate in the context of setting the limit, how to convey confidence and belief and not convey judgment, how to use your connection with your child, how to communicate clearly, and how to let yourself off the hook big time. It will be a leap of faith to think that if you use your emotion skills, you have a far better shot at changing behaviors. But that's the plan.

Remember that the first step in our boundary system was to become aware of the boundary style that is just who you are as well as the impact your style has on your kids: Are you lamb or lion? Then, we want you to embrace it. Both types can get the job done just as well as the other. But you have to work with who you are. The lamb can be too wobbly, or they can be firm but kind. The lion can be too scary, or they can be caring but strong. When you combine embracing and using your natural style with the guidelines below for limit-setting, you can still be you, but with more aces for success up your sleeve.

BE FLEXIBLE WITH YOUR LIMITS

Being flexible with limit-setting means that we are mostly consistent but that we can also loosen or tighten the limit when we see that the child needs it or because we need it ourselves. For example, some parents are convinced that children refusing to go to school should go no matter what. In this desperation, we may force our children to go, or refuse to pick them up, even when they are unable to cope with being there. This would be an example of an inflexible limit. A flexible limit, on the other hand, would be that the basic rule is "You have to go to school," but it may be appropriate to keep a child at home for a few days if there is good reason, such as the child being afraid of going. For some children, it is actually the fact that the parents loosen their grip and do not force them that gets them back on the school bus. On the other hand, some parents are very focused on conveying that school is not the most important thing in the world. They are focused on not pressuring their child and will not try to encourage their scared child to go to school or do home-work even if they have been at home for several weeks. This is also an example of inflexible limit-setting, where parents double down on an expectation even if it is not working for the child. Flexible limit-setting conveys that going to school is not the only thing that is important; sometimes, there may be a more important reason for staying home. The point is that the strategy should help the child resolve the dilemma around school. If it does not actually help the child get back to school, then we revisit and adjust, with the parents making it clear that school is not optional; that they have faith that the child will, and can, resolve the dilemma; and that the parents will help to resolve it so the child can go back.

SELF-COMPASSION: GO EASY ON YOURSELF!

It is a lot of work to set limits that are a healthy mix of flexible and firm because it means we can't operate on autopilot. We have to evaluate repeatedly whether what we are doing helps us achieve what we want for our child, and helps our child, and we have to adjust accordingly. There is no set answer, and we have to try different strategies. Problems arise when we continue to use a strategy that is not working and end up locked in an unhelpful but familiar cycle. Being good at limit-setting means that we need to be patient—not judge, not scream, and not give up. We need to keep a balance between limits that are too strict and too permissive. We need to validate before we move in to set a limit. We need to separate boundaries from conversations about character, morals, and values. No wonder we struggle and fail sometimes! Honestly, it's a minefield.

Let's be kind to ourselves and give ourselves a break. Let's remember that we come by our internal boundary style honestly as a part of the package of our personality and temperament, from our genetics and our early environment. And no one has taught us how to identify what our style is, how to understand the way it is motivated by our emotions, and how to use it for effective limit-setting. This is a steep learning curve here, folks. For the moment, suffice to say that trying to set limits with our children when we don't understand our boundary style or how it works is like driving a fast Ferrari, blindfolded and with our hands tied behind our back. It doesn't work, and we go over the cliff into a feeling trap, blaming our child, our coparent, the school, the other kids, society—and, of course, ourselves.

A ROUGH GUIDE FOR SETTING LIMITS

Let's build our limit-setting skills one step at a time.

Start With Validation

Validation comes before limit-setting, unless the child is engaging in a potentially harmful behavior that must be stopped. Validation increases cooperation. When we validate children's emotions first, we won't have to spend as much effort on setting the limit. When children feel understood, they listen and follow instructions more readily. It also makes it easier for them to make a case for what they want rather than having to act out. When children feel seen and heard and are taken seriously, this gives them the confidence to say outright why they are angry or what they need, without their feelings being cloaked behind rage and provocative behavior. Thus, even when they object to the limit, they do so in a healthier way when we validate authentically before we tell them what they must or mustn't do.

Validate Feelings, Set Limits for Behaviors

It is important for the child to understand and be able to handle their feelings, and to seek out others who can meet their emotional needs and meet those needs themselves, and to experience that their feelings are valid. Be aware of whether you say things such as "Don't be so angry!" "Stop whining!" "It wasn't so sad," "There's nothing to be embarrassed about," or "No, this is not scary," and—well, just stop saying them! Instead, validate the feeling and only then set the limit with your angry child: "Of course you get angry when I say no. And the answer for today is still no. There's no point in asking again. It will still be 'No' all day today." Or: "I can see you're unhappy. I'm not sure what it's about, but I can see there's something. Try to tell me without shouting what you need or want."

If your child is furious and hits you, you can say the following:

> Stop. I'm wondering if you're angry because I said it's bedtime and you wanted to stay up and watch the show with your

brother. I can't let you hit me, so I'm holding your hands until you get control of your body. You're allowed to be angry. Use your words, and tell me why you're so mad. You know you're not allowed to hit, so I can see you're really frustrated and you're not able to tell me what is wrong. Can you breathe calmly or count to ten? Let's count together. One, two . . .

When Your Child Needs to Do Something Hard, Consider Using Short Validation

We should not give a deep validation when the child is in a specific situation where they have to do something they dread, or think is difficult. When children who are afraid to go to school are heading out the door, when children who are afraid to go down the big slide are sitting at the top looking down, or when the child with anorexia sits with a plate of food in front of them, it makes it harder for them to do what they detest or fear if we are talking about how scary or awful it must be. In these situations, it's better to do a short, clear validation with caring but firm encouragement. For example, it may sound like this:

- "I know you dread going to school because you're afraid that Kim and the others will say mean things to you. Take a deep breath, and then let's walk out the door. Come on!"
- "I know you can do it. These big slides are scary. I can walk next to you and then you can slide down. You can do it and I'm here with you. One, two, three!"
- "I know you don't want to eat this food, and I know it's difficult. I'll sit with you until you've finished. Start with a little bite, and then you're on your way."

While we recommend using only short validations in a situation where the child has to do something they dread doing, some parents experience that deep validation also gets the kids out the door in the morning or down the long slide. There are no rules without exceptions here, either. Try it out and test what works best for you and your child.

Sometimes when we try to set clear limits and the child is not receptive, validation doesn't help us, either. Then major repair work may be needed. There could be an emotional wound in the relationship with your child that will make them unresponsive to the limits until it is repaired. Apology strengthens the relationship so that parents are in a position to validate, meet emotional needs, and set limits.

Convey Confidence in Yourself and Your Child

If we believe in ourselves and in our children—in our ability to provide the structure and limits they need, and in their wish to find and be their own best selves, and in their need and ability to develop their own healthy, protective boundaries—that belief will shine through in our nonverbal body language. Our child will see us as being confident, and the research is very clear on this: Our confidence as parents is not only what instills confidence in our child. It is our confidence that predicts the child's success, more than their own confidence does. And don't worry if boundaries have not been going great in your house and you do not have belief and confidence. If it hasn't been going well, of course you don't. That's why we have a skill set for you to learn. What we do in the meantime is "faith it till we make it." We also call this "acting as if." Academy Award time, folks. Like with validation and apology: At first have blind faith in the ingredients and the steps, and just learn and do them acting as if you know they'll work. Expertise and actual belief in yourself and in your child will come.

You need to "act as if" in the meantime because belief (or lack of) comes across loud and clear through nonverbal messages. Those of you who follow professional boxing or mixed martial arts know this: The fight is won before the fighters even enter the ring. The same is true in many sports and other competitions: How we convey our belief in our success has an enormous impact on the likelihood of being successful.

Are you a parent who makes a strong show of force when difficult limit-setting situations arise, or do you tend to back down and give up or give in? Either way, this will be evident in your nonverbal expression. It will give your child mixed messages—too much power will signal that you don't believe in them, and too little, that you don't believe in yourself. Both will lead you further from your goal. We need to adjust our nonverbal expressions in situations of conflict. Ideally, we use a firm and determined but noncritical voice when we need children to do something they don't want to do or get them to stop doing something they like. A voice that signals clearly "This is going to happen," without it being a strict command, or a question. It helps to have a noncritical expression on your face and clear body language that is consistent with the behavior you want. It's also important to be physically close to the child, especially the young ones. Be prepared for resistance and strong feelings, even when you believe (or convey) that you will succeed. You'll be less surprised and derailed if you're prepared that they won't like the limit you set, and you'll be better able to validate the resistance and feelings while holding your ground with the limit-setting.

Don't Convey Judgment

A further note on the idea of adopting a noncritical tone of voice and facial expression: There is a good reason for using the words "noncritical" here. The main thing the parents we've worked with have discovered regarding their failed attempts to set limits is that they feel and then convey or express judgment in setting limits. And the child hears it loud and clear (whether conveyed or spoken). We've seen parents discover over and over that what they thought was their child refusing to comply with the limit turns out to be the child reacting to the judgment. All of us react to judgment. Many of us react to it with shame, and remember: Anger is a soldier of shame. Anger is a cloaking device for shame because shame feels so gross. And once your child is in the anger-and-shame feeling trap, not even the best, most skilled limit-setter on earth can reach them. Their reasoning brain is offline. That is why we encourage you to use boundaries without judgment. If you get frustrated and angry yourself, it's completely understandable. Take five. If that's not realistic, accept that on this occasion your efforts might end in the same old battle.

By "noncritical," we mean withholding not only criticism but also judgment of any kind. What feels judgy is specific to your child, your relationship with them, and both of your personality types and magnets. Some of you, when you're in a feeling trap, might resort to clearly visible criticism, and that can be shaming for your child who has developed a magnet for criticism. But we don't say use a "warm" or "kind" or "friendly" face, because for those of you who have a more snowplow, rescuing, submissive style your child will have a magnet for you being "nice" and saying "please," as though you need to sugarcoat it when you need them to do or stop doing something. Sugarcoating your requests of them makes them feel like you're walking on eggshells—and children whose parents walk on eggshells end up feeling like they must be monsters if their parents are too hesitant or scared to stand up to them.

The best way to find your tone of voice and facial expression is to start by doing the opposite of the usual you. If you usually storm in like a stern, critical, cold, or angry lion, you might try softening your face and tone with a little warmth, kindness, or friendliness. If you're normally "nice" and tiptoe in smiling and all warm and fuzzy—shut that stuff down, and try to present yourself more neutrally. Get ready, once again, for your children to react to the change. And keep experimenting until you find the boundaries-without-judgment face and voice that work for you and your child.

Be Physically Near Your Child

One of the classic mistakes we make when we set limits is that we are not in physical proximity to our child, and so we can't help things get started with some physical encouragement. Many people can probably relate to shouting from the hallway up to the second floor that it's time to come down for dinner, or you've yelled from the kitchen that it's time to end computer games and get ready for bed. And how many times have you heard your child mumble or shout "Yes" and then continue with the same activity as if you had not said anything at all? Some may also relate to saying something angry like: "I've told you three times! Why don't you listen? Now!" Others give up and leave the responsibility to their better half. The problem is that many children don't actually hear what we're saying or understand the seriousness when we speak without having gotten their attention first. The same goes for adults. We sometimes hear someone asking us a question but don't really pay attention to what's being said, and then our answer ends up being vague or senseless.

We are much more likely to succeed in giving instructions if we are physically close to the child. It can also be helpful to use physical touch, such as a hand on the shoulder, or gentle movements that physically lead the child in the right direction, or stroking the child's head. It requires a little more of us in the moment, but it can save us from having to spend a lot of time on a possible conflict if we get a bit lazy. It's especially important to be physically close and to get the attention of the child if you have a child with concentration difficulties, who becomes very engrossed in a particular activity and shuts out the rest of the world, or who gets angry quickly when you set limits.

Don't Insist on Eye Contact

Don't ask your child to look you in the eye. That can be provocative and threatening for some children, especially in combination with a strict tone of voice or if they are feeling a bit ashamed (which having a limit set can do to any of us, even when it is done well). Stand or sit next to the child. You can also crouch down in front of smaller children or sit on the other side of the table when you want to give an important instruction, but don't force the child to look at you. Children with strong temperaments naturally tend to get angry when we ask them to end an activity they like, or if we say no to something they want. It's normal for both children and adults to get angry when others prevent us from reaching goals and doing activities that are important to us. Consider this when setting limits, and try to talk to the child as if they were an engaged and like-minded person.

Don't Be Abrupt or Jump to Conclusions

Sometimes it's tempting to give sudden, abrupt instructions, without any kind of introductory conversation. In a busy and stressful every-day life, it's understandable that we take shortcuts and go straight to saying that the child has to stop playing, or come and eat, or get ready for bed, or clean their room. Sometimes, it's all we can manage. But it will save us time (tons of time) in the long run if the limit-setting goes well. So when you can, start the conversation with a "Hi," or "Hey, what's up?" before "It's time to do homework." Other times, we ask our children if they've done something they were supposed to do, with the expectation that, and in a tone that says, they haven't. Let's say a child is responsible for walking the dog after school. We get home and say right away, "You haven't walked the dog, have you?" We jump to the conclusion and judgment that they haven't done it and that they had no intention of doing it. It's natural enough that we do this, arriving home after a long day's work. Also, often they haven't done it! But the child has often spent the whole day without the parent. Whatever is up with them, whether they've done their chores or not, judgment neither feels good nor helps. They now feel ashamed for having failed and disappointed us and angry at being judged and criticized. This is not a good starting point to motivate children to do things they find tedious or irksome. We also miss a golden opportunity for connecting with our child. Again, we will have more success by starting with a "Hi" or "How was your day?" before we ask, in a neutral tone of voice, "Have you taken the dog out?" or "Why don't you walk the dog while I make dinner?" (expressed as more of a statement than a question). This way we also give our child the chance to tell us if they have not done the chore they were supposed to do. In addition, we'll know if the child has had a crummy day or a good day. We can feel confident that we've shown interest before we make demands and that we're taking the child's emotional state into account in the situation.

Don't Be Hesitant

Another classic mistake is to start saying something with a sigh, or mumbling, or with a hesitant question rather than a clear instruction. We'll say, "What do you think about . . .?" "Can you go and get dressed now?" "Do you want to . . .?" when the issue is not really up for discussion. When we ask questions in this way, we're suggesting that the child has a choice. When we're not giving them a choice and we ask a question anyway, then we have to go against the answer the child gives if they say no. First, this is dishonest, and second, it leads to conflict. We're inviting the child to disregard the limit that we are trying to set. Instead, when you're not giving the child a choice, give a clear message. When you give an instruction you know the child will not like, use the words and tone that will not trigger your child.

For example, if you're usually stern, it can work to say: "Let's go upstairs together so you can brush your teeth, and afterwards I'll tell you something funny that happened at work today." Or: "Let's go clean up your toys now, and we can listen to your audiobook at the same time." If you're usually invested in being "nice" try to be more neutral: "You know the drill. Five minutes, and then up to bed."

Being too hesitant or too stern is partly due to our personality. But still there is a lot we can learn and modify, regardless of our inborn style. If we didn't realize how important clear instructions and expectations are to making limit-setting successful, we might be hesitant and unclear. We then convey that what we're saying is not important. At other times, we're vague because we're afraid or nervous about the child's reaction and expect a "No" or a massive conflict. We give up before we even try. We're afraid to get in the ring with them, and we lose before we start. It might be that we are stressed, frustrated, or angry about things not related to the situation. In this case, we need to take a moment before we tell our kids to do what we need them to do. Then stand firmly, with your legs slightly apart; straighten your back; and speak in a clear and neutral voice. Give an instruction. Do not ask.

Give Yourself Some Grace

Remember that your child is more likely to listen to you if you find the tone of voice and facial expression that are less likely to evoke their old anger at you. Let's also be realistic—we're bound to nag and scold a bit when we set limits. It's normal, and most children tolerate some nagging and raising of voices. As always, make it work for your family. Some children are particularly sensitive to raised voices and can experience a loud voice as critical or scary. In this case, we need to be extra careful. Just don't be too hard on yourself. Sometimes, when children are either in danger, or when we can't cut through the noise from the TV or siblings quarrelling, it may be necessary to raise your voice and be abrupt. We're all going to fall into our old ways, and yell . . . or say "Please," depending on your style. It's not the end of the world. Just remember that if you think you were too aggressive, or the child experiences that you were too aggressive, or they were intimidated by you, you can apologize. No child enjoys getting loud and angry instructions about what they should or should not do, but it simply doesn't always work to interrupt what is going on if your voice is too soft. This is a difficult thing to balance when setting limits, and so we'll make mistakes, and that's just fine. Parents who quickly become aggressive in an inappropriate way, and who are physical with their children, or say hurtful things, have the most amount of work to do in this area. In these cases, it is worth putting extra effort into reducing recurring conflict situations.

We find that it's much more possible to change and fix your "flaws" in limit-setting when you think about creating boundaries without judgment. Remember that it's not the limit-setting, but the criticizing or judging the child for something they have done or not done, that ruins your effectiveness. Remember that when we set limits and judge the child at the same time, they don't hear the limit. They only hear the criticism, disappointment, or contempt in our voice:

> I can't be bothered to stand here every night and nag you. I can never sit down in the evening and relax. You create problems every night. Can't you just go to bed now? You never go and get ready for bed when you're supposed to.

Some parents are critical and hostile when judging their child. Other parents beg and appeal to the child's feelings of guilt. None of this works with limit-setting. We need to use a neutral voice without judgment to be effective at setting limits.

EXPERIENCE IT: TONE OF VOICE

Imagine that you have to set a limit for your child who will not stop playing and go to bed. Practice setting the limit out loud using different tones of voice. What do you think works best?

STEPS FOR SETTING LIMITS

How can we move from judging and not being effective at setting limits, to setting limits effectively without judgment? Before the actual limit-setting, there are two things to do. We first assess whether there is an instant need for a limit, such as a child hurting another child or in danger themselves, in which case we are not going to stop and validate first! Assuming, however, that it's not a situation where you absolutely must intervene right away, limits work best if we think them through and use our emotion skills rather than act on impulse

---

Steps for Setting Limits

Pre-Step A: Assess the situation. Do you need a limit immediately, or can you validate first?

Pre-Step B: Validate. Make the connection.

Step 1. Set your body in ready mode. Make your body language strong and clear.

Step 2. Set your emotions. Avoid the feeling trap; be calm, engaged, caring, and confident. Have faith in yourself. Be empathic toward your child. Avoid judgment.

Step 3. Choose your words, and communicate the limit. Short. Succinct. To the point. No lengthy discussion at this point. No moral or character lectures.

Step 4. Hold your ground. Stick to your decisions unless new information comes up with good reasons to reconsider.

---

when we and/or our child are caught in feeling traps. Start with a quick assessment of what your child needs in the situation and what limits you need and want to set. If you can, take the time to discuss the situation with your coparent, if you haven't already developed good guidelines for this situation.

Next, validate the child's feelings about having the limit set. Validation strengthens the connection and helps your child feel seen and understood before you give the instruction. Again, the specific situation determines whether there is time to validate and whether there is a need for short or deep validation. But, if at all possible, we validate, because validation paves the way for cooperation. You will simply have much better success in setting the limit when the connection with the child is good. And helping you have success rather than frustration is what we want.

Once you have assessed and validated, you need to set your body for conveying a clear message. You need to feel strong in your legs, arms, core, upper body, neck, and head. Not angry and threatening, not too weak, but appropriately strong. Let your "pointing finger" rest, and lift your arms out to the side only when you really need to. These kinds of movements can make the child want to withdraw, maybe in annoyance or maybe in fear, depending on their temperament. Avoid flailing your arms around or fiddling with your fingers, but you can gesture a little or put your hands on your thighs or stomach. Also make sure that you have physical proximity to the child, and use your body actively by, for example, placing a hand on their shoulder; sitting next to them; or, with smaller children, carefully starting to lead them in the right direction.

Next, prepare your emotions. Make sure you're not in a feeling trap; that your Brain Boss is quiet; and that you are calm, engaged, caring, and confident. Remember the goal of limit-setting. It is important to convey to the child that you have belief in yourself and in the limit being set. Have empathy for your child. Remember that there are huge differences in power, size, and strength between adults and children. It can feel shameful when someone sets a limit for us, and it can be hard to have to stop an activity, or to have it pointed out that you've done something wrong. Be empathic toward the child in a way that avoids or minimizes them being shamed. No child is naughty or mean because they want to ruin things for others or push others away. They act that way because they are struggling to express their needs in a reasonable way, and they need help and support from us to find a new way.

When the body is strong and the emotions are in place, the third step is to choose your words and communicate the limit. Give short and precise instructions. Avoid lengthy discussions and counter-arguments, as well as explanations for why you are setting the limit. Also let go of the urge to give lessons in morals or values. Clear limits are typically set with words such as "This is how it will be now." "This is happening now." "I know." "You're right." "It's not what you want to do. It feels unfair. Still, right now, this is how it is." Other good phrases in setting limits are "It's going to be how I've decided it will be because you don't do well with lots of sugar." Or "This is how it's going to be because I need to know that you are safe." Or: "You're going to bed now. Of course you don't like going to bed when you're not tired. It's the rule. You go to bed at 8:00 every night. Come on, let's go. I'm coming with you."

The last step in setting a limit is to stay strong and hold your ground. Stick to your decision. Then include a healthy dose of flex-ibility. There are times when changing your mind and not sticking rigidly is the best option, for example, if it's a decision that turns out to be not so well-thought-out after all. It's important, if you change your mind, that you base it on new information and make a new assessment of your own or your child's needs, and not because you get tangled up in a feeling trap. It might be a good idea to say something about why you are changing your mind. For example:

I understand that you finally have the chance to play with Jonas, and you haven't played with him for a long time, and I know you've really missed that. I know you don't want to miss this chance. You know what? You can get an extra fifteen minutes. And then I want you to turn off your computer at exactly 9:15.

Or even, after hearing your child's sigh: "Good point. I said 'No' too fast. That's fine; you can go."

When you practice and master the steps for setting limits, your child is still going to have feelings! We've had plenty of parents really nail the limit-setting but then doubt themselves afterward because their child still got angry. But remember—we're setting limits on behaviors, not on feelings. You can just go on ahead and validate that! "I see. It makes you so angry that you have to do your chores before heading out with your friends." And yet there they are, doing the chores. Later, when the waters are calmer, you can add: "I appreciate you getting that job done."

In the next chapter, we look at where consequences fit into this system.

CHAPTER 13

GIVING CONSEQUENCES

We will lose credibility if we try to tell you that once you embrace your boundary style and master the steps of limit-setting, your child will never act out or misbehave. Every parent knows that they are going to have to deal with bad behavior along the way. You might even think, if you have a bit of the rebel in you yourself (or if you did when you were younger), that it isn't desirable for a young person to be compliant all of the time. You might think that could lead to being overly submissive, not having sufficient autonomy, and not having access to adequate self-assertive anger. But most of us also believe that it's our job to teach our children well, and that includes showing them that bad behavior has consequences. Let's dive in and get a better understanding of consequences and of what leads to our successes (and mishaps) in using them to reinforce the limits we set.

CONSEQUENCES VERSUS PUNISHMENT

In the context of parenting, we distinguish *consequences* from *punishment*. A consequence is something that directly follows destructive or dangerous behavior, or behavior that violates important family rules, norms, and values. It is related to the bad behavior and is designed to reinforce the underlying value that has been violated. For example, an understandable consequence for a child who smashes and breaks their phone in an angry fit may be that the child does not get another phone until they have saved up money to buy a new one. Or they have to wait 'til their birthday for a new one. Or they have to settle for a spare phone for now. When the child smashed their phone, they violated the value of caring for one's property. Thus, the consequence reinforces that phones are valuable and should be handled with care.

Another example is that your child has a friend visiting, the two end up in an argument, and your child hits their friend in the face. A typical consequence could be that the visit has to end and the friend is sent home. Since it didn't go well the last time they were together, the adults may need to be closer by on the next visit and not allow the children to play alone. If the next visit goes well, the children get another chance to play alone without supervision. These kinds of consequences should be communicated to your child alone, in order to avoid inflicting shame on your child while others are around.

A final example is the teen who is out all night without being in touch. The parents finally reach them in the early hours of the morning. A direct consequence could be that the planned trip to the swimming pool with friends the next morning is canceled because everyone needs to make up for lost sleep. If, on the other hand, your teen comes home at five in the morning and you react with a ban on watching TV and playing computer games for a week, that would qualify as a punishment. Taking away TV or game time is not an evident and direct consequence of being out for a long time without permission. In the same way, it's a punishment if the reaction to your child hitting another child is being grounded or taking away pocket money, because that reaction is not a direct result of hitting.

WHAT'S SO BAD ABOUT PUNISHMENT?

Punishment may seem to work in the short term in specific situations, at least in that we succeed in our children not being allowed to continue with an activity that they want to do or get them to refrain from aggressive acts. But there is extensive research telling us that punishment is not particularly useful and that it can be harmful to the child's development (Assor et al., 2004; Gershoff, 2002; Grolnick, 2002).

Punishment can regulate the child's behavior, but it does not teach them to develop good internal boundaries and to become good at setting protective limits in relation to others. Children subjected to frequent punishment may come to rely excessively on their parents regarding what is right or wrong and not learn to rely on their own ability to know the difference. Punishment, threats, and consequences that are too harsh can also take a severe toll on the relationship between parents and children. Children can become more oppositional, and increasingly aggressive, as they try to push past the limits. Punishment can lead to emotional pain and anger, and contempt for the parents who have inflicted the pain. Anger at the parents can then turn inward in the form of self-harm, drug and alcohol abuse, eating disorders, or mental health struggles. This is especially the case if the parents do not respect and validate the child's assertive anger and need for their own boundaries. If children are unable to use their healthy anger to help them solve the difficult situation they're in, they end up with increased emotional discomfort and will turn to more inappropriate strategies, such as self-harm or drugs and alcohol.

Each family has their own way of doing things, and we're not telling you how to discipline your children. We're inviting you to examine your actions with two questions that we believe will serve your own goal of smoother and more effective limit-setting. This way can also lead to more skill with anger and with your child learning important lessons. The goal is for them to have better internal boundaries and fewer angry outbursts:

1. Is what you did punishment (not related to their misbehaving)? If so, this will usually make them angrier, causing thinking and learning to go offline.
2. Or is what you did a consequence that they can link to the behavior? If yes, then they have the chance to learn from their mistake.

Let's take another classic example. The children can't stop playing on their phones and computers in the evening, after they've gone to their rooms, and it affects their sleep. The kids are simply not mature enough to have the responsibility they have been given, and although they understand the rationale—that they need their sleep— their competing motivation to be onscreen wins out. They need the parents to take charge. Because the draw of screens is so powerful, the parents will be more successful if they stick to consequences in the way we've discussed, not only in terms of the parents' firmness but also, and equally, in being related to the issue and not ones that the children will instinctively know do not fit "the crime." The parents introduce a new routine, which is that the kids hand over their phones and computers before going to bed, with the intention that the children will get enough sleep to be able to function the next day. The kids, however, sneak out of their room after bedtime, find the devices, and the parents discover them playing at midnight. The parents react by confiscating the electronics and banning their use for a week. This is a punishment. We're not saying it's severe. That is not the issue. We're saying that it will not serve the purpose because it doesn't have the lesson in it. It's not addressing what the failure or need of the kids is—which is that they play on the devices too late into the night.

When kids say, "It's not fair!," sometimes it's just a way of expressing, "I'm angry!" But other times, it's from that instinct of theirs that says, "This doesn't fit what I did." And we can hear that *if* we listen, and engage, and hear their point. "Unfair" punishment (remember, that is not saying you're too strict or that the punishment is severe) contributes to making kids angry, and makes angry kids angrier. There's that inherent sense they have that although they need you to be at the helm, they need you to share power so that they can internalize your guidance and live by it for themselves. In the above example, a consequence would be locking the devices away at night, to prevent them ruining the children's sleep and, when they're ready, helping them to gain the internal control to balance nighttime habits and daytime needs.

Another reason that makes this distinction between punishment and consequences so important is children's motivation. Children, like adults, are highly motivated by certain things, and this motivation helps them do necessary but unpleasant tasks to get to what they love. If your child loves to game, then taking away gaming as a punishment for not complying with a rule can further lower the motivation to comply. Some parents take away the child's right to play their sport as a punishment. If the child lives to play hockey, often hockey will be a motivator—get homework done to be able to get to the rink. Even—do homework because Coach has a rule: Keep your grades up to stay on the team. And even—do homework to get good grades and get a scholarship to play hockey on a university team. Just as when teachers keep kids inside at recess as punishment, denying kids their chance to play, run, and do sports will *not* help their behavior or reduce their angry outbursts, whereas playing, running, and doing sports will.

Let's think of other examples where we can try to keep the consequences in line with the situation and not too much or too little. If a teen gets drunk and isn't home by curfew one evening, being grounded on weekends for the rest of the year is not a consequence that is in line with the situation. It also doesn't help the child to grow. What could be a natural consequence for parents of a teen who won't respect curfews is that the parents start by following up with them more closely over the next couple of weekends, with curfew times, pickup times, or checking in during the evening. The purpose is to ensure that the teen is safe and gets home in one piece. If it seems to be going well, and the teen adapts to the parents' tightening of the limits and keeping a closer eye, then the limit can be loosened again. Young people need to be given new opportunities to handle a greater responsibility for themselves relatively quickly.

WHEN POSSIBLE, AVOID MAKING YOUR CHILD AFRAID OF A CONSEQUENCE

Threatening consequences is different from actual consequences. We can let our child know that a certain behavior will have consequences, and why, so that the consequence doesn't come out of the blue. But we find that using consequences as a threat can lead to the child behaving a certain way only to avoid, or out of fear of, the consequence. It doesn't help the child's development to behave a certain way out of fear of consequences; it can even be harmful. We try to avoid sentences like "If you do not . . . then. . . ." Instead, say: "I need you to . . ." or "We're doing this now," or "When you lose control and hit your little brother then I have to move you away." Or, when yesterday they wouldn't brush their teeth when you asked, and it dragged on forever, and then you felt resentful reading a story when it's so late, the next day you can say at the outset: "You have 10 minutes to brush your teeth. Get to it and we'll have time to read a whole chapter before bed." Incidentally, we don't say, on the night that it went badly: "It was so difficult to get you to brush your teeth that now it's too late for more than two pages of your book." That might sound the same as the previous one, but there are kids who have a very strong sense of these "internal scales of justice." It's as though they see it as us letting them dawdle, then blaming them when they do and when it's too late to turn back the clock and get it right. It's fascinating to us—it's like the child is saying, "I know I fight it. But that doesn't mean I want to win." and "Please don't let me win the battle, and then make me pay in guilt and regret. Even though I fight, I want it to go well."

WHY SOME PARENTS AVOID GIVING APPROPRIATE CONSEQUENCES

Some parents are afraid of escalating the conflict or losing connections with their children if they impose consequences for aggressive or unfortunate behavior. Other parents are busy, sick, or in the middle of a difficult life situation, so they don't have the capacity to monitor the children as needed. It obviously requires more of us adults when the children can't manage on their own, or with little supervision. In that case, ideally, and if we can manage it, we'd stay closer and be more watchful when it comes to their own boundaries. If you are in a particularly difficult and demanding situation, it's great if you can get more people to help: grandparents, aunts and uncles, neighbors. We know this can be really hard for some parents, both out of reluctance to ask or fewer options in terms of who you can ask. We just suggest that it's better to ask for help when you see that your time and resources are limited rather than letting things go and then trying to address the situation later, when it has become more serious. At that point, it will be more difficult to change the behavior. You'll need much more help, and it will take much more of your own time, energy, and even money if things escalate and you need to seek professional help.

While fear may prompt some parents to avoid giving consequences, it can prompt others to give excessively strict consequences
as punishment. It's perfectly understandable that parents get frightened. It's just that fear is not the best guide to parenting when it is feeling-
trap fear. If we can recognize and work with our feeling traps, that
will help us recognize when it is not a feeling trap and there is in
fact a more serious situation where parents do need to step in more.
The issue is therefore how we handle our fear and whether, why, and
how we act on it!

Let's talk first about when fear may be a feeling trap. Something
may have happened in our own life or in our child's life that makes
us hypervigilant and overly concerned, and we might use excessive
control to try to manage the fear. This fear-based parenting and need
for control over the child's behavior can become an overly narrow
focus that damages the relationship.

Imposing strict consequences and punishment do give the parent
a sense of control over the child's behavior; in some cases, it can even
control it. The problem is that the child may lose trust in the parent
in the process. The child can get angry at the excessive control and
avoid seeking connection and care in the future, for fear of being
controlled. We need a good relationship with our children, one that
has a high degree of trust and respect, so that we can maintain effective influence in their lives, to guide their values, boundaries, and
choices, and not just to manage their behavior. Too much control
can come at the expense of the child's autonomy, the feeling of being
a separate person who can decide for themselves and influence their
own life. All children have the right to autonomy (appropriate to
their age), and it is precisely good autonomy that will enable the child
to live life independently and productively as an adult. Restricting
autonomy has greater direct negative consequences for teens and
young adults (e.g., those still in our care) than for young children. It
can also be exacerbated if what the teen wants in life deviates from

what the parents want for them. If we try to push the youth into our vision of what is good for them, we can compromise their ability to have success in pursuing their own wishes and independent values. We can end up pushing our teen away from us emotionally, and sometimes also physically.

Often, parents threaten punishment or give out punishment in the heat of the moment, without thinking or planning. Some end up going to their child afterward with their tail between their legs, taking it back and removing the punishment. Others feel that they must follow through on what they said in order to be consistent and not lose credibility and respect—even if they regret it terribly. If you punish in the heat of the moment, the best solution is to talk to the child and apologize, using the steps for apologies as described in Chapter 10. If you manage to apologize and take back the punishment, it won't damage the relationship, even though you decided that what you did was a mistake. On the contrary, apologies in such situations will be able to restore trust and strengthen the relationship. Taking radical responsibility in such a situation will also feel more empowering for us as parents than the embarrassment we feel when we try to hide our mistake and claim that we just randomly changed our mind.

Often, when we give out punishment impulsively, it's because we get scared or angry. The next time your child breaks your rules or misbehaves, give yourself time to think about it. Let them know that you need to discuss what happened with the other parent, or that you need to think about what the consequence will be. When you've given yourself some time, have thought calmly, and possibly discussed things with others, you can let your child know about the consequences for breaking the rules or engaging in negative or risky behavior. Also inform the child about the purpose of the consequence, which is that you are looking out for the child's needs and well-being because that is your job.

SHOULD YOU EVER FORCE YOUR CHILD TO END
A RELATIONSHIP?

Some parents will stress themselves with worry about the potentially catastrophic things that could happen to their children. They can be terrified of negative influences if their teen starts up a relationship with someone who drinks or does drugs, doesn't go to school, or hangs out with a bad crowd. (Teens also have their finger on the pulse of this one. One teen told us, "My parents don't get it. I AM the bad crowd. I'm the one who's a bad influence on the friend who they think is 'bad for me,' not the other way around.") Parents' first impulse may be to limit contact and prevent their child from seeing that person at all. Preventing or limiting contact may work in some cases, but it can also make the situation worse and last longer. First, strict measures at an age where young people are seeking freedom and independence can contribute to them putting more energy into doing what we've forbidden. It then becomes all about finding ways to meet the person they're not allowed to meet and finding clever solutions for getting together without anyone knowing. Second, limits that are too strict in this context can lead to conflict and distance in the relationship and weakened trust between the child and the parents. The child may "go underground" and not tell their parents about their friends or romantic partners, and next time they won't let their parents know if they've met someone who they think the parents may not like.

Sometimes, as challenging as it is for us as parents, we have to allow relationships that worry us. We have to concentrate instead on helping the child to function as best as possible in a risky relationship and teach them to have healthy, protective boundaries and make good choices for themselves. In fact, it is more likely that the young person will be able to have a friend with risky behavior (e.g., drinking, using drugs, cheating, fighting, stealing), without starting the same behavior themselves, if they receive good support and help at home to set limits and take care of their own needs. In addition, it is more likely that we get to preserve the child's trust, and the child will be wiser going into the next relationship.

In extreme instances where a young person is regularly abusing drugs or alcohol, is engaging in a sexual behavior that could be harmful, or is spending a lot of time in a stressful and risky environment, it can be necessary to take drastic measures to help them out of the situation. These kinds of measures may include taking them out of an environment and trying to end certain relationships. It is important to explain to the child why we're using such drastic measures and to spend a lot of time validating and showing understanding for the fact that it is extremely difficult for them to lose their right to decide. Some young people will understand the need for this when they have exposed themselves to danger, and some may even want the parents to rescue them, even if they express a lot of ambivalence. Other young people will not be able to understand the consequences of their own behavior and will have little understanding that adults need to take such measures, even if, for example, they drink or get high daily and end up in trouble with the law. In these cases, it's very tough for the parent to stand firm on boundaries and at the same time accommodate the young person's feelings. Most parents in such desperate situations will benefit from professional help.

There is a big difference between a young person who doesn't go to school and engages in destructive behavior on a daily basis and a young person who is mostly at school but who is in a problematic relationship, experiments with drugs at parties on the weekends, or gets in a fight once in awhile. In the case of the latter group, it usually helps more if we guide and support them if they start to get into problem behaviors, such as self-harm or drugs, instead of forcing them to break off relationships that are important to them. Helping

275

children without taking them out of challenging situations or relationships requires us to keep our cool. It is often with our hearts in our throats that we choose to guide children in difficult situations rather than try to take them out of them.

REMEMBER THAT SERIOUS MISBEHAVIOR IS A SYMPTOM OF EMOTIONAL PAIN

In this chapter, we have written a bit about serious behaviors such as self-harm and drug and alcohol abuse. We would like to finish by pointing out that self-harm and addiction are symptoms of underlying emotional pain, in the same way that aggression and violence are. Parents are often frightened by their children's behavior; they panic and want to change the behavior; and they might think that as long as they change the behavior, they have saved their child. This is understandable. It is also not how it works. If we get rid of an unwanted or risky behavior without helping the child with the underlying emotions, new problematic behaviors will show up to replace the old. It's the painful feelings and unmet needs that are the cause of the destructive behavior, and that is what needs attention. Children and adolescents can turn to destructive behavior when they actually need to feel belonging, recognition, love, or safety.

Sometimes there are clear underlying causes for the pain, such as the child being bullied or subjected to violence or abuse; or the child has difficult close relationships with family or friends; has difficulty at school; or has experienced serious trauma, such as death or illness in the family. Other times, there are more diffuse and complex causes, and in some cases the difficulties are due to chemical or neurological conditions, which are difficult to figure out. In any case, our children need us to see them, to be there for them, to try to understand and to follow them closely, without blaming them for their unwanted behavior.

WHAT ABOUT REWARDS AND PRAISE?

Rewards can work well with children who are acting out, if used correctly. But there are also many potential pitfalls. If we don't use rewards correctly, then when there is no reward, the child can see this as a form of punishment. Reward is not included in emotion focused skills training for parents, because we emphasize other parenting skills that we believe are more essential and more important and that make rewards in the form of stickers, gifts, or treats unnecessary. This does not mean that we don't think it can work, or that we think it's bad for children if you enforce limits by using rewards. If it's working for you, that's what counts. Then we can give you options for when your child is angry and what you're doing is not working.

With a focus on validating anger and setting limits for aggression, the goal is that the child will behave in such a way that shows they can be responsible for tasks, follow rules, and eventually be able to take care of their own needs for safety and health, mental and physical. These outcomes are intrinsic rewards. *Intrinsic rewards* are rewards that the individual feels inside, such as the feeling of mastery, pride, and enthusiasm kids get when they handle challenges, apologize when they mess up, and are able to express their anger in a self-assertive way. Providing external rewards can derail and undervalue the more lasting power of intrinsic rewards. "I do it for the candy, not for the mastery and good feeling I get on my own from doing it."

In emotion focused skills training, we give praise and validate and reinforce useful feelings and actions when they are already activated in the children. For example, if a child does not feel self-assertive anger, it is not easy to get them to assert themselves when others treat them badly. Instructing the child to stand up for themselves does not work. But if the child already feels angry, and tries to express it even mildly, we can praise the child for being brave enough to let us know. There is then a greater probability that the child will take in the praise and that the feeling of mastery will become stronger. Feel free to praise your child when they are able to establish and express their own boundaries and other emotional needs, even when it happens in relation to you. That is how you really help them become wise about their anger and teach them to take care of their own boundaries and their own need for healthy self-assertion. If we reward children's behavior or efforts with encouragement and praise, they will want to do more of the same. Praising, validating, or showing pride when children express anger and other feelings and needs in a good way, or when they take responsibility for their own bad behavior, has a great effect on their behavior going forward.

It's also important to praise the effort rather than the result. For example, it's important to praise the child's intention and attempt to apologize and not give praise on the basis of the outcome. The child hasn't done a better job if the other child with the black eye forgives and they become friends again than if the hurt child remains angry and the animosity continues. In the same way, it's important to praise the child's attempt to stand up for himself, and the courage it required, and not the result of the situation that arose. It can also help to praise the intention to want to do something good, or to want to talk about something that was unfair, even if the child has not yet done it. We can also praise children for doing tasks and activities they find difficult, such as going to kindergarten when they are dreading it, or participating in their first theater production even though they were very nervous beforehand. Just remember that praise has the greatest effect if pride is already a feeling that is activated in the child. When teaching therapists about emotions, "Dig where the ground is soft," says Leslie Greenberg, who developed emotion-focused individual therapy, suggesting that therapists should stay empathically with their clients in their pain. The same metaphor can be used about parenting and raising children. Praise the children when the ground is soft and it is easy to dig out the good feelings.

The use of praise also has a cautionary tale, and we offer the same guideline we did in regard to the tone of voice and facial expression to use in limit-setting. The essence of the guideline is: The thing that you usually do and find easy to do is likely the thing you need to alter. Parents who have always apologized a lot and find apologizing easy will end up, as we said, "apologizing for the weather." They lose credibility, and their apologies lose their healing power. Parents who struggle to apologize and have to step way outside their comfort zone to do so are likely to give great benefit to their child with it. Parents who are easily warm and nice need to wipe that smile off their face when setting limits or the child gets the message that the parent is afraid of upsetting them, as though they are flawed and need handling with kid gloves. That parent needs the courage to stay more firm and neutral, whereas the usually stern or more reserved parent will increase the effectiveness of their limit-setting with a warmer, friendlier approach.

For those of us who praise easily, we have similarly been likely to praise when praise is not warranted. Inaccurate praise, where we praise our children without them having achieved or mastered something, ends badly. Children will experience the praise as not true because it doesn't match their experience. They will then conclude that we, their parents, can't be trusted when we give praise. There can be thoughts such as "Dad says I'm kind, but I'm not kind. I couldn't say sorry." If the child is often praised for being assertive, kind, apologetic, or good at setting limits, and the child does not recognize it in themselves, then mistrust of parents can contribute to the child developing a harsh inner critic. The praise ends up having the opposite effect and contributes to the child being self-critical. The child may then turn to their inner critic for guidance and help to ensure they don't make mistakes or, for example, seem mean, or weak, or stupid, or selfish. Our inner critic functions as a blunt instrument, cracking down on anything that can be construed as bad behavior. The child can become self-critical about even minor misdemeanors.

The challenge for us is that it's not the actual situation or behavior that determines whether the child can accept praise, or whether the praise has a good effect, but rather whether the child feels that they deserve praise or not. The child's sense of worth does not have to depend on the objective situation but comes from a complex interplay between learning history, temperament, and the relationship to their own feelings. This emphasizes that not everything is straightforward, and there are a number of factors we need to keep in mind that are not always so obvious. We may do everything correctly but still not achieve the desired result. This can result in us having our own feelings of self-criticism, anger, and frustration. If you start praising the child, and you see that the child dismisses the praise, leave it. Find another way to reach them, or try the praise again at a later time when you can see the pride in your child's body or hear it in their voice.

EXPERIENCE IT: RECEIVING AND GIVING CONSEQUENCES

Take a moment to draw on your own experiences with punishment versus healthy consequences. Think of a specific time when you were young and you misbehaved. Maybe you hit someone, stole something, or broke a rule. Look back and imagine yourself at that time. What happened? What did the adult do? Try to get a clear picture of what happened as a result of your behavior. Play it out in your mind like a film.

Did you get away with it? Did you get punished? Or did someone give you a consequence that made sense and that you can see now had your best interests at heart? Try to get a clear sense of the adult's reaction. Once you've grappled with that, imagine yourself back to being you as that child, at that age. What does it feel like inside your chest and stomach to get the reaction or lack of reaction you got? What emotions come up?

Are your needs met in the situation? Did your caregivers set healthy, flexible limits and give consequences that helped you move forward? Or were your needs for safety, approval, boundaries, freedom, company, sleep, food, or love overlooked? Check inside. What does it feel like right now? What can you learn from this experience that you can carry with you? How can it guide you in being there for your child?

Now try something different. Think of a specific time when your child misbehaved. Maybe they hit you, stole something, or broke a rule. Imagine your child and yourself in the situation. What happened? How did you react? Try to get a clear picture of what happened as a result of your kid's behavior. Play it out in your mind like a film.

Did your kid get away with it? Did you punish them? Or did you set a limit and give them a consequence that made sense and that you can see now had your child's best interests at heart? Try to get a clear sense of your reaction. Once you've grappled with that, imagine being the child—being your child at that age in that specific situation. What does it feel like inside your chest and stomach as you imagine being your child? What's it like to get the reaction or lack of reaction they got from you? What emotions come up? Are your needs met in the situation? Or are your needs for safety, approval, boundaries, freedom, company, sleep, food, or love overlooked? Check inside "the child's" tummy. What does it feel like?

Now, switch back to being you, and again sink into your stomach. What's going on inside you right now, having done this exercise? What can you learn from this experience that you can carry with you? How can it guide you in being there for your child? If you feel like you did well, let yourself sit with that pride for a minute. If you feel some remorse or self-criticism about how you reacted, try to be curious. Is there a link between the experience you had when you were a child and how you reacted as the parent?

It might be weird, but imagine the younger or little you (from the memory you thought of above) reacting to and trying to parent your child's misbehavior: you as a child, parenting your own child. Now, what do you feel toward yourself, when you think of it as "little you" trying to be the parent? When you see it in this light, is it possible to have more empathy and compassion for yourself regarding any flaws in what you did?

CHAPTER 14

TROUBLESHOOTING WHILE SETTING LIMITS

Some of you are still wondering how all this is going to work when your child is exhibiting more serious behaviors. In fact, for all parents, there will be times when it's hard to imagine this system of limit-setting being effective when what your child is doing seems out of their own control and out of yours and where it is destructive physically and emotionally to themselves, others, and to you. The first thing we want to say is: Don't bail on the plan too fast. We have seen and heard extraordinary outcomes when parents stayed the course, even when they felt at their wits' end. The two-part boundaries-without-judgment system we discussed in Chapter 11 has power even if the results come gradually. But let's also talk specifically about the reality of some of the difficulties you may be facing.

WHAT IF MY CHILD IS PHYSICALLY AGGRESSIVE?

Sometimes children can act out so violently that we have to restrain them physically so that they don't harm themselves or others. Ideally, we would use physical restraint as infrequently as possible—only when it is absolutely necessary. We might need, and make good use of, physical restraint in situations where there is a threat of self-harm or harming another person, or a threat to damage or break something. In some cases, it might even be preferable to let the child break something—a glass, for example—than to restrain them. If we do need to restrain them, we want to do so for as short a time as possible, and let go as soon as the child has calmed down. We do best to restrict their freedom of movement as little as possible. If it's enough to secure the child's hands so that their legs can be free, that's good. The best way to restrain your child is to wrap your arms around them and hold on to your own hands or wrists. This is less likely to hurt them physically than holding their body and is the least uncomfortable way to restrain someone.

For most children, being restrained feels like an affront, and more so if we hold them longer and harder than necessary. Age, of course, plays a big role. It is less of an affront for a toddler to be physically lifted and held back. But by early school age, physical restraint can be seen as offensive and contrary to the child's important development of autonomy. For teens, the threshold for when we should use physical restraint is even higher; fortunately, in most cases a child's physical acting out decreases with age. There is never a need to use physical restraint for verbal aggression or empty threats. It is when the child has already begun to act out against themselves or others, or the threat of that happening is very likely, that we turn to physical restraint.

There are factors for each individual child, including their temperament and history, that will have an impact on how they react to physical restraint. If they have experienced violence, abuse, or physical bullying, being physically restrained and held tightly will be more distressing. Some children also have painful experiences from playing that have gone too far, whether they have been trapped, squashed by a mattress, wrestled, or ended up in situations where they couldn't breathe or get free. In these cases it is especially important to explain what is happening, preferably before it happens, or at least while it is happening. We should explain what we are intending to do, and why we are doing it, and assure the child that they will not be hurt.

As a general rule, it is better to hold a child in a tight hug than to put them on the ground or push them against a wall. Some children, though, will feel like they're being suffocated even when they are held, usually because it's associated with a previous painful experience of violence or violent play. For others, a firm hug, where the parent holds only the upper body and prevents the arms from moving, can feel positive and good. They realize that they are out of control and want help to stop, and they like the feeling of safety. But it never feels good to be put on the ground, with a knee in the back, or to have one's arms bent around the back. We've talked to several children who have described these differences in the experience: With one parent, being forcefully put on the ground feels like the police would treat a violent criminal during an arrest, whereas with their other parent the actions felt more like a hug. Children describe being held physically in these two different ways as very different experiences. And there's no doubt about which the child will prefer.

Allow as much freedom of movement as possible. Restraining both arms and legs can feel too restrictive and like a violation, and it is usually unnecessary with a small child. When holding the child in a tight hug, always do it as lightly and for as little time as possible. Say what you are doing and why, and let them know that you will let go as soon as you feel they have better control. Validating the child's feelings about being restrained can help to soothe the child. If holding your child is not enough, then they can be guided, firmly but not roughly, into sitting on a sofa or chair. As much as possible, avoid putting them on the ground. If you cannot prevent a large, strong, enraged teen from harming themselves or others, and you have to put them on the ground, then it is important that the child be placed on their side, never on the stomach or back. This allows them as much control as possible over their legs and arms and ensures that you keep the airways open. There are different techniques and grips that can be learned, and if you have a large child who acts out regularly and violently it is recommended that you get professional help to learn proper holding techniques. If you have a large and violent teen who may also be intoxicated, and who is also resisting you, it's difficult to avoid being harsh if you are alone. If you have a dangerous teen in an intoxicated state that you are unable to protect yourself or others from, you can call the police for help.

Talk to your child after you've had to use physical restraint. If they're at an age where it should no longer be necessary to restrain them physically, validate how awful it must have felt. Validate and help them to put their experience of it and their feelings into words. Check if something was particularly scary, painful, or okay. Talk to your child about the fact that a certain type of behavior will mean that adults have to hold on to them, so that they are aware of it in advance of them acting out, in case it happens again. Let them know that you want to avoid having to restrain them, and ask them if they have input on what can be done to prevent such situations from recurring. Ask your child what *they* want, the next time they become this aggressive, that will stop them from harming themselves or others. This can give you options for adjusting how you restrain them the next time, should it become necessary.

Some of you might be shocked by this discussion of restraining a child who is no longer a toddler, or a teen or adult child. Or you might wonder how it fits with a discussion of emotion skills. This is a book about anger. Angry kids can become physically aggressive. It is a hallmark of our approach that parents need to put their own oxygen mask on first in order to be there for their child. They need to protect their own well-being. The best gift we give our own children is our own well-being. This is the only way we will be able to attend effectively to our child's needs. It is good for neither us nor our child when the child feels they can be physically aggressive with us. It is therefore important for both parent and child equally that physical aggression toward the parent must stop. We strongly believe parents can stop their aggressive child from hurting them. We also believe in parents' ability to do their best for their child. If things have gotten to the point where your child is physically aggressive, we hope you will be able to take radical responsibility (because that is going to give you the best platform for being empowered to stop it), and we hope you will forgive yourself for any role you had in modeling it, or allowing it, or in not stopping it before. And we want to give you all our support in stopping it now. For some, things haven't reached this point in your home, and this is not relevant. For others, it has reached that point. We want to empower you to make it stop.

Remember, pretty much all of us, when confronted with anger, and even more so with aggression, naturally power up like a lion or power down like the lamb. We're inviting you to use every ounce of wisdom you can squeeze out of all the boundary and limit-setting information and skills we've provided, to use the power you have and mix it with validation and empathy to stop your child from ever being physically aggressive with you again. Or, for the lambs among you, we invite you to consider that your child needs you to power up. It is not hurting them to stop them physically from hurting you or being aggressive with you. It is hurting them to continue to allow it. Children whose parents can't stop them can end up feeling like monsters. "I'm so bad that even my strong adult parents, the ones meant to guide and protect me, can't stop me." Take a breath. You can do it. Power up. Or soften your own aggression with empathy. And give your child this all-important gift of stopping them from hurting you and from having to define themselves as someone who hurt their parents.

WHAT IF MY CHILD IS MANIPULATING ME?

Some children pretend to be angry even when they don't actually feel angry, because they learn that anger, sometimes along with aggression, can work to get a certain result. We call this *instrumental anger*.

That means they can have aggressive behavior without feeling angry, in order to get that result or to get their way. Some of these children can end up running the show in families where the adults do not set sufficient limits and the children are allowed to act as they please with both adults and siblings. Other instrumental emotions can also manipulate adults, such as the classic crocodile tears that make us give in to the nagging for another ice cream, or pretend fears that make us stay a little longer in our child's bedroom at night. It is not necessarily the case that children who have a lot of instrumental anger also have other instrumental feelings. Because this is a book about angry children, we want to focus on instrumental anger.

First of all, it is important to say again that children who have a lot of instrumental anger and use it seemingly manipulatively do not do this with malicious intent or on purpose. Children who use anger to get their way lack competence with emotion. They have trouble understanding and communicating their feelings and needs. For that reason, we often see instrumental emotions in younger children. They haven't had enough experience with their emotions and needs yet to develop that competence. Biology plays a role here, in that some children mature later than others. The environment, especially the family environment, also plays a role. Children learn instrumental anger in their relationship with us, their parents, and with other family members. They may see that adopting the stance of anger works to get what one wants in the family. It also can develop as a result of ineffective limit-setting.

When boundaries are too porous and loose, it's as though the parents yield control to the kids. But children don't actually want to be little dictators who smash through our limits and put themselves in the seat of power. They may act as if they do, but it's really us who let it happen. If we catch it quickly and set it right, it doesn't have to become an issue. Most of us have had an occasional experience of our children taking too much power—that feeling of tiptoeing around the child, not wanting to push the button that will prompt a scene of exaggerated emotion. But it only becomes problematic if it becomes a pattern, and the only one who can stop it and free the kids to be kids and not bosses anymore is—you guessed it—you. The parent. Brace yourself. There will be struggles when you tighten the limits and take back the helm.

In families where it's not just a difficult period, but where the child frequently and regularly adopts the stance of anger and uses it as power, and the adults are not aware of what is happening, the parents can end up feeling manipulated. If the parents continue to be ineffective in setting limits and taking charge, children can become extremely aggressive. They may intimidate family members, threatening to hit a little brother if he doesn't give up his candy, or threatening to make life a living nightmare for their parents if they aren't allowed to stay out as late as they want. If the family dynamic becomes a negative cycle of threatening, angry, and aggressive children, scared siblings, and adults with blurred boundaries, then these children will be seen as tyrants. We can lose empathy, distance ourselves, and withhold care from them. This is a dangerous development for children, and it can lay the groundwork for more serious antisocial behavior as adults. When children experience that their parents don't like them, can't handle them, and distance themselves from them, the aggressive behavior will often increase. They can feel disappointed as well as more and more frustrated that there is no room for their angry feelings and react by dialing up the intensity of their angry expressions in a desperate attempt to be seen and get help.

You can use everything you have learned in this book so far to deal with your child's behavior and your feeling of being manipulated when your child has taken the reins. As always, you have to start with yourself. What does your Brain Boss tell you when you tiptoe around your child and don't dare to say what you want? What is that about? What does it tell you, to make you afraid to intervene and set limits? What does it say is the worst that can happen? Raise your awareness of how you got here. Then follow the steps in setting limits. The only thing that is different about instrumental anger is that it is not as necessary to validate the emotion that the child shows because it is not as genuine and the child can more easily be freed from it. If you are in doubt about whether the anger is instrumental or whether it is cloaking anger, it is never wrong to validate. But if you are absolutely sure that this is instrumental anger, you can start with taking responsibility for this happening. "It wasn't okay that we didn't figure out what was up and that you had to show so much anger to make us listen. We're listening now." You can suggest that the anger is about something that they need or something they feel, and you can ask the child to tell you in a calm voice what they're unhappy about.

Another strategy is to use humor. You can hand out yellow cards for adopting the stance of anger or find other ways to make the situation less serious. Just be careful not to let humor come across as ridicule, and try to figure out what works for your child. Keep in mind that as you tighten the limits, the child will likely increase the amount that they adopt an anger stance in an attempt to test whether the limits will hold. It's important to stand in it and stay strong and to have faith that limits work well over time.

WHAT IF THERE IS AGGRESSION AMONG SIBLINGS?

Parents can find it difficult to navigate limit-setting with siblings, especially if the children have different temperaments and different ways of doing things. It can feel difficult always to be setting limits for one child and not the other. It can feel unfair, and it can be painful for the child who has the most challenging behavior and who gets in the most trouble. It's easy to fall into the classic trap that the "difficult" child always gets the blame, or that we become unreasonably strict with them because we lose patience over time. It's not often we have two children who are exactly the same when it comes to temperament and aggressive behavior, so most parents know about this issue to some degree, at least in difficult periods. Many people wonder how they should make up for the fact that they yell so much at one child. And sometimes we end up with unclear boundaries for things other than aggressive behavior, as a kind of compensation for the fact that we often yell at, and nag, the child for their disobedient behavior. It's easy to see how we can end up in a negative pattern of interaction.

The first step in fixing limit-setting between siblings is to take a step back and try to look at the interaction from an outside perspective. What can I see in me that triggers my child to become angry and aggressive, how do I react emotionally to my child's behavior, and then what do I do? How does what I do further reinforce the child's feelings and behavior? This is how the interaction cycle goes around and around. We affect each other and react to each other, and then unfortunate patterns can be created, even though we really like each other and we want the best for our child. In the same way, a pattern develops with the child who has the calmer temperament. Many of the "easygoing" children can feel that they are overshadowed by the more outspoken children who get a lot of space and on whom we spend a lot of energy and focus. Those with a lighter temperament can even feel that there's no room for them to get angry and oppose something, even if they need to. They may also feel unloved. They are often afraid to add extra weight to their parents' burden. And it's easy for us as parents to think it's so wonderful to have a child who listens that we end up being okay with the child not expressing their needs and their anger. It may feel like that's the only way to cope. When negative cycles of interaction develop between us and the kids, the same thing often happens between siblings. It can show up as arguing and jealousy, or as distance in the relationship.

In these cases, both the temperamental and the quieter children need a lot of validation. It can really help to apologize for the way we may have contributed to them not getting along, or because we yelled at one child too much and ignored the others. If the dynamics go awry, we can end up with more children who feel unloved, for completely different reasons, and who need very different apologies. The child who has been overlooked, given too much responsibility, and who is not allowed to express difficult feelings often needs the adult to take responsibility and apologize, so that the circle of interaction will change. As part of the apology, it's important to say something like the following:

> No wonder you feel like I don't love you as much, because I never ask you how you really feel. And I think you have an expectation that you always have to be kind, and if you're not, then I scold you. It's really unfair that you haven't been allowed to be angry and that we haven't spent as much time with you.

The temperamental child, who often feels like the bad guy and who ruins things and is unlovable, needs other feelings validated: "No wonder you worry that I don't love you as much, because I yell at you so much and we always argue."

It's also important to be aware that different children actually need different limits. They cannot be treated equally. Some children handle a lot of responsibility and want it, while other children want close follow-up and know there is a lot they can't manage on their own. Some children could handle a lot of responsibility but don't want it, while other children handle responsibility poorly, even though they want to be independent. We need to adapt to all of these nuances when it comes to limit-setting. If siblings think of fairness as everything being the same, they will never see limits and rules in the family as fair. We have to come to terms with that and explain it to the children. It's important to validate the feelings the children have when they realize that the rules for each of them might be different. It's not fair for some children to have unnecessarily strict limits simply because we feel they should be the same as those needed for the more temperamental child. And it's not good for children who need a lot of clear rules and limits if things are too loose, just because we don't want to treat them differently. Our goal is to give our children what they need, and they have different needs. We can explain this to them, and we can acknowledge their feelings about it feeling unfair. Then we are much freer in doing what is best for each and for the whole family, and we can set limits with a greater degree of confidence.

A final point related to limit-setting among siblings is that, even within the family, it can be shameful to be reprimanded in front of others. It's kinder to speak privately to each child about limits and consequences.

WHAT IF THE AGGRESSION HAPPENS OUTSIDE THE HOME WHEN I'M NOT THERE?

Aggression outside the home is definitely a difficult topic. We can't protect ourselves or our children from every conflict and challenge that arises when they are away from home. We can help by addressing a bad environment at school or outside school, and we can try to reduce everyday stress, but we can't protect our children from all the hurtful things in the world. By working with the home/family environment, connecting with the children emotionally, and helping them deal with their own emotions, we can, however, quite quickly bring about changes that also allow us to set limits for our children when they are out in the big world so that they learn to move about with healthy boundaries. If the family environment improves, and we help our children to deal with their emotions, that's a good starting point to get the ball rolling. If, when they're at home, children receive understanding, acceptance, and love, as well as limits and expectations that are firm and flexible and communicated clearly, then outside of the home they will engage in less unwanted behavior and will be better at protecting themselves. If this doesn't work, we follow the same principle of assessing and addressing the situation, validating before setting limits, communicating clear limits, and holding our ground. To a certain extent, we can follow up with our kids when they are out, by phone, by contact with other parents, or by driving and picking them up in situations where their boundaries seem sure to be pressed by others. When necessary, we can introduce appropriate consequences, to ensure that their safety and needs are taken care of. One area many parents find demanding is school or day care. It is especially challenging to set limits for children's behavior at school or day care if they behave differently at home, or if you as a parent disagree with the way the school or day care handles things.

When it comes to different behaviors in these two places, the most challenging communication and limit-setting seems most often to occur when the child is aggressive at school or day care but not at home. At home, the parents are close by and have better control. But it's difficult to understand what's going on and how we should help the child when the challenges are mainly related to school. In this book, we mostly talk about aggression as the problematic behavior, but it can of course be just as difficult to set limits outside the home if, for example, your child only has problems going to the toilet when they're at school, is bullied, or is extremely shy and quiet or lonely at school. So what do we do when our kid acts out and is a menace at school or in day care but behaves just fine at home?

First, it's important to validate the child's anger and at the same time try to find out if there are other emotions lying underneath. It's easier to guess what the other emotions are than to guess what the anger is about. So, start with your child's feelings. This is where the key lies. Maybe they are actually overwhelmed by something, scared, ashamed, or upset, and the anger is a cloaking emotion. If there is not a lot of trust between you and your child, and they don't want to open up and tell you what's happening, you may need to repair something in the relationship or improve the trust through gradual validation and healthy boundaries so that you can eventually reach your child.

There can be many reasons why aggression shows up only at school or in day care. Some children are more vulnerable to large environments with lots of other kids and a structured schedule. Other children are sensitive to various stimuli, such as light, sound, and touch, and are easily stressed or overwhelmed when there are lots of children around them, who bump into them and shout loudly. Many children react with anger when they are physically stressed, and it can be difficult for them to understand the connection between too many things stimulating them and their anger. For some children, light and heat from the window, which they can't avoid without leaving the room, irritates the senses and the body. Other children are socially stressed by school or day care. It's not suitable for all kids to be with many other children all day. Some kids like it best when they are with only one other child, or with a few. If your child went to a small day care, the social anxiety when they get to school can come as a shock when there are suddenly large classes, nowhere to hide, and few adults with whom to seek refuge. In addition, there is an increased risk of bullying, or of the child making friends with someone who is dominating and they're afraid of. The aggression of the dominant friend could, for example, be about the desire to have some control at school, where you typically have little influence on limits and rules. In playing with other children, some kids may get an experience of this long-awaited control. Other students are afraid of the teacher, or they feel small and stupid in the classroom and develop performance anxiety. Some children become quiet when they are socially stressed, while others become aggressive.

Painful life events or stressors can also be more difficult to deal with at school than at home. For children experiencing grief, school can be a difficult place. It's hard to grieve that your parents are getting divorced, that your dog died, or that someone in the family is ill, at the same time as having to be at school and try to learn. Many children struggle to conform to a system that ultimately does not consider individual differences and needs. For many children, it creates huge frustration, which often leads to aggression, over having to function within the difficult system that school can sometimes be. For some kids, it's difficult to function in the classroom setting, to follow a timetable, to play and work alternately when the bell rings, to switch on and off, to raise their hand and talk only when they're allowed, to find friends and navigate socially, to perform academically at school and at home with homework, and to experience a much more limited freedom of movement than at home or in day care. There are, therefore, many good reasons why children are aggressive at school, and the above are only a few.

The consolation is that even if we don't know exactly what it's all about, we can still validate their feelings about being at school or day care, whatever those feelings are. We can wonder out loud with them about what the difficulty might be. A curious and nonjudgmental attitude is the first step toward helping your child feel better away from home. When your child has done something wrong at school or day care—for example, stolen or damaged something, or been aggressive—it's important to address the problems and talk to them. As always, start by validating your child's feelings and see if they tell you what happened. You're pros at it now, right? While it is very important to work the best you can with the day care or school that your child attends, there are huge differences in the resources available at different schools to communicate and collaborate as we might wish.

Doing everything to foster that relationship, from home to school, and to find joint solutions for children, is essential. But given our unending belief in and wish to empower parents, we also encourage you to see yourselves as the answer. Validate. Keep working on improving the connection between you and your child. "Faith it till you make it." And decide that whatever is going on in your child's life, if at all possible, you will do the work at home to smooth the way in the other settings where they spend their days.

AFTERWORD

We've set out to show how important it is to understand, validate, and work with not only our children's anger but also our own. Actively dealing with children's emotions, and trying to help them understand and utilize their emotions, is one of the most valuable things we as parents can do for our children when they are angry or aggressive. With help from us, children can learn that anger gives them important information about other feelings and about their needs. They can listen to their anger and use it as a guide in life. When we are good emotional guides for our children's anger and underlying painful feelings, they learn to handle their feelings, even the painful and unpleasant ones. With an understanding of anger—and with tools such as validation; apology; and healthy, protective boundaries—every parent will be better equipped to meet their child's challenges. But what about when our own anger takes over and steals the show? Our own powerful and painful feelings can get in the way: They can come between us and our children, competing for our attention and preventing us from helping our child. Time and time again we will stumble into a feeling trap and have a hard time climbing out. But with courage and curiosity, we can do it. We can tolerate being faced with our own painful feelings, just enough so that we can choose to follow the motivation to validate, apologize, and reset the family boundaries.

Remember that even with all the knowledge and wisdom and skills we learn, we are still going to make mistakes as parents. The ideal is *not* to be the perfect parent who never messes up. The fact that we fail is actually an absolutely essential part of our children's development. We will hurt them, yell at them, and dismiss them, and some of the time we will apologize and fix our mistakes. Children's enormous resilience, and the strong bond between parents and children, gives us every opportunity to help our children with all the difficult experiences life offers, such as heartache, conflict, being unpopular, self-harm, anxiety, depression, and aggressive and violent behavior. We can protect our children from both addiction and destructive behavior by not avoiding difficult emotions, by taking radical responsibility, and by apologizing for what is still unresolved. We can learn to reconnect with our children and help them reconnect with their emotions, so that emotions again become a valuable source of information, and we become an important supporter. We cannot prevent suffering, and some children have congenital vulnerabilities that can make it harder to help them. The point is not to make our children feel better but to help them so that they get better at feeling.

An enormous amount of research has been done on emotions over the past 20 years, and a lot of research has examined emotion-focused therapy. Emotion focused skills training for parents is a relatively new method of parental counseling, and much more research is needed in this field. But the research that exists has shown good results. There is still a huge amount about being good parents and helping children who are struggling that we don't know, and probably a lot we have not yet come up with to investigate or make models for. The same goes for emotions. We have a lot of knowledge, but we are still far from solving the mystery of being human and knowing what it takes to avoid, and heal, emotional and relational wounds and various traumas.

We hope that this book has given you some useful information about emotion. We hope it has helped you tap into the important emotion wisdom you already had in you. We hope you've gotten answers to questions you had about your child's anger, and your own. We hope you're taking away some new emotion skills. We know there is probably a lot left unanswered and untried. It is one thing to learn something by reading a book; it is another to try it out in the relationship with your child. Maybe you completed some of the exercises, maybe you skipped them, and maybe you've figured some things out. Whatever the case, we encourage you to have the attitude that your child is a wonderful being who is trying to find their place in the world and who wants to belong. If you have an angry child, then you have a strong-willed child. A powerhouse! We believe you deserve the chance to enjoy and appreciate the upside of that. See the strength in a fiery temperament. And remember that none of the bad behavior—kicks, punches, swear words, or threats—are about the child wanting or setting out to be horrible or wanting to ruin things for themselves or for you. Our fiery and outspoken little, adolescent, and adult children are just struggling to tell us what is painful and what they need. Their brain fires quickly and gives orders for them to act, and they're not able to think of the consequences in the moment. The brain and the emotional system are not fully developed until they are well into their 20s. Your child needs you. You are the one who is best able to help your child, and it's your child's deepest wish to have that help come from you.

We believe you can get closer to answers for your unanswered questions if you continue to explore your own feelings as well as your child's. Maybe one day you can look back on your family's life now and be proud of the effort you put in. We hope you can also look back and see that you made changes, maybe some big and maybe some small changes, as a result of your changing course. Maybe you became kinder to and more curious about yourself and forgave yourself. (That's big.) Maybe you began to sit with your child in their pain. (That's big, too.) Maybe the relationship to emotions will be completely different in your family in the coming generations, and your contribution will be an important part of that. In the same way that violence and emotion avoidance are inherited, wisdom and knowledge about emotions will also be inherited and help prevent emotional pain and mental difficulties for future generations.

REFERENCES

Al Majali, S. A., & Ashour, L. M. (2020). The negative consequences of poor emotion management (anger, anxiety and frustration) on the brain and body. *Talent Development & Excellence*, *12*(2), 3410–3419.

Ansar, N., Hjeltnes, A., Stige, S. H., Binder, P.-E., & Stiegler, J. R. (2021). Parenthood—Lost and found: Exploring parents' experiences of receiving a program in emotion focused skills training. *Frontiers in Psychology*, *12*, 559188. https://doi.org/10.3389/fpsyg.2021.559188

Ansar, N., Nissen Lie, H. A., Zahl-Olsen, R., Bertelsen, T. B., Elliott, R., & Stiegler, J. R. (2022). Efficacy of emotion-focused parenting programs for children's internalizing and externalizing symptoms: A randomized clinical study. *Journal of Clinical Child & Adolescent Psychology*, *51*(6), 923–939. https://doi.org/10.1080/15374416. 2022.2079130

Assor, A., Roth, G., & Deci, E. L. (2004). The emotional costs of parents' conditional regard: A self-determination theory analysis. *Journal of Personality*, *72*(1), 47–88. https://doi.org/10.1111/j.0022-3506.2004. 00256.x

Baron, R. A., & Richardson, D. R. (1994). *Human aggression* (2nd ed.). Plenum Press.

Beebe, B., & Lachmann, F. M. (2013). *The origins of attachment: Infant research and adult treatment* (Vol. 60). Routledge. https://doi.org/ 10.4324/9781315858067

Dolhanty, J., Hjelmseth, V., Austbø, B., & Hagen, A. H. V. (2022). *Emotion focused skills training for parents—A guide for clinicians*. Empty Chair.

Ferris, C. F., & Grisso, T. (1998). *Understanding aggressive behavior in children*. Psychiatry Publications.

Foroughe, M., Stillar, A., Goldstein, L., Dolhanty, J., Goodcase, E. T., & Lafrance, A. (2018). Brief emotion focused family therapy: An intervention for parents of children and adolescents with mental health issues. *Journal of Marital and Family Therapy, 45*(3), 410–430. https://doi.org/10.1111/jmft.12351

Gershoff, E. T. (2002). Corporal punishment by parents and associated child behaviors and experiences: A meta-analytic and theoretical review. *Psychological Bulletin, 128*(4), 539–579. https://doi.org/10.1037/0033-2909.128.4.539

Greenberg, L. S. (2002). *Emotion-focused therapy: Coaching clients to work through their feelings*. American Psychological Association. https://doi.org/10.1037/10447-000

Greenberg, L. S. (2017). *Emotion-focused therapy* (Rev. ed.). American Psychological Association. https://doi.org/10.1037/15971-000

Greenberg, L. S., Auszra, L., & Herrmann, I. R. (2007). The relationship among emotional productivity, emotional arousal and outcome in experiential therapy of depression. *Psychotherapy Research, 17*(4), 482–493. https://doi.org/10.1080/10503300600977800

Greenberg, L. S., & Goldman, R. N. (Eds.). (2019). *Clinical handbook of emotion-focused therapy*. American Psychological Association. https://doi.org/10.1037/0000112-000

Greenberg, L. S., Warwar, S. H., & Malcom, W. M. (2008). Differential effects of emotion-focused therapy and psychoeducation in facilitating forgiveness and letting go of emotional injuries. *Journal of Counseling Psychology, 55*(2), 185–196. https://doi.org/10.1037/0022-0167.55.2.185

Grolnick, W. S. (2002). *The psychology of parental control: How well-meant parenting backfires*. Psychology Press.

Havighurst, S. S., Duncombe, M., Frankling, E., Holland, K., Kehoe, C., & Stargatt, R. (2015). An emotion-focused early intervention for children with emerging conduct problems. *Journal of Abnormal Child Psychology, 43*(4), 749–760. https://doi.org/10.1007/s10802-014-9944-z

Jaffe, J., Beebe, B., Feldstein, S., Crown, C. L., & Jasnow, M. D. (2001). Rhythms of dialogue in infancy: Coordinated timing in development. *Monographs of the Society for Research in Child Development, 66*(2), i–viii, 1–132.

Johnson, S. B., Blum, R. W., & Giedd, J. N. (2009). Adolescent maturity and the brain: The promise and pitfalls of neuroscience research in adolescent health policy. *The Journal of Adolescent Health, 45*(3), 216–221. https://doi.org/10.1016/j.jadohealth.2009.05.016

Lafrance Robinson, A., Strahan, E., Girz, L., Wilson, A., & Boachie, A. (2013). "I know I can help you": Parental self-efficacy predicts adolescent outcomes in family-based therapy for eating disorders. *European Eating Disorders Review, 21*(2), 108–114. https://doi.org/10.1002/erv.2180

Meloy, J. R. (1988). *The psychopathic mind: Origins, dynamics, and treatment.* Jason Aronson.

Miller, W. R., & Rollnick, S. (2012). *Motivational interviewing: Helping people change* (3rd ed.). Guilford Press.

Siegel, D. J. (2015). *The developing mind: How relationships and the brain interact to shape who we are* (2nd ed.). Guilford Press.

Thomas, S. P. (1997). Angry? Let's talk about it! *Applied Nursing Research, 10*(2), 80–85. https://doi.org/10.1016/S0897-1897(97)80141-3

Treasure, J., Smith, G., & Crane, A. (2016). *Skills-based caring for a loved one with an eating disorder: The new Maudsley method.* Routledge. https://doi.org/10.4324/9781315735610

Tronick, E. (2007). *The neurobehavioral and social-emotional development of infants and children.* W. W. Norton.

INDEX

ABOUT THE AUTHORS

Anne Hilde Vassbø Hagen, cand.psychol, is a psychologist and leader of The Institute for Psychological Counseling (IPR) and the Norwegian Institute of Emotion Focused Therapy and a publisher at Empty Chair Publishing. She is the mother of 10-year-old twin girls and welcomed a baby boy to her family 2 years ago. She has further education in emotion-focused skills training for parents, emotion-focused therapy for individuals and for couples, clinical adult psychology, and work with children. IPR's work includes therapy, training and supervision of therapists, expert work, research, and conferences, as well as the dissemination of the emotion-focused approach. Ms. Hagen is the writer, creator, and producer of the popular Alfred & Shadow educational film series, which was made in collaboration with The Norwegian Council for Mental Health. The films are produced in Norwegian and English and can be found on the YouTube channel #aboutemotions. Widely used in teaching and therapy, the films have more than 2 million views. Ms. Hagen has written three books and received two book scholarships from the Norwegian Association of Authors and Translators.

Joanne Dolhanty, PhD, CPsych, is a supervising and consulting clinical psychologist and the mother of two young adult sons. She has a doctorate in clinical psychology from York University in Toronto, Ontario, Canada, and has extensive training in the emotion-focused approach. She is a certified supervisor with the International Society for Emotion Focused Therapy and provides trainings to individuals, parents, professionals, and organizations through her Emotion Training Institute (https://www.emotiontraininginstitute.org/), the Emotion-Focused Therapy Clinic at York University, and through institutions in countries around the globe. With Dr. Leslie Greenberg, she developed the application of emotion-focused therapy to eating disorders. She is the developer of an emotion-focused skills training (EFST) program that brings the benefits of emotion-focused therapy to the broader population in a simplified format. EFST promotes transformations in difficult feelings, in relationships, and in stubborn behaviors via short-term experiential learning of emotion-focused skills. Dr. Dolhanty is known for her ability to reach, relate to, and have a positive and lasting impact on hugely diverse populations of parents all around the world with her delivery of EFST online or in person. She is also the developer of Powered by Emotion, a simple three-step transformative emotion-focused personal and professional growth program for organizations, leaders, teams, and individuals.

santa clara
county
library district

Renewals: (800) 471-0991

www.sccl.org